George Washington and
American Constitutionalism

American Political Thought
edited by Wilson Carey McWilliams
and Lance Banning

George Washington and American Constitutionalism

GLENN A. PHELPS

 UNIVERSITY PRESS OF KANSAS

Published by the University Press of Kansas (Lawrence, Kansas 66049), which was organized by the Kansas Board of Regents and is operated and funded by Emporia State University, Fort Hays State University, Kansas State University, Pittsburg State University, the University of Kansas, and Wichita State University

Library of Congress Cataloging-in-Publication Data

Phelps, Glenn A., 1948–
    George Washington and American constitutionalism / Glenn A. Phelps.
        p.   cm. — (American political thought)
    Includes bibliographical references and index.
    ISBN 0-7006-0564-9
    1. Washington, George, 1732–1799—Views on the Constitution.
    2. United States—Constitutional history.   3. United States—
    Politics and government—1783–1809.   I. Title.   II. Series.
    E312.29.P44   1993
    973.4′1′092—dc20   92-21824

British Library Cataloguing in Publication Data is available.

Printed in the United States of America
10 9 8 7 6 5 4 3 2 1

Contents

Preface:
The Intentions of a Framer

George Washington remains a problem for students of American constitutional history. Few would challenge the notion that Washington was probably the most beloved public figure of his generation. Although Lincoln, Jefferson, and even Franklin Roosevelt have perhaps since surpassed Washington's standing in our civic pantheon, much of their veneration developed after their deaths. Their popularity in their own times was more attenuated. Yet if Washington was truly "first in war, first in peace, first in the hearts of his countrymen," we should expect to see his mark on the political institutions and practices with which he was so intimately involved. In particular, our Constitution and the traditions that grew out of it should show some evidence of his having been on the scene, first as presiding officer of the Constitutional Convention in Philadelphia and second as first president of the newly constituted United States.

But assessments of Washington's accomplishments rarely address his substantive role in American constitutional development. Most accounts applaud his military accomplishments, commend his strength of character, and acknowledge his importance as a rallying point for American nation building. But these same accounts are often reluctant to portray him as anything more than a symbolic contributor to the founding of an American Constitution—an "indispensable man," to be sure, but indispensable in ways more instrumental than substantive. They see Washington as a conduit through which the ideas and aspirations of the "great" framers, men such as Hamilton, Madison, and James Wilson, acquired political legitimacy. Although this would be no small achievement in its own right, Washington's *substantive* constitutional contributions are deemed negligible.

At first glance, this assessment does not seem unfair. As a political philosopher Washington certainly lacked the erudition and sophistication of Jefferson, Hamilton, Madison, or any of a dozen other of his contemporaries. His reading leaned toward natural history and heroic biographies rather than the political treatises favored by others of the founding generation. Moreover, many of the letters and speeches for which he is most famous (e.g., the Farewell Address, the Inaugurals, the Circular Letter to the States, and his resignation from the army) were written with the help of talented ghost writers such Madison, Hamilton, David Humphreys, and Tench Tilghman—each the possessor of a political personality and agenda of his own. Finally, while in the chair at the Philadelphia Convention and again as first president under the new Constitution, Washington is portrayed as an honest broker between contending viewpoints, concerned with achieving a consensus on national affairs and dedicated to creating a stable system of government. But his own constitutional aspirations are downplayed. His seeming passivity in the face of intense partisan conflict is often interpreted as a sign that he cared little about the shape and direction of national policy, that he was a mere empty vessel into which the political cant of others was poured. Thus, so the argument goes, Washington ✓ was not so much a "founding" Father as he was a "facilitating" Father.

A close reading of his letters and papers has led me to a different conclusion. Washington's political thought may have lacked the originality and richness of his contemporaries—he wrote no extended essays on politics or public affairs, preferring to express his views in private correspondence and in a handful of significant state papers—but his ✓ writings reveal a clear, thoughtful, and remarkably coherent vision of what he hoped an American republic would become. These notions began to emerge early in the 1770s, took on a sharper, clearer perspective during the Revolution, and changed little thereafter. His words, many of them intended only for friends and family, reveal a man with a passionate commitment to a fully developed idea of a constitutional republic on a continental scale, eager to promote that plan wherever and whenever circumstances or the hand of Providence allowed.

This interpretation challenges the conventional view of Washington in several other ways. First, I maintain that Washington's political values changed very little over time regardless of who his "secretary" was; the various messengers seem not to have affected Washington's message. He was no political chameleon willing to change his colors to conform to the interests and ideas of his brilliant counselors. The contributions of his better-educated ghost writers, steeped in philosophy, certainly improved upon his stolid prose, but the substance remained distinctively Washington's.

Second, Washington's constitutional vision—drawing on elements of classical conservative republicanism and continentally minded commercialism—developed years *before* he ever met Hamilton, Madison, and the other Founders under whose spell he was supposed to have fallen. Thus, claims that Washington was a mere figurehead for the nationalist movement that emerged early in the 1780s underestimate Washington's contribution. The nationalists did not merely capture Washington's growing national reputation to lend authority to a cause of their own making. Rather, they looked naturally to him for leadership because his views were already well known and firmly established. Indeed, many of his ideas presaged the nationalist program.

Finally, no other American was situated as advantageously as George Washington was to affect, and perhaps in a few instances even direct, the development of the American constitutional tradition. Washington used his unique opportunities—as commander-in-chief of the Continental Army during the Revolution, as presiding officer at the Philadelphia Convention that drafted the federal Constitution, and as the first president of the United States—to promote his own enlarged notions of a constitutional republic. He did not always succeed in grafting his "intentions" on that constitutional tradition. No single Founder could ever hope to claim such comprehensive parentage. But this work, I hope, will restore Washington's rightful place as one of this nation's most important constitutional Founders.

This restoration would not have been possible without the support of others. The early stages of my research were supported by faculty colleagues on the Organized Research Committee of Northern Arizona University and its chair, Henry Hooper. The Earhart Foundation graciously provided funds that allowed me to travel to the "dustbins of antiquity" (in reality, the airy, modern Manuscripts Division of the Library of Congress). Earl Shaw, the chair of the Political Science department, and Earl Backman, the dean of the College of Social and Behavioral Sciences, arranged to free up time for me to write at a particularly critical stage in the project.

My intellectual debts are even more numerous. Lance Banning's careful reading of the manuscript saved me from my most egregious errors and more than once showed me the way. His enthusiasm for the project often exceeded even my own and confirmed for me that historians and political scientists *can* still talk to each other intelligibly and productively. At various times Hal Bass, Dan Cothran, Tom Cronin, Edward Dreyer, Joseph Farry, Tom Greene, Fred Greenstein, Carey McWilliams, Thomas Pangle, Larry Preston, Earl Shaw, Paul Sigmund, and Jeffrey Tulis offered insights that proved invaluable. From beginning to end my colleagues in the Department of Political Science provided moral support and encouragement when they were most needed. Finally, in Fred Woodward I was able to acquire both a publisher and a friend.

Two folks deserve a special note of appreciation. Leonard Ritt, without having the slightest interest in George Washington (or, indeed anything that occurred before 1933), offered his wise and funny counsel over innumerable coffees and lunches and more than once replenished my intellectual juices with his infectious curiosity. My wife, Cathy, had the most thankless job of all. Gentle critic and firm supporter, she assumed the daunting task of explaining to our children why Daddy had to go to work on Saturdays. Thank you, Cathy.

1 / The Conservative Revolutionary

American political thought is not, at its core, an exercise in intellectual abstraction. This is not to say that no Americans have made their mark on the world of political ideas. Our history as a colony and nation has never lacked for interesting, provocative, or even on occasion original political ideas. From the founding generation, Thomas Jefferson, James Madison, Alexander Hamilton, John Adams, and James Wilson, to name just a few, deserve to be included in any accounting of people whose thoughts have contributed to that vast reservoir of ideas we call Western civilization. These men all took the business of politics seriously and tried to think and write systematically about the aspirations and hazards of self-government. That they approached the problems of political life with sophistication and even elegance surely qualifies them as "American originals."

But to characterize even these few American statesmen as political philosophers misses the essential quality of American political thought—its reliance upon experience. Political ideas, like most other useful notions, are not the result of undiluted acts of pure reason. Nor are they delivered full-blown from some epiphany of insight. To the contrary, Americans, even those who do think seriously about their political world, have always been skeptical of ideas that are not grounded in the hard-tilled soil of practical experience. While John Dickinson's remarks at the 1787 Philadelphia Convention ("Experience must be our only guide. Reason may mislead us."[1]) best illustrate this attitude, his sentiments reflected the prevailing view of most Americans of his generation. George Washington himself often expressed the opinion that reason could go only so far in animating political principles. People (and his reference here is almost certainly to Americans) "must *feel* before they will *see*."[2]

Some might be tempted to interpret this attitude as yet another example of the anti-intellectualism that recurs in American culture.[3] But this conclusion would seriously misread the mindset of the founding generation. Many of Washington's contemporaries were children of the Enlightenment. They were committed to reason and reflection as the path to the good life, especially the good public life. But reasoning meant something other than mere abstraction or broad theorizing. It meant reasoning by example—reasoning that sought to derive practical wisdom from the accumulated knowledge of their own individual and collective experiences, reasoning that was focused on the resolution of real political problems in their own times.

When the delegates arrived in Philadelphia for the Constitutional Convention of 1787, they brought with them not only their substantial intellectual talents, but also their own experiences, great and small, in the business of governing. Most had served as representatives in their state legislative assemblies, as delegates to Congress, or as judges or magistrates at the local level. As plans and proposals circulated through the convention the delegates evaluated them in substantial part by reference to their own rich and varied experiences. If a delegate made an assertion (for example, that the legislature should be able to remove an executive officer for malfeasance in office) the debate often proceeded from broad theoretical claims (for example, that executives, like all men, were inherently susceptible to the blandishments of power and therefore must be checked by the threat of perfunctory legislative removal) to a consideration of how each of the delegates interpreted those claims in light of his own political experiences.

George Washington was no exception to this experiential, culturally constrained model of American political thought. His constitutional vision was not conceived whole and new in Philadelphia. Nor can we attribute his insights to the effects of only one great seminal moment in his life. Rather, his vision for an American constitutional republic emerged over a long period and was shaped by the social and political community in which he was raised and by the numerous events in which he was an active participant or interested observer.

There is always a risk in trying to explain human behavior. We can observe what a person does and make inferences about the effects of that behavior. But when we venture into the realm of personal causation (that is, when we try to understand why a person behaved a particular way or said particular things) social scientists and historians get rather glassy-eyed. And with good reason. The elements that influence what we say and do are always maddeningly just beyond the reach of normal investigation. We simply cannot know with perfect confidence precisely what was in someone's head at any given moment. And even if we could (a rather horrifying prospect!), we still would confront the equally daunting task of determining *which* value, *which* experience, *which* (mis)perception truly influenced the person's behavior.

Nevertheless, two sets of experiences resonate again and again in Washington's pre-Constitutional writings: his immersion in the social, economic, and political life of his native Virginia and his unique vantage point as commander-in-chief of the Continental Army during the Revolution. There were other influences on Washington's thought, to be sure; but the role that these two factors played in shaping his political outlook cannot be ignored. From 1754, when his correspondence begins, until his departure for the Philadelphia Convention in 1787, nearly every letter that Washington wrote on public affairs can be best understood within the context of these two experiences.

Virginia's Politics of Deference

We must guard against assuming too readily that an American political tradition or even a distinctive American identity existed before the Revolution. There were, indeed, important commonalities. By the eighteenth century most American colonists spoke a common language: English. By the 1750s legal procedures were becoming standardized throughout the colonies and provided a framework for an expanding network of commercial and civil transactions. A Boston merchant could trade with a Virginia planter within a legal structure that made the contractual obligations of each party quite clear.[4] Most of the colonies had political institutions that mirrored those of Britain. Colonists had even adopted many of the rhetorical forms common to British politics. For example, colonial political factions often referred to themselves as Whigs or Tories, though what those labels represented varied from colony to colony, and used language in their everyday political discourse (e.g., references to ''court'' and ''country,'' the ancient constitution, political liberty, and the rights of Englishmen) that Americans almost anywhere in the New World would immediately recognize. Thus a Georgian traveling from Savannah to Boston could stay at any tavern along the way and join an after-dinner discussion on issues of the day without needing any special knowledge of the local political climate.

Yet in spite of this growing commonality of experience in the eighteenth century, each of the colonies retained its own unique political culture. By the middle of the century the patriotic object of most Americans was increasingly the colony in which they lived. Most colonists still, of course, swore allegiance to and in many cases retained strong emotional ties to the Crown or other British institutions such as the Church of England. But by the 1750s, if you asked someone from Williamsburg or Alexandria or Richmond what his country was, he would most likely reply, "Virginia."

Washington's first appearances on the public stage, as a commander of Virginia militia and later as a volunteer staff officer serving the British expeditionary force commanded by General Edward Braddock, illustrate this shift in patriotic focus. Washington continually sought the approval of his superiors by emphasizing service to his country, service that he distinguished from service to "His Majesty" the king. For example, when he wrote to Virginia's governor to recommend a particularly meritorious subordinate, Washington took special note of the young man's "readiness to serve his Country. (which I really believe he looks upon Virginia to be)."[5] Even more dramatically, to obtain his country's favor Washington was willing to expend much of his personal energy, embark on reckless military enterprises, and engage in an embarrassingly self-interested pursuit of personal honor.

Most of these early events in Washington's public career, as well as much of his developing political character, can be best understood in the context of Virginia's politics of deference. Virginia society exhibited a remarkable degree of cohesion in the 1700s. This was particularly true of the privileged class that dominated political, economic, and religious affairs.[6] To be sure, Virginia's aristocrats were not exempt from the personalistic squabbles, backbiting, maneuvering, and petty corruption that arise within any ruling elite; but they presented a united front on many of the big questions of their day, e.g., support for a hierarchical social order and preservation of the colony's increasing political independence from the Crown in local affairs.

More so than in any other colony most Virginians, including the small farmers, artisans, and merchants who were not part of this ruling aristocracy, acknowledged the legitimacy of these arrangements—a social consensus that provided Virginia with a remarkably long period of political stability. The quiescence with which most Virginians accepted the leadership of this elite suggests that the state's politics of deference was premised on more than the traditional claims made by feudal aristocracies. On the contrary, Virginia's aristocrats rarely argued that deference was due them because of some nobility of birth, or because God had established a Great Chain of Being that required obedience from those of low birth, or because they were naturally endowed with wisdom and talents that exceeded those of ordinary men. Instead, they believed that it was their right and obligation to provide political leadership for their communities because of four interconnected principles: land, wealth, independence, and self-government. Much of George Washington's nascent political ideology can be attributed to his growing understanding of how these four principles defined Virginia's politics of deference.

An Avarice for Land

In Virginia, at least, land was the principal measure of a man. Social and political standing were determined in large part by the acreage that one was able to accumulate, or by the trappings of the estate that one established on one's lands. Washington's attitude toward acquiring land bordered on the obsessive and was governed by three principles: buy (or claim as a bounty for public service) as much good land as possible, trade poor land for better land whenever possible, and never sell land for cash.[7]

If this acquisitive fever for land was an obsession, though, it was an obsession common to several generations of Virginia's wealthiest and most talented citizens. What accounts for this extraordinary focus on land as the currency of accomplishment and reputation? One clue can be found in the rise of "Country" ideology; its ascendance explains much about the political culture of Virginia in the 1750s. Ironically, to speak of "Country" as a distinctive, well-integrated political ideology is a bit of a reach. Those who were identified with the Country way of thinking in Virginia, like their counterparts in Britain, often did not agree on a specific set of political principles and public policies. Indeed, for many of the important issues of the day (e.g., western expansion, internal improvements, taxation) Country ideology provided little or no guidance. On those issues Virginia's political and social elite was far more likely to divide on the basis of where one lived (the Tidewater area or the Northern neck) or who one knew (friends of the governor in Williamsburg or friends of the magistrate in one's home county) than on the basis of ideological factions. Instead, it is more useful to think of the Country ideology as a set of attitudes or fears about political power and its consequences held in common by many Virginians.[8]

Most of the Virginia gentry shared a firm commitment to socially conservative principles. They believed in stability and social order. They promoted private property and the rule of law as the linchpins of that social order. They insisted that only the "right sort of men" were entitled to govern. And, perhaps most importantly, they conceived of the community as an organic whole whose collective interests could best be advanced by social harmony, institutional cooperation, and a heavy infusion of public virtue.

Where Country men departed from their more "metropolitan" brethren was in their respective notions about which sorts of political arrangements were best suited to promoting these values.[9] If, indeed, the devil is in the details, Country men saw far too much of the devil in distant Williamsburg or in even more distant London. Each viewpoint conceded that institutions such as the monarchy and the church were necessary instruments for maintaining the social equilibrium. But where "metropolitans" were satisfied to entrust the protection of their cherished rights and privileges almost entirely to the good offices of the king and his ministers (or, in Virginia, the governor and his councillors), Country men retained a profound skepticism toward political power. Like most conservatives they believed power exercised an almost irresistible allure for the self-interested and ambitious. Human character was surely capable of virtue, public-spiritedness, and disinterestedness, but, just as surely, it ought not to be tested too severely.

Corruption was the watchword of Country ideology. Political power, especially centralized power, was a corrupting vortex that, like a great sun, sought to bring all into its orbit. Even when acting for good purposes, such as maintaining the social cohesion and harmony deemed essential to a virtuous community, those in power would tend in time to enrich their own authority by coopting all who might oppose them.

Corruption would inevitably ensue. The virtue of prominent citizens would be eroded by offers of government positions (e.g., tax collectors, magistrates, councillors) or by offers of charters and franchises granting oligopolistic economic privileges to a few favored fellow travelers. To assure the continuing loyalty of these placemen, they had to be provided for. Meeting those demands meant a greater and greater burden on the people, especially those within the landed gentry still loyal to Country principles, and a greater and greater loss of the liberty that wealth and social station were intended to promote. All forms of government, whether monarchical, aristocratic, or mixed (no one seriously spoke of democracy as a legitimate option—it lacked all of the conservative qualities noted earlier), were subject to these same corrupting tendencies. Even a government populated by erstwhile Country men could not long prevail against the centripetal forces of political power. Indeed, for this reason alone Country ideology can be thought of more as an ideology of opposition than as a philosophy of governance.

Fear of corruption, then, best explains the linkages between land, wealth, independence, and self-government that characterized the Country ideology and the politics of deference in which Washington was steeped. Land, especially the possession of vast quantities of land, was at the heart of the Country ideology. Country proponents' concern, one is tempted to say avarice, for land was not rooted in the sort of romantic agrarianism often ascribed to the Jeffersonians. Theirs was not an endorsement of "sweat of thine own brow" industry as a builder of character. (By that criterion, the slaves, indentured servants, and tenants who worked the land and constructed the great estates were the most virtuous members of society!) Washington, at least, never took seriously the claim that the land was endowed with mystical properties that imbued those who worked it, or possessed it, with a kind of liberty that mere tradesmen or men of money could never understand, much less enjoy.

Rather, Washington and many of his fellow Virginia aristocrats had a more functional regard for land. Land was, first of all, a constant. It was not subject to the changing fortunes of paper money inflation, royal mercantile policies, the loss of political favor, or the decline of one's skills through age or poor health. The whims of public taste or the interdependent and therefore unreliable nature of business enterprises seemingly posed no threat to the great landowner.

This preference for "realty" over "personalty" can be seen in Washington's paternal concern for John Parke Custis.[10] Washington had developed a deep and abiding affection for his wife's son, but he was constantly vexed by "Jacky's" poor head for business. When Custis determined to sell a substantial portion of his landed inheritance, Washington implored him not to. But Custis persisted and his stepfather finally assented, though not before Washington pleaded with his stepson to reinvest the money in other land, because "lands are permanent, rising fast in value, and will be very dear when our Independancy is established, and the importance of America better known." Money, on the other hand, "will melt like Snow before a hot Sun, and you will be able to give as little acct. of the going of it."[11]

There was a self-deluding quality to this notion of land as a symbol of economic and therefore political independence. Scorned though it was, money was still indispensable in building a proper Virginia gentleman's estate. Most of the trappings of the good life had to be imported and usually could only be purchased with cash. Unless one was engaged in land speculation, mere possession of land, then, was not enough. It had to generate money. Thus young Washington, striving within this deferential culture to attain the honor and recognition that he so deeply craved, had to manage his lands with an eye toward productivity—productivity sufficient to generate hard cash.[12]

Ironically, the prices Washington got for his tobacco, wheat, corn, and hemp were often disappointing. He complained to his London agent, hinting that the "pitifully low" prices at which they sold his "Sweet-scented Tobacco" were the result of inattention to his interests rather than the fickle fortunes of the market.[13] In truth, Washington, like many of his planter friends, was periodically in debt. From time to time a few were even ruined. Wealth in land did not automatically provide the wherewithal needed to maintain the lifestyle expected of a Virginia gentleman. But most Virginians *believed* that land was the most sure sign of wealth and personal success, and in the end that is what really matters.

The Virtues of Disinterestedness

Wealth in land was central to Country ideology because of its political as well as its economic and social significance. Deference was due to Virginia's landed gentry because their wealth provided them with a quality essential to opposing corruption—disinterestedness. Many of these well-educated aristocrats had read Mandeville's *The Fable of the Bees*.[14] Its protoliberal philosophy suggested that the pursuit of private interests (Mandeville referred to it as "vice") might, if properly directed, be a means of improving the public welfare—an argument that should have been well received in a society structured on commercial expansion and a seemingly boundless appetite for acquiring land. Virginians admired virtue and went to great lengths to be seen as virtuous in the eyes of their peers. So the temptation of the fable is obvious. If true virtue could be attained by blurring the distinctions between pursuit of private advantage and contributions to the community interest then surely one could, to employ a phrase not in the Founders' lexicon, have one's cake and eat it too. Self-aggrandizement could be clothed in the garments of public virtue.

Interestingly, though, Mandeville was not highly regarded by his American readers.[15] We recognize the language of Mandeville's fable more readily today than Washington would have. The language of self-interest and individual enterprise is *our* language. The vocabulary of private consumption and limited state regulation is *our* vocabulary. Washington and his contemporaries still used the language of classical republicanism to define "interest."

To the Virginia aristocracy of 1750 all men had interests. Men could no more ignore their passions, lust, ambitions, and avarice than they could avoid eating or drinking. It was, therefore, no sin to pursue one's self-interest. But in addition to these private interests there was a separate, identifiable public interest. Just as individuals had to be self-interested in order to prosper and even survive, the commonwealth (or public good) demanded that its collective interest be served. It was understood, in the language of classical republicanism, that only those who were "disinterested"—that is, those who could at least temporarily set aside their own self-interest—were capable of acting in ways likely to promote the commonweal. To act disinterestedly, in fact, was the sign of true virtue and honor for a citizen.[16] It was part of their conservative world view, however, that only those with substantial property and wealth or, in Virginia, land were good candidates for exhibiting such virtue. Their wealth and social standing gave them an independence—an ability to view things from above the hurly-burly of self-interested factions—that no person of lesser means could maintain for long. Those with little money or property lacked this independence. All men naturally had interests, but ordinary men were especially susceptible to having their public responsibilities seduced by the serpent of corruption.

Paradoxically, disinterestedness was the manifestation of a different kind of self-interest. Fame and glory were aspirations, or interests, of a peculiar kind because they could be attained only by acting on behalf of the public interest. Fame's special allure was that it converged with classical notions of the virtuous republican widely held by the Virginia aristocracy. Today we view fame as a by-product of notoriety. Michael Jordan is famous, as are Madonna, Dan Rather, Lee Iacocca, and even high-profile criminals like Bernhard Goetz. But in Washington's time fame meant something very different from mere celebrity. Fame was an accolade reserved for those who had served their fellow Virginians with distinction. To call a Virginian virtuous was to pay him the greatest tribute to which a citizen could aspire. Not wealth, not piety, not education, not even property could elevate a man's standing in the community so much as the exhibition of public virtue. To achieve that fame a man had to demonstrate his willingness to promote the well-being of the community without regard for its effect on his private interests.[17]

Fame's close cousin was glory. Here virtue could be exemplified by one who sacrificed, or at least set aside, personal fortune in order to protect the interests of king and country. The more heroic the service, the greater the glory. The greater the responsibilities one exercised (e.g., the higher one's rank), the greater the glory. The greater the personal interest (fortune) that one risked on behalf of the common interest, the greater the glory.

A Monument to Corruption

Even though fame and glory were the most admirable of human achievements, self-conscious *ambition* for fame and glory offered great opportunities for corruption. The outward manifestations of fame and glory—political office and military rank—could often be obtained on the cheap, without providing the tangible evidence of genuine public service that virtue demanded. Where government or a ruling faction was able to dispense rank and office without regard to real merit, corruption was sure to follow.

Washington's own early career was as much a monument to this corruption as it was to genuine virtue. In his youth Washington was only a peripheral member of the Virginia gentry. His landholdings were modest, and he had no immediate prospects for increasing them. Had he entertained any political ambitions, of which there is little evidence, his status as a minor planter would have severely constrained them. But Washington was not without powerful friends. The greatest landholder in Virginia was Lord Fairfax, whose family Washington had become closely connected to through his brother Lawrence's marriage to Anne Fairfax and by Washington's subsequent friendship with George William Fairfax and his wife, Sally. When Washington was only twenty-one, with little military training or experience, Fairfax used his substantial influence to garner a colonel's commission for him in the Virginia regiment. This was the highest rank available to a colonial officer in Virginia.

In short, Washington's first entry onto the public stage did not result from any display of exemplary public service or virtue. Rather, it came unmerited from political patronage—the very sort of seductive corruption Country ideologues warned against. Washington was not unmindful of the debt he owed the Fairfaxes and the governor for his quick, one might even say premature, elevation to a post sure to offer great opportunities for glory and status. Washington's letters to Lieutenant Governor Dinwiddie, Speaker of the House John Robinson, and the Earl of Loudoun, supreme commander of the king's forces in British North America, have an obsequious, toadying quality that goes beyond the normal deference and respect due to a superior. To Dinwiddie he wrote, ''nothing is a greater stranger to my Breast, or a Sin that my Soul more abhors, than that black and detestable one Ingratitude. I retain a true sense of your kindnesses, and want nothing but opportunity to give testimony of my willingness to oblige you, as far as my Life or fortune will extend.''[18]

Even more disingenuous were his entreaties to the Earl of Loudoun. Loudoun had arrived in Boston to coordinate the efforts of all His Majesty's forces in the colonies—regular army regiments, colonial troops, and militia. At this time (1757), Washington's military leadership had fallen under something of a cloud because of his inability to protect the frontier settlements from Indian raids. Dinwiddie, in particular, had become increasingly critical of his actions. In an effort to restore his reputation Washington decided to appeal directly to Loudoun, thus bypassing his immediate superiors, Dinwiddie and the Virginia assembly. He penned a lengthy summary of Virginia's military predicament to Loudoun before their face-to-face meeting. After chronicling his frustrations of the previous months he proceeded to lay the blame at the doorstep of Dinwiddie and the assembly. He was especially critical of the assembly's passage of a military code "in order (I suppose) to improve upon the act of Parliament . . . but such a one as no military discipline could be preserved while it existed."[19] What he neglected to tell Loudoun was that these were changes that Washington himself had remonstrated for again and again. The assembly seemed not always to fully comprehend Washington's situation or the specific nature of his requests. Thus, the irony of Washington's complaints was that he often got what he asked for, then discovered that it wasn't what he really wanted or needed.

There was ample blame to go around for the mess on Virginia's frontier, but Washington was especially sensitive, even thin-skinned, about his own reputation. He could never escape the tenuousness of his rank and its dependence on the patronage of others. Thus, he once again resorted to flattery of the most sycophantic and self-serving kind to attract the support of Lord Loudoun: "Your Lordship's name was familiar to my ear, on account of the important services performed to his Majesty in other parts of the world. Do not think, my Lord, that I am going to flatter; notwithstanding I have exalted sentiments of your Lordship's character and respect your rank, it is not my intention to adulate. My nature is open and honest and free from guile!"[20] Indeed!

The pursuit of rank and its perquisites was a constant quest for Washington. Not only were his superiors blistered by his complaints, but letters to his friends railed against his ill-treatment. First, he complained that his initial appointment made him subordinate to a more senior colonel of, in Washington's mind, less merit. (The issue became moot when the infirm Colonel Fry died before assuming command.) Then he was offended at the common colonial practice of divorcing colonial commands from those of the regular British army. In particular, when a contingent of British troops commanded by a Captain McKay was attached to Washington's regiment, McKay refused to acknowledge Washington's command. He argued that permanent royal commissions were superior to temporary colonial commissions regardless of relative rank. McKay's view was correct according to the military protocols of the day, but Washington nevertheless complained that colonial officers "have the same Spirit to serve our Gracious King as they have" and that the inferiority of colonial rank "will be a canker that will grate some Officer's of this Regiment beyond all measure to serve upon such different terms when their Lives, their Fortunes, and their Characters are equally . . . as . . . exposd as those who are happy enough to have King's Commissions."[21] Washington offered the grievance on behalf of all colonial officers, but his stake in the complaint was more personal than corporate.

Rank, then, was important to Washington. Rank symbolized one's relative position within Virginia's deferential society; it cemented one's social and political reputation; and it was the outward manifestation of a person's capacity for honor. Without rank and the preferments that went with it, no honorable gentleman could be induced to serve his country. When Washington complained that the pay of Virginia's officers was insufficient, that it was "the most trifling pay, that ever was given to English officers," and that it amounted to little more than an ordinary soldier's pay, his complaint was not really concerned with considerations of equity and a living wage.[22] No colonial officer saw the military as providing enough income to enter the gentlemanly life. Most served in the hope of attaining glory, not for the wages. Rather, Washington believed that the worth of one's rank, and therefore its standing in the community's eyes, was measured by the differences in compensation between officers and the enlisted ranks, as well as by the relative pay among the officers. If a colonel in Virginia were paid less handsomely than a British captain, the implication was that the Virginia colonel was less capable of offering useful service to the king.

That social status, not rank or pay, was the crux of Washington's persistent whining can be seen by his offer, made on several occasions, to serve as a volunteer rather than accept the ignominy of a rank or pay beneath his station ("if you think me capable of holding a Commission that has neither rank nor emolument annexed to it; you must entertain a very contemptible opinion of my weakness").[23] Eventually he did serve as a volunteer aide-de-camp to General Braddock when he correctly perceived that no permanent British officer was obliged to acknowledge the superiority of any rank bestowed by a Virginia commission, a circumstance unlikely to provide Washington the honor he craved. Ironically, it was Washington's heroism under fire during Braddock's ill-fated campaign that first brought the young Virginian to the notice of his countrymen. Popular accounts noted with approval that he had served out of love of glory and country rather than for mere pay.[24] To one who aspired to be a gentleman, what greater honor could there be than this?

The purpose here in documenting Washington's early military career is not to suggest that his self-serving maneuverings for rank reveal serious flaws in his public character. Such behavior was hardly unusual or even exceptionable in his time. Instead, these episodes are symptomatic of a political culture in which social rank was everything. So long as one's rank or station in life was *dependent* on the patronage of someone else, status anxiety and political unreliability were sure to be the result. The landed aristocracy in Virginia, therefore, claimed the right to exercise power on behalf of the whole community because they lacked for none of the inducements (land, wealth, position, status) that corruptible government could offer an ambitious young man like George Washington.

When Washington acquired ample lands through his marriage to Martha Custis his unseemly supplications about rank and pay disappeared. Never again did Washington write in the conniving, ingratiating way that permeates these early letters. Never again did he need to rely on patronage and political intrigue for the public honors he craved. As an *independent* landed gentleman of considerable means he was now prepared to play his part as a disinterested, virtuous public citizen.

Washington's startling change of demeanor between the 1750s and the 1770s—from a hot-tempered, fawning, reckless, young court pleader to a reflective, somewhat diffident, and politically astute leader—has baffled many of his biographers. Douglas Freeman, for example, resorted to near-mysticism in his account: "Many other men matured after 25; Washington was almost transformed."[25] But the notion of independence provides a simpler explanation. So long as Washington remained on the periphery of the great circle of Virginia's planter aristocracy, the honor and fame that he so desperately craved was dependent on currying the favors of others. He shaped his actions, whether noble or self-serving (and most would say there is ample evidence of both), to conform to the expectations of men who were socially and politically his "betters." But once he obtained the independence provided by land and wealth his betters became his peers; Washington was now self-confident enough to pursue his own notions of public virtue free from the need to please the governor or his patrons. The Virginia elite's claim to political deference was based on the superior virtue to be found in a wealthy, landed, independent, and therefore disinterested aristocracy. Washington's early career exemplifies the validity of those notions.

A Constitutional Revolutionary

How, then, could the politics of Virginia culminate in revolution? How could this aristocracy, full of the collective arrogance of social place and privilege, committed to the most conservative principles of good government, and allied in defense of the rule of law and of property, come to the point of actually leading an armed struggle against the Crown—that very symbol of order and stability? One could understand Massachusetts. There, the discontents of a rising petite bourgeoisie explained much. But Virginia?

There is no simple answer to the question. We cannot presume that the factors that animated each of Virginia's patriots were identical. People can unite toward a common goal, including even a political revolution, with quite different grievances and aspirations in mind.[26] We can say with some confidence that Virginia's aristocrats became increasingly self-assured and increasingly protective of the economic and political liberty that their wealth and independence had purchased. Collective assessments that purport to explain more than that, however, tend to gloss over the shifting motives and political ends of individual Virginians.

But the principles that governed one Virginia aristocrat, George Washington, can be clearly discerned. His words and deeds on the eve of revolution reveal a Patriot with a well-defined sense of purpose and a coherent, if limited, set of political ideas. Added to the opposition instincts nurtured by the Country ideology he shared with many of his fellow Virginians was now a strong strain of constitutionalism. These pre-1775 constitutional principles go far in explaining how a man so politically and socially conservative, so much an embodiment of the aristocratic Virginia culture, could become a committed revolutionary. Indeed, it is clear that at least at the beginning of the struggle with Britain, Washington defined his role almost exclusively in constitutional terms.

As early as 1765, during the Stamp Act crisis, Washington had written his wife's British uncle that the act was an *"unconstitutional* [my emphasis] method of Taxation" and a "direful attack upon their Liberties."[27] At the time, the comment was something of a throwaway. The bulk of the letter contained a carefully reasoned critique of colonial economic matters and Washington's confession of bewilderment at Parliament's insistence on pursuing such obviously counterproductive policies. At this point, he still perceived the growing conflict between Parliament and the American colonies as a misunderstanding. If their British brethren could more fairly appreciate the practical realities of living in and doing business in America, then surely they would refrain from this burdensome heavy-handedness.

But subsequent events led Washington to abandon this accommodationist stance. The Stamp Act had only signaled the opening volley in a parliamentary effort to assert its sovereignty over British trade and taxing policy. Subsequent salvos included the Quartering Act, the Declaratory Act, the Restraining Act, and the Townshend Acts. These continued "misunderstandings" made no sense, unless one concluded that Parliament knew very well what it was doing and that, sooner or later, the center would induce the periphery into a closer orbit.

For most of these prerevolutionary years Washington was a member of the Virginia Burgesses. And as he listened to the arguments of Patrick Henry and George Mason and observed developments in Virginia and other states he began to realize that the "troubles" were not the result of a mere misunderstanding. They resulted, instead, from increasingly divergent, and incompatible, visions of the Anglo-American constitution. Like many other Americans, Washington had come to believe that the American version of that constitution was morally and legally superior to Parliament's version. If the "old" constitution were not restored, by resistance if need be, then the "new" (parliamentary) constitution would strip away the rights and liberties that independent Virginians like himself had grown accustomed to.

We can see the outlines of Washington's emerging constitutional ideas in his efforts on behalf of the Fairfax Resolves. In the summer of 1774 Washington actively campaigned for these Resolves and even may have helped to write them.[28] The resolutions, although amounting to little more than unofficial statements of community outrage, asserted in highly provocative terms that the abuses heaped upon the people of Boston threatened the very fabric of American constitutional liberties and would be resisted, with force if need be, by Virginians as well as New Englanders. The resolutions also included several specific provisions (e.g., no trade with Britain until she nullified the acts directed at suppressing the people of Boston, a day of fasting in support of their Massachusetts brethren) that, while voluntary, were intended to mobilize the citizens of Fairfax County—in 1774 already a hotbed of sedition.

Particularly revealing of Washington's constitutional principles at this time was a series of letters he wrote to Bryan Fairfax, the son of his old friend, William Fairfax. Given the closeness between the two families there is no reason to think that the ideas that Washington expressed here were disingenuous or in any way intended as propaganda or public posturing. It pained Washington to oppose the interests of his great benefactors, but he candidly revealed the heart of his revolutionary convictions and why those principles dictated his support for the opposition cause.

His more conservative friend entreated Washington to go slowly, to continue to work toward some accommodation with the British. But Washington had had enough of appeasement. "Have we not addressed the Lords, and remonstrated to the Commons? And to what end?"[29] Now was the time for men of true "virtue and fortitude" to be put "to the severest test."[30] Further petitions to the king and his ministers were not only futile, they were becoming increasingly unmanly. "What hope then from petitioning, when they tell us, that now or never is the time to fix the matter? Shall we, after this, whine and cry for relief, when we have already tried it in vain? Or shall we supinely sit and see one province after another fall a prey to despotism?"[31] To Washington, honor and virtue demanded that Americans not kowtow to the sort of intimidation that had become business as usual for the king's ministers.

Washington's conservative sensibilities had been especially shaken by events in Virginia that immediately preceded the Resolves. The colony's royal governor had refused to accept any more ''insulting'' petitions from the Burgesses and had dissolved the assembly. Now, not only was Virginia's government prevented from dealing with pressing legislative matters, the assembly had been dissolved before it could authorize any appropriations. With no source of revenue, the governor closed the courts. To a law-and-order constitutionalist like Washington this abdication of official authority threatened the very security of Virginia society. ''This Dissolution . . . has left us without the means of Defense'' against the ''cruel and blood thirsty Enemy at our backs [the Indians].''[32] Washington believed that the one unalterable principle of Britain's ancient constitution was that the sovereign was obliged to do all in his power to protect the people and assure their safety. The closure of the courts was to Washington a monstrous violation of that constitutional obligation. Colonial subjects were thus not only justified in submitting meek and respectful petitions to their king for a restoration of these fundamental constitutional principles, they were bound by honor and virtue to ''assert our rights, or submit to every imposition, that can be heaped upon us, till custom and use shall make us as tame and abject slaves, as the blacks we rule over with such arbitrary sway.''[33] A people who willingly acceded to the corruption of their constitution deserved subjugation.

Fairfax was perplexed by Washington's confident insistence that the patriotic opposition was grounded in constitutional principles. If the Patriots could be satisfied with arguing that Parliament had no power to lay revenue taxes on the colonies (as opposed to taxes related to trade or collective defense), then Fairfax would be happy to join their cause. This principle of no internal taxation had an honorable lineage and had served the colonists well in many of their previous constitutional disputes with Parliament. But Fairfax saw something new and frightening in the Resolves. The second resolution suggested that Parliament had no authority in the colonies; that it was the king in conjunction with his colonial assemblies, not Parliament, that exercised constitutional authority in America. Fairfax could not bring himself to such a sweeping repudiation of the old order. Pointing out that the Patriots' claims went beyond the ''no taxation without representation'' argument, he appealed to Washington's conservatism: ''Whatever we may wish to be the case, it becomes good subjects to submit to the Constitution of their Country. Whenever a political Establishment has been settled, it ought to be considered what that is, and not what it ought to be. To fix a contrary principle is to lay the Foundation of continual Broils and Revolutions."[34] Conform this second resolution to good constitutional principles, Fairfax intimated, and the patriotic cause would have more supporters.

Washington refused to take the bait. His support of the Resolves and other patriotic activities was based on two interconnected principles. First, he believed that objection to all parliamentary taxation really *was* the core of America's constitutional case. If taxation by Parliament were a legitimate part of the constitutional scheme, then resorting to further petitions made perfect sense. As subjects of Parliament they would only be entitled to appeal to the wisdom or paternal sentiments of their lawful representatives—"we should then be asking a favor, and not claiming a right."[35] But Washington was confident that Parliament had no such constitutional power. "I think the Parliament of Great Britain hath no more right to put their hands into my pocket, without my consent, than I have to put my hands into yours for money."[36]

Second, when Fairfax appealed for loyalty to the "constitution of our Country"—a request calculated to appeal to one so steeped in the language of Virginia's politics of deference—he was surprised to find that its effect was quite the opposite of what he expected. Washington insisted that he *was* loyal to the constitution of his country, but, as noted earlier, Washington, like a generation of his fellow Virginians, had come to define his country as British Virginia, not Britain itself. The constitution that he wished to defend was not the British Constitution, but the constitution between the king and the colonial governments created by royal charter. The people of Britain were represented by the British Parliament, and they were subject to its laws and its taxes. But the people of Virginia were represented in the king's domain not by Parliament, but by the Burgesses. Parliament, by this view, had no more sovereignty over the internal affairs of Virginians than it did over the French. Thus it was the extraconstitutional aggressions of Parliament, not the actions of Virginia's dissidents, that undermined the "constitution of our country." It was Parliament that sought to coerce the people to give up their ancient constitutional rights and privileges; it was Parliament that abolished the charter government of Massachusetts (and by doing so threatened to impose unconstitutional arrangements on all of the colonies); it was Parliament that sought to undermine lawful order at the point of a sword. Washington believed that his actions were dedicated to saving the constitution and to conserving the political and legal principles that had served his country so well.

Washington was a Patriot, but he was also still a conservative and a constitutionalist. For example, he opposed that part of the Fairfax Resolves that called for complete nonexportation of goods or revenues to Britain. Many Virginians, including himself, owed substantial sums to English merchants. Some had imported goods from those merchants on credit; others had already sold their tobacco or grain through their agricultural agents in Britain who were now awaiting shipment. But the resolutions urged Virginians not to export anything to Britain, including money to pay lawful debts, until the miseries of Massachusetts were resolved satisfactorily. Washington thought this recommendation unjust and dishonorable. Like many Patriots, he insisted that Britain respect the ancient rights to life, liberty, and property. Washington's dilemma was that he took those admonitions seriously. Just as the British government could not use "the troubles" as an excuse to diminish the property rights of Patriots, neither could legitimate opposition activities by Americans absolve them from an obligation to respect the property rights of British citizens: "Whilst we are accusing others of injustice, we should be just ourselves; and how can this be, whilst we owe a considerable debt, and refuse payment of it to Great Britain, is to me inconceivable."[37] A true Patriot loved not just liberty, but honor and virtue as well; and honor demanded that a man deal justly and fairly with everyone. The high ground of virtue seized by the Patriots would be undermined, Washington thought, if their resistance could be portrayed as little more than a handy excuse for avoiding their obligations. Patriotism could then be characterized by its opponents as merely the pursuit of self-interest, not the disinterested defense of sacred principle that would do honor to a virtuous gentleman.

Washington's conservatism and commitment to constitutional principles can also be observed in his attitude toward political independence in 1774. He was troubled by reports that certain Massachusetts men were set on nothing less than total independence and, to that end, were terrorizing good men of property who did not share their dire assessment of affairs.[38] Washington's understanding of the constitution at that time assumed that each state would maintain its connection with the Crown. Thus, it was right and just (and constitutional) to resist parliamentary usurpation of colonial rights and privileges (the rights of Englishmen in America), but like most Americans he was reluctant to renounce the historic relationship between the king and his loyal subjects that characterized the "old" constitution he wished to conserve. He assured his correspondent that "no such thing is desired by any thinking man in all North America; on the contrary, that it is the ardent wish of the warmest advocates for liberty, that peace and tranquility, *upon constitutional grounds* [my emphasis], may be restored, and the horrors of civil discord prevented."[39]

Nevertheless, he insisted that the constitutional crisis had been precipitated by Parliament. Patriots were merely reacting to this provocative assault on the political rights and liberties guaranteed them by the "old" constitution. Restoration of that constitution was the goal of many within the Patriot opposition. And Washington made clear his feeling that if Britain persisted in its efforts to impose this new political order (Washington hesitated to call it a constitution) by intimidation or force, then these same loyal, constitutionalist Patriots might well come to the conclusion that Britain no longer wished to govern under a constitution and that Americans would, of necessity rather than preference, have to go their own way. Thus, while Washington could claim that few of his fellow Virginians were advocates of independence from Great Britain, he also warned that "this you may at the same time rely on, that none of them will ever submit to the loss of those valuable rights and privileges, which are essential to the happiness of every free state, and without which, life, liberty, and property are rendered totally insecure."[40]

Independence was a foreboding step for a man of Washington's conservative predilections. But it was a step he was clearly prepared to take if Britain continued in its obstinate behavior. An honorable constitutionalist had to have a constitution to honor—ordered liberty was impossible without one. And if Britain refused to live up to her own constitution, then Washington was willing to join a revolution to defend a new one. In this sense, George Washington was both truly conservative—and truly revolutionary.

As the conflict with Britain escalated and Washington prepared to move onto the national stage, it is useful to remind ourselves that his vision for the continent was essentially grounded in the political values of his native Virginia. He believed in self-government, but only by the "better" sort of men—men who, through the education, experience, and independence provided by their property, could act disinterestedly on behalf of the community. He evinced many elements of the deferential culture and Country ideology common in his social circle: a belief in virtue as the measuring stick against which all governments and citizens were evaluated, an abiding distaste for corruption, a love of liberty (especially liberty in property), the desire for a social order based on harmony and a sense of one's place, and a deeply felt need for a constitution to serve as the glue that held society together.

As his experiences in public life expanded his political horizons beyond the woods of bucolic Mount Vernon to the courts of the Old World, his constitutional vision took on, of necessity, more complex layerings. Virginia politics, rich though it was, could never fully prepare him to cope with all the problems inherent in building a new nation and a new constitutional order. Yet while Washington was to add many new rooms to his constitutional edifice, he never abandoned the foundation he had laid in Virginia.

2 / The Republican General

The War for American Independence was the second great influence on the development of George Washington's public philosophy.[1] One measure of the degree to which Washington was consumed by prosecuting and winning that war is that from June 15, 1775, when Congress selected him to serve as the Continental Army's commander-in-chief, until December 23, 1783, when he formally returned that commission to Congress, Washington took not a single day off. That seemingly mundane observation tells us much about his dedication to the cause. It was common for his fellow officers to take extensive furloughs to look after private business, to recuperate from injuries and fatigue, or sometimes just to remove themselves for a while from the dreary shabbiness of the army's encampments. Washington was compelled to grant these furloughs, some of them coming even in the midst of critical military campaigns, in order to maintain the morale of the officer corps. But Washington never furloughed himself. For eight and a half years he stayed at the helm, dealing daily with the grinding frustrations of leading a Patriot army, mediating the never-ending disputes over rank, pleading to Congress and the states for food and clothing for the army while imploring those same troops to be patient as they starved, reviewing the verdicts of hundreds of general courts-martial, trying to settle squabbles between his troops and local civilians. Occasionally, he even fought the British. But for most of those eight and a half years Washington was far more the administrative captive of headquarters routine than the daring field general of American legend.

Yet despite the camp drudgery and political infighting that caused most of his subordinates eventually to resign, Washington stayed on. When victory finally came, he was rewarded with honors far beyond those of even his great hero-ideal, Cato.[2] The merest rumor that Washington might be passing through town was sufficient to trigger spontaneous celebrations in Pennsylvania and New Jersey as enthusiastic and adulatory as any in Virginia. These sentiments toward Washington ran so deeply into every stratum of American life—rich and poor, farmer and shopkeeper, frontiersman and mechanic, Northerner and Southerner—that his critics (and there were still plenty who believed his military abilities were overrated and his politics suspect) felt it necessary to hold their tongues lest they be deemed unpatriotic.

This near-deification of Washington can be attributed in large part to his standing as the one national symbol of the struggle for independence. Other Americans were more central in leading the political movement toward independence. Indeed, while Washington was sympathetic to the movement's goals, he remained a peripheral player at best; his leadership of the army prevented any substantial involvement in revolutionary politics. Yet because he stood at the head of the one constant, visible symbol of the independence effort, the Continental Army, many Americans came to see Washington as the embodiment of all those complex aspirations that represented the Revolution.

Americans hailed Washington as the great soldier of liberty—a man whose exceptional patriotism and virtue assured final triumph over a corrupt king's mercenaries. Nor was his fame confined to unthinking Americans brainwashed by the propaganda of revolutionary pamphlets. Even many contemporary British accounts spoke favorably, if begrudgingly, of his character and military talents.[3] In short, his standing as the "Father of the Country" (and that phrase was already being widely used in pamphlets and sermons) derived from his wartime leadership, not from the popularity of his political beliefs. Few Americans were even aware that Washington was developing a distinctive vision of an American republic. For most it was enough to know that he was a Patriot.

Yet he *was* developing an increasingly sophisticated understanding of the kind of constitutional government that he felt most comfortable with. The influence of Virginia was still evident in his thinking, but the war both expanded and sharpened his understanding of what worked and, as often as not, what did not work. There is a striking measure of the impact of the war on his thinking. Of the thirty-seven volumes in the Fitzpatrick edition of Washington's collected writings, his wartime output, about 8 1/2 years worth, begins with volume 3 and ends in volume 27. By contrast, the eight years of his presidency fill less than six volumes. There is, to be sure, much in these wartime volumes of little interest to the political detective: marching orders, assessments of the military situation, recommendations regarding the color and style of continental uniforms, the daily issuance of passwords and countersigns. But the Washington who accepted command of the army in 1775 was not the same Washington who in 1783 anticipated a quiet retirement to the life of a Virginia gentleman. The war was a stern teacher, and Washington learned much.

Deference and Democracy

George Washington was a thoroughgoing republican both before and after the war. Unfortunately, that description does not tell us very much about his political ideas. By 1776 nearly everyone who supported independence (and even some who did not) called himself a republican.[4] Indeed, the term was virtually synonymous with the equally generic "patriot."[5] There were certain core values that all republicans shared: an aversion to hereditary and arbitrary power, government by popular consent, the promotion and protection of liberty (especially liberty in property), a commitment to constitutionalism and rule of law, a notion that government existed to provide for the common interest of the community, and the encouragement of public virtue. But endorsement of these general sentiments was not enough to bridge the ocean of political differences that separated republicans. Thomas Paine was a republican, but so was John Adams. Thomas Jefferson, Alexander Hamilton, Gouverneur Morris, John Dickinson, George Mason, Richard Henry Lee, Benjamin Rush: they all considered themselves republicans. There is a long tradition in American politics whereby the distinctive qualities between and even within ideological camps are blurred and intermingled. Republicanism in the late eighteenth century was no exception. It was something of a muddle even to its adherents.

The important question, then, focuses not on whether George Washington was a republican, but rather on what *kind* of republican he was. For example, republicans of all shadings believed that constitutional government could only be legitimated through the instrument of popular consent. But how much consent was required? By what means? And what were the instruments through which popular consent was registered?

Revolutionary-era republicanism was a house of many rooms; Washington was firmly situated within its conservative wing. If we compare Washington's republicanism with Abraham Lincoln's later model of democratic government ("of the people, by the people, and for the people") we can say that Washington readily acknowledged Lincoln's first principle—consent clearly had to come from the people. Even in class-conscious Virginia, Washington accepted the notion that the people's representatives had to be chosen by a broadly based electorate. And he most certainly endorsed Lincoln's third principle—republicans of almost all ideological shadings believed that public virtue was to be obtained by pursuing the interests of the whole community. Government was not to exist for the benefit of a privileged few. But the second of Lincoln's principles was anathema to Washington. He could never bring himself to accept the notion that all men were equally endowed with virtue, experience, and disinterestedness. Political liberty was a natural right and therefore held equally by all men; but political virtue was neither inherent nor held in equal measure by all men. Some men were clearly more virtuous than others and could more safely be entrusted with the people's business. Government by the self-interested, uneducated, propertyless masses might be democratic, but it could not be republican.

One of the best illustrations of his conservative republicanism can be seen in his relationship with his troops. He regularly made distinctions between his officer corps and the ordinary soldiers that underlined his hopes for the former and his fears about the latter. Popular mythology often portrays the American soldier as a receptacle for all of those virtues we wish to see exalted in times of national crisis. The American soldier (the "GI") is motivated by duty, loyalty, and patriotism. He is willing to sacrifice everything, including his life, to defend the principles underlying the "cause," whether it be independence, union, making the world safe for democracy, or rolling back the tide of communism. Washington harbored no such ideals about the capacities of the ordinary soldier. On the one hand, his addresses to his troops included the usual encomiums to the virtues of a Patriot army: men fighting for their liberty were morally superior to men who fought only for the king's silver; each soldier had the opportunity to earn the approbation of his fellow countrymen; the commander-in-chief was confident that every man would do his duty with great spirit. That was the official Washington.

Privately, and to Congress, he was far more skeptical of the virtues of the ordinary soldier. In a protracted war (and Washington was convinced early on that the conflict would be a long one) patriotism could go only so far in eliciting good behavior from soldiers. "When men are irritated, and the Passions inflamed, they fly hastely and chearfully to Arms; but after the first emotions are over, to expect, among such People, as compose the bulk of an Army, that they are influenced by any other principles than those of Interest, is to look for what never did, and I fear never will happen."[6] He believed that only a professional army under the firm discipline of competent officers could defeat the British in such a protracted war. Obtaining that discipline among liberty-loving American soldiers would be no mean feat: "Men accustomed to unbounded freedom, and no controul, cannot brook the Restraint which is indispensably necessary to the good order and Government of an Army; without which, licentiousness, and every kind of disorder triumphantly reign."[7]

Upon his arrival in Boston in 1775 he was shocked at the behavior of the Massachusetts provincials. For an aristocrat reared in a culture of deference, these New Englanders seemed far too democratic and far too willing to erase the social barriers between gentlemen and the masses. He reported to some of his Virginia friends that the army was composed of "an exceeding dirty & nasty people."[8] They exhibited an "unaccountable kind of stupidity" that one could only expect from the "lower class of these people."[9] He was astounded at the degree of "familiarity between the Officers and Men" in the New England regiments, convinced as he was that such leveling was incompatible with discipline and good order.[10] And he took special exception to the common practice among New England units of having the enlisted men elect their officers. Washington's conservatism would not permit him to envision an army in which republican virtue was equally distributed among all citizens, especially among the rabble of the common soldiery.[11]

A good soldier, in Washington's view, was not necessarily one filled with the spirit of liberty. State militia units, objects of Washington's scorn for much of the war, often served as prime examples of this belief. He observed that militiamen were too "accustomed to unbounded freedom" and thus resentful of the kind of control and discipline necessary for a successful long-term campaign.[12] Bravery and spirit were surely desirable, but in a soldier these qualities were a double-edged sword. The spirited soldier could as easily be turned to mutiny (a problem that nagged the Continental Army from 1779 until the end of the war) as to the defense of his country. Washington believed that only training and discipline could create an army for the long haul. To this end he encouraged the "Activity & Zeal" of his officers while asking only for "Docility & Obedience" from the common soldiery.[13] Militiamen who bore arms when enemy troops approached their homes and farms but returned to their civilian lives as soon as British battle flags disappeared over the horizon could never be docile and obedient. They could never be the foundation of a permanent Continental Army. Washington wanted to command soldiers deferential to his vision of the common good, not a band of freedom-loving individualists bent on protecting their own interests.

Washington's hierarchical vision of military society becomes even more apparent when we contrast his attitudes toward the ordinary soldiers with his expectations for and treatment of his officer corps. While in his view enlisted men were crude, ignorant, and motivated largely by their immediate self-interest (poor metal indeed for the making of military steel), officers ought to be "men of character" actuated by "principles of honour, and a spirit of enterprize."[14] The key word here is *ought*. Washington did not presume that rank alone endowed men with these virtuous qualities. New England's elected officers were his principle case in point: "Their Officers generally speaking are the most indifferent kind of People I ever saw. I have already broke one Colo. and five Captain's for Cowardice . . . there is two more Colos. now under arrest, & to be tried for the same Offenses."[15] In Washington's estimation there could be no democracy in the organization of a republican army, for democracy took no account of the social values he most cherished: order, discipline, virtue, and most of all, deference.

Washington's idealized officer corps was to be composed principally of gentlemen. As in Virginia, gentlemen had the sort of social and economic independence that permitted them to look beyond their immediate self-interest toward the public good and freed them to pursue a more noble aspiration than wealth—glory. This did not mean that all

gentlemen were inherently virtuous. Without appropriate inducements they could be just as susceptible to the allure of money and position as the privates under their command. The endless disputes over
rank served to remind Washington of the capacity of some of his officers to act out of "interested" motives. He expressed profound disappointment over this unseemly behavior. Even when he pointedly questioned some of the complainants' commitment to the cause, words
clearly intended to embarrass the aspirants, his appeals were usually
futile.

Nevertheless, he remained committed throughout the war to building a cadre of elite officers—young men (mostly) who shared a common commitment to private honor and public virtue, young men who
were committed equally to independence and to republican government and who were as loyal to Congress as they were to Washington
himself. With such men, he hoped to shape this undisciplined "democratic" army into an instrument for winning the war and for protecting
the liberties of all the people. He envisioned his officer corps as nothing less than an example to the world of the kind of leaders that a republican society could nurture.

By and large Washington's officers were a remarkable group, as astute
politically as they were enterprising militarily.[16] Many would provide
the core of national political leadership for a generation after the war.[17]
But it would be a mistake to think that this outcome was in any way
foreordained or natural. While the bulk of the officer corps were "Gentlemen and Men of Character," such men were still not immune to
"low and dirty acts."[18] They had families to feed, careers to pursue, and
interests to promote. Washington was no idealist when it came to human nature. He understood that it was one thing to promote a regard
for public virtue in his officers; it was quite something else to expect
virtue to survive for long unrewarded. To ask officers to serve in the
public interest without regard for their private fortunes was acceptable
(fame, after all, would provide the real compensation for service); but it
was unrealistic to expect them to accept diminution of their personal
fortunes so that other, more "interested" citizens could better themselves at the officers' expense.

Washington came to realize that virtue alone was too shaky a foundation upon which to construct a republican army; the notion of interest
was too deeply imbedded in American character to simply wish it away.

Experience taught Washington that virtue could only be promoted on a broad scale if it could be reinforced by interest. If there was one principle that Washington retained throughout the remainder of his political life it was this: *In republican government, virtue must always be tied to interest.*

To create this cadre of officers, then, Washington first had to recruit and retain the best sort of men—men whose military talents and political loyalty would bring honor upon them all. Rank (and its perquisites) was one means of announcing the public worth of his officers. The commander-in-chief regularly petitioned Congress to be frugal in giving out rank. Washington believed that for rank to be respected and pursued by men of character, it had to be scarce.[19] Appointing too many generals not only confused an already chaotic command structure, it devalued those who already held the rank. He also protested against the proliferation of foreign officers. Washington conceded that many of them were capable, especially as engineers and artillerists, in military specialties in which American officers had limited experience. However, he argued that these commissions limited the opportunities for American officers and pointed out that, in the long run, the republic would be better served by promoting ''home-grown'' officers.[20] In addition, he defended the practice of allowing officers to use soldiers as personal servants against criticisms that the practice was inconsistent with the egalitarian spirit of the Revolution.[21] Finally, whenever the military judgment or the character of any of his officers was assailed Washington came to their defense, even when he confided privately that, in a few cases, the public criticism was probably deserved. Washington did all of these in order to establish a sense of common cause and *elan* among his American officers.

But to have a republican officer corps one more thing was necessary. Washington had to attach the individual and collective interests of the officers to the success of the republic and its principal agent, the Congress; he had to somehow make the national interest congruent with their own. The usual appeals to high principle (e.g., patriotism, honor, duty, liberty) could only go so far. Officers had to be convinced that there was something in the war for them—that its successful conclusion would serve them individually at least as well as it served the larger community. As Washington put the problem to Congress: ''The large Fortunes acquired by numbers out of the Army, affords a contrast that gives poignancy to every inconvenience from remaining in it. The Officers have begun again to realize their condition and I fear few of them can or will remain in the service on the present establishment."[22] Washington recommended several measures during the course of the war intended to improve the morale of his officers: pay increases for each rank that corresponded to pay scales in the British Army, a provision for a bounty to be paid in western lands, a pension for their wives and families, payment of all officers' wages in specie rather than the deflated, virtually worthless Continental currency, a promise of half-pay for life (a proposal that was later modified to provide a lump sum equal to full pay for seven years payable upon demobilization of the army). Washington believed that the more "respectable" the standing of an officer, the more he could be relied upon to act properly. "I have not the least doubt, that until Officers consider their Commissions in an honorable, and *interested point of view* [my emphasis], and are afraid to endanger them by negligence and inattention, that no order, regularity, or care, either of the Men, or Public property, will prevail."[23]

The message-within-the-message lurking in most of these appeals was that the mass of ordinary soldiers was a cauldron of bubbling resentments whose vitriol was directed as often at Congress and the states as it was at the British. Washington was too thoroughly conservative (and probably too politically astute as well) to deliberately play the "army card," but he often hinted to his friends in Congress that the only thing that prevented soldiers from looting the countryside and endangering the liberty of the people was the firm, guiding hand of the officer corps. Trying to purchase competent, loyal officers on the cheap was a policy guaranteed to undermine all of the aspirations of the great republican experiment.

By contrast, Washington opposed giving economic incentives to the soldiery as a whole. He believed the practice tended to break down the distinctions between officers and enlisted men, strained public credit beyond the breaking point, and, perhaps most dangerously, raised the expectations of the soldiers without any real prospect of making good on those promises. "[Raising soldiers' pay] is a doctrine full of dangerous consequences, and which ought not to be countenanced in any way whatever. . . . All that the common soldiery of any country can expect is food and cloathing. . . . The idea of maintaining the families at home, at public expense is peculiar to us; and is incompatible with the finances of any government."[24] Washington was right, of course. The depleted national treasury could only have met the soldiers' demands with promises as worthless as its paper currency. Nevertheless, the anecdote again highlights the elitist, deferential quality in Washington's notion of republicanism. A republic could not long survive by relying solely on the virtue of its citizenry at large. It was likely to prosper only when the better sort of men could be induced to defend public virtue against a jealous, self-interested, liberty-loving people. Republicanism could only be constructed from the top down, not from the bottom up.

Republicanism and a Professional Army

A capable officer corps was also important because it was the principal instrument through which Washington could demonstrate the trustworthiness of a republican army. His problem was as much practical as it was political. Many Americans believed that the war could be effectively prosecuted by militia and by provincial troops loyal to the state governments. They envisioned the sort of conflict that has characterized many twentieth-century wars of liberation. In this model a large colonial army of occupation could be defeated not by a decisive set-piece engagement fought in traditional European fashion, but rather through continual harassment by small bands of irregulars who would skirmish with the enemy, destroy their lines of supply and communication, and then melt away into the forests and farms of the hinterland. These bands would avoid direct combat with the enemy's main forces whose advantage in discipline and firepower would probably overwhelm them. It was supposed that this guerrilla-style warfare would frustrate the British, both in the field and at home, and eventually bring them to the view that the war was unwinnable.[25]

Washington thought this scenario was absolutely wrongheaded. Guerrilla tactics might be appropriate for a peasant people who would have little to lose from a long, drawn-out conflict and the social upheaval that would inevitably ensue. But Americans were neither a peasant society nor a society that lacked indigenous social and political institutions worth defending. Once again revealing his conservative sentiments, Washington believed that Americans had more to lose from a long, populist war than did the enemy. In his view British troops could occupy the main commercial centers of America (New York, Philadelphia, Charleston, and Boston) almost at whim. Marauding by guerrilla bands might inconvenience the British, but it could never dislodge them. If this occupation went unchallenged by a concerted American effort, the effect on the American economy would be disastrous. As economic disruption deepened, American support for the war would falter. The treasuries of state and local governments, dependent on continued economic expansion, would be strained beyond their capacities. Patriot governments would be faced with a Hobson's choice—impose confiscatory and decidedly "unrepublican" taxes on the people in order to pay for a long *and* expensive war, or issue increasingly worthless paper currency, permanently undermining public confidence in the great republican experiment.

Washington believed that irregular forces simply lacked the military capability to remove the British. Pester them? Make life difficult for them? Inflict significant casualties on them?—Yes. But remove them?—No. He believed Britain's superior economic resources could outlast the states' in any war of attrition. "In modern wars the longest purse must chiefly determine the event. I fear that of the enemy will be found to be so. . . . Their system of public credit is such that it is capable of greater exertions than that of any other nation."[26] A long war, even one fought by small irregular units, would eventually pit an increasingly constricted American economy against this British leviathan and so impoverish the states that either the war effort would collapse or the newly emerging republican governments would be transformed into something far less worthy of defending. Washington believed that only the defeat of British arms in the field could induce Parliament to consider peace; only an army built on a permanent establishment under centralized leadership could pose that credible threat to the British forces. For more than six years his entreaties to Congress, often delivered in the midst of mutiny and starvation, carried the same urgent message: Stop dissipating valuable resources for temporary expedients (e.g., bounties for state militia); raise funds sufficient to establish and maintain a professional national army large enough to drive the British Army from American soil once and for all. Not only would the war be won more quickly, it would be less expensive in the long run. Moreover, a quick victory would not jeopardize nascent political institutions or existing American social structures—a matter of no little consequence to a conservative revolutionary like Washington.

Washington's formula for victory seems orthodox enough today. Use a superior, well-trained army to destroy the enemy's military capabilities and peace will quickly follow. Yet many Americans feared their own army nearly as much as they feared the British; opposition to Washington's insistence on a professional national army was widespread. The very idea of such an army ran counter to widely accepted republican principles. Ironically, suspicion of the Continental Army was particularly deep-rooted among the same Country ideologues who had so influenced Washington's early political views.[27]

After an early period of enthusiasm for the notion of a national army, these older suspicions reemerged.[28] First, a standing army would have to be fed. Moreover, because it was a permanent establishment the army would have to be fed and clothed even when not fighting—a condition more common to the life of the Continental Army than even Washington would have liked. Some republicans feared that provisioning such a large body for an extended period inevitably would strain the public treasury. As the gap between the soldiers' expectations and the public's pockets widened, the army would be tempted to extort satisfaction from the government, e.g., "Tax yourselves to feed us adequately or we will take what we need from the property of the citizens." Republican government thus would be lost to the predations of its nominal defenders.

A second republican concern about a professional army focused on the "loaded gun" scenario. Many Americans believed that armies were blunt instruments capable of directing their force against whatever objects were chosen for them by their officers. Well-trained, well-disciplined troops loyal to their military commanders might prove an irresistible temptation to a clique of officers bent on pursuing their own political agenda. Cromwell's army was still near enough in the historical memory of most Americans to make them cautious about a permanent military establishment. In addition, many of these critics believed that there were always enough corruptible men in government, even in a republic, capable of enlisting the army as leverage for obtaining political advantage, thereby substituting force for the republic's commitment to government by reason. State leaders were especially concerned that the Continental Army would look to Congress for support, thereby strengthening the hand of centralist elements within the Confederation.[29]

Finally, many republicans feared the rigid hierarchy of obedience within a military order. They understood the military necessity of a clear command structure, but they worried about its potential for mischief if the army remained large and permanent. The social logic of any military organization was to look to its head, particularly to its general officers. Republicans thus believed that armies were innately susceptible to monarchist tendencies. Soldiers offering up to their general the mantle of Caesar was a standard element in republican demonology.[30]

Washington was thus faced with a war on two fronts. He not only would have to defeat the British, he would also have to convince American skeptics that the army, and its commanding general, could be trusted to behave as good republicans. This was no simple task. Both publicly and privately he implored the army, and especially his officers, to be paragons of virtue, to prove their worth in the defense of liberty, and to show that a Patriot army could endure more hardships than mercenary troops.[31] But Washington recognized that wishing for virtue was not enough.

The Deferential Dictator

Washington could not guarantee the conduct of every one of his soldiers. The army was too scattered and command too decentralized to expect strict adherence to his orders. Yet his own thirst for fame and glory ("The approbation of my Country is what I wish. . . . It is the highest reward to a feeling Mind; and happy are they, who so conduct themselves to merit it."[32]) was inextricably tied to the army's behavior. Washington therefore tried to impress upon his fellow officers that deference to civil power would do as much to establish the army's reputation as any number of battlefield victories. If the army were found wanting politically, then no amount of military success could retrieve its honor, or Washington's.

Washington attempted to ensure that at least his own republican credentials were above reproach. If his conduct could serve as a model of republican rectitude and respect for civilian authority, then perhaps the army and its officers could be persuaded to govern their own behavior accordingly. As a standard for his political conduct (his military conduct was something on which he took no instruction) Washington looked to his commission from Congress. The commission stipulated that his office was awarded to him by "The Delegates of the United Colonies" and that he should "observe such orders and directions, from time to time, as you shall receive from this, or a future Congress of these United Colonies, or committee of Congress."[33] His authority was neither personal nor grounded in his military rank; it derived from Congress and the states—from the people's representatives.

The commander-in-chief went to great lengths to prove his republican reliability by deferring to civil authorities on many matters whose ambiguity might well have justified his own independent action. People submitted all manner of petitions to him, assuming that as commander-in-chief he had great political influence. Some asked for civil appointment to the army; some asked to pass through British lines; some sought to do business with the army. Even his own officers brought their personal and political grievances to him. In every instance in which even the remotest question of civil authority was raised, Washington passed the petitions on to Congress or to the appropriate state governor. The cumulative impact of Washington's perspicacity in these matters was tremendous. Jealousies and suspicions toward Washington gradually melted away.

Among the many incidents that illustrate Washington's deference to civil authority, three stand out. In July 1776, shortly after independence had been declared, the British Admiral Lord Howe sent emissaries to Washington with hints of a peace offer. But his first message to the American commander-in-chief triggered an almost comical dance of protocol. Howe addressed his letter to "George Washington, Esq." Washington had instructed his aide to accept no communication unless Washington's official title was acknowledged. After much diplomatic to-and-froing the British aide returned with a letter addressed to "George Washington, Esq., &ca, &ca." Again the letter was refused. Finally, Washington was asked whether "His Excellency, General Washington" would receive Lord Howe's adjutant. Washington consented.[34] Some might be tempted to attribute this episode to Washington's self-conscious vanity, but there was much more at stake. Washington, in consultation with his staff and other officers, recognized that Howe might try to deal directly with Washington and bypass Congress altogether. If the army could be induced to make a separate peace, Congress would be left without the military arm on which the Revolution depended. By refusing to accept any British overtures to him that did not formally recognize his *congressional* authority, Washington made it clear to his British counterparts that his leadership of the army was not personal, but constitutional—it was delegated to him by Congress. Moreover, the only constitutional body in America entitled to entertain peace offers was Congress, not a general in the field. When Washington emphasized that all such proposals had to be directed to Congress, the British commander dropped the whole idea. Throughout the episode Washington had insisted on defending Congress's prerogatives. His actions on their behalf went far in establishing Washington's credentials as a military man sensitive to republican values. Congress subsequently endorsed his conduct in the following resolution:

> That General Washington, in refusing to receive a letter said to be sent from Lord Howe, and addressed to "George Washington, Esqr." acted with a dignity becoming his station; and therefore, this Congress do highly approve the same, and do direct, that no letter or message be received, on any occasion whatsoever from the enemy, by the commander in chief, or other, the commanders of the American army, but such as shall be directed to them in the characters they respectively sustain.[35]

The second set of incidents illustrates his equally respectful posture toward the civil powers of the states. A problem endemic to all military campaigns is that soldiers and civilians do not always behave like brethren in the same cause. Contact with the army often leads many civilians to perceive soldiers as violent beasts who trample their fields, butcher their cattle, and molest their persons. Soldiers often hold civilians in equally low regard, viewing them as ungrateful wretches who profit from the misfortunes of the army and seek to gyp the common soldier at every opportunity. The Continental Army was no exception. Soldiers often stood accused of "outrages" and "violences" against local citizens. In every instance, Washington ordered the accused soldiers to be turned over to the civil authorities of the state in question. In a few cases he went further, dispatching a personal letter to the Governor expressing his willingness to support state authority in such matters.[36]

Nor did Washington make any distinctions between officers and soldiers. When General Benedict Arnold was summoned by the state of Pennsylvania to answer certain charges about his official conduct as military administrator of Philadelphia, Washington told the mercurial Arnold, one of his favorite field commanders, that he would have to respond to those accusations in a civilian court. Moreover, when Joseph Reed, the president of Pennsylvania, complained that Congress would not subpoena any of the military witnesses in Arnold's case, Washington assured him that Congress's intercessions were unnecessary. "Where any person in the military line is summoned . . . it is *my* duty to order their attendance, which I shall of course do. With respect to these therefore the interposition of Congress would be unnecessary."[37] Privately, Washington professed that many of these prosecutions were unfounded; but individual justice was less important than establishing a pattern of good republican conduct and respect for the rule of law by the army's commander-in-chief.

What most cemented Washington's reputation as a republican general, however, was his conduct during the periods of his "dictatorship." Twice, in 1776 and again in 1777, Congress was compelled to flee Philadelphia to escape the advancing British troops. They feared that such an ignominious abandonment of the seat of national government might signal the collapse of the war effort, or at least the part of it directed by Congress. To prevent this, Congress, in each instance, delegated extraordinarily broad powers to General Washington. These powers were not merely administrative; they authorized Washington to "direct all things relative . . . to the operations of war."[38] Washington, in essence, was expected to assume powers and responsibilities closely akin to those typically granted to Roman dictators. In republican Rome a dictator was appointed only in a time of military crisis and was empowered to do whatever was necessary to save the nation from military defeat. His political power was plenary and unlimited during the duration of the grant. After the military crisis was alleviated the dictator was expected to return his extraordinary powers to the republic, or so Roman practice anticipated. In Roman republican theory, dictatorship was never intended to be anything more than a temporary expedient to preserve the fabric of civil society.[39] Yet looming behind even the most benign of dictators was the specter of tyranny and the abolition of republican principles. Many Americans, including most members of

Congress, shared those misgivings about dictatorship. Thus, the willingness of Congress to endorse such a dangerous course is a mark of just how desperate those times were.

Ironically, these periods of dictatorship only served to further cement Washington's republican credentials. His political ideals had insisted all along that a proper respect for the rule of law was the cornerstone of any constitutional order truly worthy of the name. Granted these vast powers by a panicky Congress, Washington chose to exercise, or, in several noteworthy cases, *not* exercise, these powers in ways that stamped him as a man with more than a token commitment to republicanism.

For the most part Washington continued business as usual. He forwarded items for Congress's consideration even though it was fully within his own authority to deal with them. For example, when the army's chief surgeon suggested a plan providing for military hospitals Washington responded that "altho' the Congress have vested me with full powers . . . and I dare say would ratify whatever appointments and Salaries I should fix; yet I do not think myself at liberty to establish Hospitals, upon such extensive plans and at so great an expense, without their concurrence."[40] On another matter, his dictatorial powers should surely have given him summary power to deal with desertion. After all, desertion was a problem uniquely military. Yet while Washington assumed power under martial law to deal with deserters in eastern Pennsylvania, where civil government was in chaos, he refused to extend that power into those areas in New Jersey that fell within his seventy-mile military zone of authority. He assured Governor William Livingston that New Jersey's powers were quite sufficient to deal with deserters; he would gladly defer to civil authority wherever it was well established.[41]

"Dictator" Washington did commit an excess or two that elicited controversy. At one point, he ordered all of the farmers within seventy miles of his headquarters to harvest, thresh, and deliver their grain to him according to a specific timetable. Farmers who refused would have their grain seized by the army. Instead of a fair price for their grain, these recalcitrants would be paid only the price for straw.[42] Several months earlier he had proclaimed that all persons were to take an oath of loyalty to the United States within thirty days or be deemed "enemies of the American States."[43] Both of these actions raised criticism—criticism that focused primarily upon Washington's supposed insensitivity toward personal liberty. The controversy stung Washington sufficiently that while he never formally recanted the loyalty-oath order, he chose not to enforce it. Most American leaders understood the difficulties that inspired Washington to issue each proclamation. In the end, nothing came of the criticism.

Caution was more typical of Washington's dictatorial periods than enterprise. If anything, the experience made him warier than ever of exercising political power through the military arm. When one of his most enthusiastic allies in Congress, Gouverneur Morris, proposed that the army be empowered to levy direct assessments on the city of Philadelphia during a period when the city was under military protection, Washington was quick to disassociate himself from the plan: ''A measure of this sort, in my judgment would not only be inconsistent with sound policy, but would be looked upon as an arbitrary stretch of military power, inflame the country as well as city, and lay the foundation of much evil.''[44] It may seem a paradox that the chief advocate of a centralized professional army should also be the nation's most visible example of republicanism in action. Yet that is precisely what Washington's ''dictatorship'' established.

Disorder in the Ranks and the Doctrine of Civilian Supremacy

Congress came to trust Washington's republicanism. But their fears about the threat of a professional army were well-founded. As the war lumbered on, many soldiers came to believe that Congress deliberately starved them, that it refused to clothe them, that it failed to pay them on time, that it allowed their wives and families to be impoverished and dispossessed. Congress, they believed, did not trust its army and therefore avoided doing justice to its soldiers.

Many officers shared those resentments. But they added to them the sort of grievances brought on when men of means and social standing are subjected to unaccustomed slights and inconveniences. When they were paid at all (which was infrequently) the amount was often deemed insulting. Promised bounties of money and land seemed little more than congressionally summoned phantoms. The appointment and promotion of officers generated continual internecine squabbling, made worse in the eyes of some officers by the clumsy favoritism found in Congress and most of the states. Men and officers alike grew increasingly restive toward revolutionary political leadership, believing that it was unwilling or incapable of dealing with the army in good faith.[45]

By early in 1780 Washington was warning Congress that without redress of some of the army's grievances he could not guarantee its conduct. Men had not been paid for five months. There were widespread food shortages. The spirit of mutiny was in the air, and Washington pleaded with Congress to offer some sort of palliative. Without relief the army might disintegrate or, worse, loot the countryside.[46]

His warning was prophetic. On January 1, 1781, men of the Pennsylvania Line killed an officer, armed themselves, and began marching in the general direction of Philadelphia. The soldiers had the usual complaints: no pay, poor food, and resentments against some of their officers. They also believed that their enlistments, originally for three years but later extended by Congress for the duration of the war, had expired. Without more pay or a new enlistment bonus they believed they were free to go home. Why they chose to march in military formation toward the capital and not merely desert individually to their homes (a fairly common practice) is not clear. The soldiers seemed not to have had any explicit political agenda or plan of action. Their precise motives remain unknown even to this day, but their imminent arrival struck fear into Congress and the state legislature of Pennsylvania. Washington urged Congress to do what it could to address the mutineers' grievances (they were, after all, grievances common to most of the army). But he also assured the delegates that he and the other officers were firmly aligned with the constitutional government and would do what they could to suppress the fever of mutiny.[47] He exercised restraint in dealing with the Pennsylvanians and through the mediation of some of their officers eventually convinced them to give up their enterprise.

But within two weeks another mutiny erupted, this time in the New Jersey Line. Washington now reversed his course entirely. Rather than patiently letting passions subside, rather than using the event to underscore his own continued effort to secure a commitment from Congress for a resolution of the army's rightful complaints, rather than negotiating with the mutineers, Washington chose this time to suppress the uprising with decisive force. He authorized General Robert Howe, head of the detachment sent to quell the disturbance, to demand outright surrender by the mutineers and encouraged the summary execution of its leaders as an example to the troops.[48]

We might attribute Washington's iron-fisted reaction to panic. Perhaps he feared that he was losing control of the army, that once again unseen forces were seeking to undermine him and replace him as commander-in-chief. Perhaps he felt that the second mutiny was a sign that many troops had lost confidence in his ability to serve as their representative to Congress and were now prepared to make their case directly. Whatever his private thoughts, the mutinies provided Washington an opportunity to once again demonstrate his commitment to conservative republican principles.

As a conservative, he could not allow the army to violate every good order of discipline. The Revolution could not be permitted to descend into anarchy. Washington's decisive action, especially regarding the New Jersey mutiny, assured the political leadership in Congress and the states that Washington and his still-loyal officer corps could be trusted to keep the everworrisome soldiery on a short leash. As a republican, he could not allow the military to subvert civilian government. No republic could exercise genuine self-government while casting anxious glances over its shoulder at its military leaders. As sympathetic as Washington was to the genuine sufferings of the army he could never condone using it to undermine republican government and the rule of law. This would be a betrayal of his oath to Congress and also of his own reasons for supporting the Revolution in 1775.

Many of his officers shared similar sentiments. But not all. In 1782 Washington received a private letter from Colonel Lewis Nicola. In bemoaning the plight of the army Nicola wrote in terms much like those used by Washington in his own petitions and memorials to Congress and the states; Washington's headquarters received similar letters almost daily. But Nicola went further. He offered a proposal that so alarmed Washington he immediately struck off a reply. Nicola had argued that the government was in such disarray that Washington should, with the support of the army, seize control of the reins of power.

This war must have shewn to all, but to military men in particular the weakness of republicks. . . . [I]t will, I believe, be uncontroverted that the same abilities which have led us, through diffi-culties apparently unsurmountable by human power, to victory and glory, those qualities that have merited and obtained the uni-versal esteem and veneration of an army, would be most likely to conduct and direct us in the smoother paths of peace.[49]

Nicola was not the only American with monarchist leanings, nor would he be the only American ever to suggest a Caesarian role for Washington.[50] But such views ran counter to the republican hegemony that dominated revolutionary discourse. Nicola seemed to grasp this truth and conceded that "republican bigots will certainly consider my opinions as heterdox, and the maintainer thereof as meriting fire and fagots." He pleaded with Washington not to disclose his plans to any-one else.[51]

It was a quixotic gesture on Nicola's part. Washington had not the slightest intention, even in those moments when he most despaired over the weakness of America's governments, of being an instrument of republicanism's failure. He was unsure of the noble experiment's fu-ture (indeed, he was to be haunted at times throughout his public life with private fears that republicanism was an unattainable aspiration), but if it was to fail it would not be because of treason by himself or the army. But Washington feared that Nicola's offer cloaked a more wide-spread erosion of support for constitutional government among other officers. (Nicola, later seeking to salvage his reputation, admitted as much.) He enclosed his reply to Nicola the same day—an urgency in-tended to impress Nicola and whatever supporters he might have among other junior officers with Washington's unequivocal feelings. Washington invoked classical images of military virtue and honor sure to have an effect. Acknowledging their justifiable grievances he insisted that "no Man possesses a more sincere wish to see ample justice done to the Army than I do, and as far as my powers and influence, *in a con-stitutional way* [my emphasis] extend, they shall be employed to the utmost of my abilities to effect it, should there be any occasion." But he then implored that "if you have any regard for your Country, con-cern for yourself or posterity, or respect for me, to banish" any further discussion of such "painful," abhorrent, mischievous ideas.[52]

Washington's reply elicited a series of nervous, face-saving missives from Nicola, but we simply do not know whether Nicola shared the commander-in-chief's views with like-minded officers. We do know that dissatisfaction among the officer corps continued to ferment. Late in 1782 feelings were running so high that the officers, with Washington's tacit permission, were sending emissaries to Congress. (It is likely that Washington wanted to impress upon the delegates that he was not crying wolf, that the officers' discontents were, if anything, more profound than he had represented.) These discontents became so acute that by the following spring a conspiracy emerged against the republic so convoluted that, to this day, we cannot be certain of the intentions of all of the players.[53] But it culminated in a moment of high drama at Washington's Newburgh headquarters where the general made clear in one final gesture of republican heroism that no honorable army could permit itself to threaten, much less replace, the duly constituted authority of the people.

Washington had long lobbied Congress to recognize the special situation of the officer corps. Washington believed that most of these men had suffered severe economic hardship. Not only were they required to support themselves and their retinue from insufficient salaries that were rarely paid, they also resented the effects that service had on their private fortunes and their hopes for future prosperity. A provision of half-pay for life had been enacted by Congress in 1780, but by the winter of 1782–83 many officers doubted Congress's capacity to raise the revenues necessary to pay the pension. Peace was expected any day. What, the officers grumbled, would prevent Congress from dissolving the army and then, free of the looming presence of an armed soldiery, reneging on the half-pay promise? Perhaps, some officers thought, the army ought *not* to stand down unless concrete assurances were made. Many officers now insisted that a lump-sum payment be substituted for the less certain promise of half-pay for life. Washington thought the idea a good one, but he was reluctant to push Congress and the states too far. He had, after all, been a delegate to Congress himself and understood the political difficulties that the national legislature faced. He cautioned his officers to be firm, but patient.

In March came the spark that kindled the final crisis of the war. A cabal of younger officers, probably looking to Horatio Gates for leadership, circulated a letter written by John Armstrong, Gates's aide-de-camp. The letter asked for a meeting of all field officers to discuss their standing grievances. Officers were encouraged to reject "moderation" and to consider "bolder" measures for dealing with Congress. Among the boldest of these measures was a suggestion that the army refuse to lay down its arms until its distresses were relieved: "What have you to expect from peace, when your voice shall sink, and your strength dissipate by division? When those very swords, the instruments and companions of your glory, shall be taken from your sides, and . . . [you,] retiring from the field, grow old in poverty, wretchedness and contempt?" Soldiers should not shrink from tyranny even if it cloaked itself in "the plain coat of republicanism." Make one last petition to Congress, but if it were rejected the army should pledge: "If peace, that nothing shall separate them from your arms but death: if war, that courting the auspices, and inviting the direction of your illustrious leader [the recalcitrants still hoped to attract Washington's support], you will retire to some unsettled country, smile in your turn, and 'mock when their fear cometh on.' "[54]

Washington immediately sensed that something "irregular" was afoot and called his own meeting of officers for March 15.[55] This move would allow him to control the agenda and give him time to ferret out the motives of the conspirators, some of whom he suspected were political figures seeking to use the army for their own as yet unknown purposes. Washington insisted on speaking first at the meeting and, by doing so, completely disarmed the incipient conspiracy. After attacking the author of the Newburgh Address for appealing to the "feelings and passions" of the soldiers Washington proceeded to take the same tack. Responding to the veiled threat of armed resistance against Congress, Washington pleaded that

> this dreadful alternative, of either deserting our Country in the extremest hour of her distress, or turning arms against it, (which is the apparent object, unless Congress can be compelled into instant compliance) has something so shocking in it, that humanity revolts at the idea. My God! what can this writer have in view, by recommending such measures? Can he be a friend to this Country? Rather is he not an insidious foe? Some emissary, perhaps, from New York [British headquarters], plotting the ruin of both, by sowing the seeds of discord and separation between the Civil and Military powers of the Continent?[56]

But the passion that Washington now appealed to was not the anger and frustration of a hungry, unappreciated army. Instead, he drew on the classical republican images that had so instructed his own life. He argued that threats such as those suggested by the address would "lessen the dignity" and "sully the glory" of the army. He implored the officers "as you value your own *sacred honor* [my emphasis], as you respect the rights of humanity, and as you regard the Military and National character of America, to express your utmost horror and detestation of the Man who wishes, under any specious pretenses, to overturn the liberties of our Country, and who wickedly attempts to open the flood Gates of Civil discord." The officers' perseverance in these difficult times might, instead, "give one more proof of unexampled patriotism and patient virtue."[57]

At the end of this brief speech Washington attempted to read a letter from a member of Congress describing that body's most recent good-faith efforts. Before doing so Washington fumbled a bit and then said: "Gentleman, you will permit me to put on my spectacles, for I have not only grown gray, but almost blind, in the service of my country."[58] The moment, by most accounts, left many of the officers in tears. The cabal disintegrated, and the meeting returned to the orderly business of planning the next petition to Congress.

The conspiracy had an air of unreality about it from the outset. The army probably would have dissolved rather than march as a unit into the wilderness. The state militias might have posed an effective rejoinder to any effort by the Continentals to extort money from the states. But Congress thought the threat real. Therefore, Washington's firm stand against military interference in civilian government has enormous constitutional significance.

In modern history the tradition of the "man on horseback" has a lineage and staying power at least as long as the tradition of constitutionalism. Revolutions begun for republican ends have often been undermined by the authoritarian, military means necessary to achieve them. Perhaps the American constitutional tradition was already sufficiently rooted that these recalcitrant officers would have found themselves cast adrift in a sea of republicanism whether Washington had acted or not. But many of the nation's leaders (including Washington) thought otherwise. They believed the very survival of republican self-government was a day-to-day proposition. Forced in its infancy to accommodate the coercive influence of its military arm, the American political system would have found it difficult to establish a workable constitution based on principles of republican self-government. For where there is a powerful, highly politicized military, there can be neither self-government nor a constitutional tradition. In this sense, George Washington's greatest, most lasting contribution to our constitutional tradition occurred years before his presidency—indeed, years before the federal Constitution itself.

National Interest versus Local Interest

The War for Independence, however, did not merely serve to reaffirm the conservative republican views that Washington held in 1775. There was at least one profound, immensely significant change in his thinking that came about as a result of his wartime experience. Orthodox republican ideology presumed that only small republics could long retain their virtue and commitment to liberty. Republican governments had to guard against the centrifugal forces of corruption, power lust, and centralism. A carefully crafted constitution could serve republicanism as a partial bulwark against these disintegrationist forces. But most importantly, republicanism required a vigilant people prepared to defend their individual and corporate liberties against the slightest insult. By this criterion the notion of a large republic was an oxymoron. Only in a small republic where the customs and traditions of the people were relatively homogeneous could one hope to generate a consensus about the meaning of virtue and common interest strong enough to stand fast against corruption. The likelihood that a republic could maintain itself *as a republic* diminished as its territory enlarged, as its population became more diverse, and as the variety of interests its people pursued expanded. Small republics lived in constant peril; but large ones were doomed from birth.[59]

There are a few signs that Washington was not wholly comfortable with this conventional republican wisdom before his appointment as commander-in-chief. During the war with France he had come to see that the military theater of operations should be continental, not provincial, in scope. He subsequently campaigned unsuccessfully to convince his superiors to give him military command over the entire western frontier—an appointment that would have expanded his authority beyond the boundaries of Virginia.[60] In addition, his extensive land-holdings in the West, as well as his frequent surveying expeditions to the frontier, had placed him within a circle of Virginia politicians with somewhat more enterprising, expansionist, westward-looking interests than their tidewater brethren.[61] Finally, Washington's early enlistment in the revolutionary cause suggests that like many other Patriots he was able to conceive that *some* interests could be held in common by *all* American political communities. The Fairfax Resolves, after all, found Virginia making common cause with Massachusetts in defense of the great republican principle of liberty.

Still, in 1775 many republicans of Washington's generation looked to their states as their country. They conceded that some sort of voluntary, limited confederation of states might be necessary to coordinate the war effort. Republicans were practical men capable of realizing that thirteen separate wars for independence—wars on behalf of thirteen distinct political cultures—were doomed to fail against an integrated, administratively centralized enemy. Republican virtue alone was no match for the British Army. Nevertheless, many Patriots tolerated Congress only because it was an expedient instrument for defending the sovereignty of the newly independent republican state governments. They trusted Congress about as far as they trusted the Continental Army. So long as those bodies worked to protect the interests of the states, they elicited grudging support. But there was enough lingering distrust of corruption and centralism to make most "small republic" advocates suspicious of even the slightest misstep by either body.

By the late 1770s Washington had come to view the world quite differently from these localist republicans. Because these localists dominated government in most of the states, the breach widened to the point that Washington lost almost all confidence in the supposed advantages of small republics. The careful deference to the states that had characterized the early years of his command came more grudgingly as his army's sufferings increased. He placed more of the blame for his difficulties on the lassitude and self-interest of the state governments than on the military resources of the British.

A single-minded vision governed his actions during the war. Only military victory over the British could bring the war to a successful conclusion; only a well-disciplined national army could accomplish that victory; and only constant support by all patriotic Americans could maintain that national army. No half-measures could carry the day. Whatever the merits of other republican principles, Washington believed they were secondary to the achievement of this greatest of all public goods—independence. Many Americans, especially many of his republican friends in the state governments, did not share his single-mindedness about the war and its purposes.[62] As their doubts increasingly obstructed Washington's goals, the general abandoned the mildly unionist sentiments of his early revolutionary days and became more and more an ultranationalist with a profound skepticism toward the virtues of state sovereignty. His grievances against the states read like a "long train of abuses."

He was especially discouraged by the unwillingness of the state governments to support the Continental Congress. Each state was supposed to send and maintain a delegation to the Congress. In the first years of the war attendance had been regular and the membership had included men of great reputation and ability: John Adams, Richard Henry Lee, John Dickinson, Benjamin Franklin, Thomas Jefferson. As the war dragged on enthusiasm for congressional service waned. The great debates about liberty and independence were behind them. Now came the hard business of administering the day-to-day details of the war effort. Many of the country's most distinguished men chose to forgo national service for state politics. More fame, not to mention greater rewards, was to be found in state government than in the distant, relatively ineffectual Congress. As a result, Congress often lacked a quorum precisely at those moments when Washington transmitted some of his most desperate requests. He complained to Benjamin Harrison, governor of Virginia:

the States separately are too much engaged in their local concerns, and have too many of their ablest men withdrawn from the general Council for the good of the common weal: in a word, I think our political system may, be compared to the mechanism of a Clock; and that our conduct should derive a lesson from it for it answers no good purpose to keep the smaller Wheels in order if the greater one which is the support and prime mover of the whole is neglected.[63]

He urged Harrison "to exert yourself in endeavouring to rescue your Country by . . . sending your ablest and best Men to Congress." Men of virtue and talent "must not content themselves in the enjoyment of places of honor or profit" in the states, "while the common interests of America are mouldering and sinking into irretrievable ruin."[64] But his pleadings went unheeded, and he was left to complain bitterly, "Where is Mason, Wythe, Jefferson, Nicholas, Pendleton, Nelson, and another I could name [Harrison himself]?"[65]

But there was worse. In Washington's eyes the states stood accused not only of nonsupport of Congress, but also of active interference with the national war effort. A Congress reluctant or unable to act, often because of reservations from particular state delegations, was one thing; state defiance of Congress (and, thus, the *national* interest) was quite another. Washington was cautious in his early criticisms of the states. They were, after all, his nominal superiors through the agency of Congress. But desperation eroded that caution until, by the end of the war, he openly called for measures to compel the states either to do their duty or give up some of their powers.

The problem that most vexed Washington was supply. During the course of the war Congress tried various methods for supplying the army. At first Congress levied assessments on the states and supplemented those funds by the issuance of Continental paper money. But the assessments fell short, and the printing press currency became virtually worthless. Congress then adopted a system of specific supplies. On its face, the system promised to reintroduce sound republican principles to the army supply process. There had been much criticism of the previous money-based system because it had been rife with corruption and the profiteering of middlemen—two traditional bugbears in republican demonology. Under the system of specific supply each state was expected to provide a requisition of a commodity (e.g., shoes, beef, gunpowder) at a given time and place. Specific supply was good republican theory, but it was bad military policy. When the requisitions were fulfilled, which was infrequently, distribution was chaotic. The system broke down in the periods between campaigns. Troops encamped for the winter were never able to obtain even the marginal levels of support provided them when they were in the field. State politicians successfully justified these actions with the usual anti–standing army rhetoric; but Washington thought it utterly dishonorable and against the common national interest for state legislators, many of them far from the smoke and grapeshot of battle, to starve the army at pleasure[66]: "If the States *will* not, or *cannot* provide me with the means; it is in vain for them to look to me for the end, and accomplishment of their wishes. Bricks are not to be made without straw."[67]

Incidents of delay or noncompliance by the states kept Washington's army on the brink of disaster and dissolution for much of the war. But the states' perfidious conduct did not end there. A few states even "appropriated" supplies for their militia that were intended for the Continental Army. In one instance, New York troops seized twenty-six bales of clothing intended for Washington's army. The commander-in-chief was livid: "This I look upon as a most extraordinary piece of conduct, and what involves me just at this time in the greatest difficulties; for depending upon that cloathing, I have not applied elsewhere and the troops in the field are now absolutely perishing for want of it."[68] These were strong words for a Virginia gentleman; in that era challenges to a person's honor less pointed than this often resulted in a duel.

Whatever the reality of the situation (and there is considerable evidence that most of the states strained mightily to meet their military obligations), Washington was convinced that state cooperation varied with the proximity of British battle flags. When enemy troops threatened the state, few efforts were spared to help the army. But when the British moved their operations elsewhere, local enthusiasm waned. Washington found himself in a curious, double-edged political game in which the army's status, and thus the national interest, was constantly jeopardized. State governors often failed to meet their supply obligations and recruitment quotas in large part because they feared the local political consequences of using their limited resources to benefit other states or a distant army.[69] Yet when the enemy posed an immediate threat to the state its leaders employed every art of persuasion to have Washington bring the Continental Army to its immediate defense.[70]

Even when the states sought to support the war effort Washington found their attempts inconsistent and meddlesome. Especially harmful to the cause, he believed, was the states' insistence on fighting the war as much as possible with militia. Washington was convinced that these "short-termers," raised by increasingly expensive bounties, were a detriment to the national interest. They were undisciplined, unreliable, and subject to recall by the states at times that made strategic planning extremely difficult for Washington and his staff. The militia, moreover, was usually better paid and better fed than the Continental troops—a condition that worsened the discontents already rampant within his army.[71] He also resented his lack of control over the militia. Although militiamen were nominally under his command, his options were constrained by state prerogatives and jealousies. He believed that militia could only be counted on to help in local campaigns; the merest inkling of a major campaign in a distant state sent many governors scurrying to recall their militia for the defense of "important local prizes."

The states also disrupted his unity of command. Authority, Washington believed, should be commensurate with responsibility. He complained of having "*powers* without the *means* of execution when these ought to be co-equal at least."[72] Because Washington was commander-in-chief of all the armed forces arrayed against the British, he naturally presumed that his authority would be fully competent to meet that enormous undertaking. He was wrong. He did not even have the authority to appoint his own officers or to recognize extraordinary merit with promotions. Washington often found himself saddled with generals too old, too independent, or too incompetent to do him much good, yet too politically well connected in their states for Washington to remove. This system caused endless wranglings and jealousies among the often better-qualified junior officers. Indeed, the seed of Benedict Arnold's treason is often attributed to his disappointment in not attaining a rank suitable to his military deeds in the war—a rank that Washington lacked the authority to give. Without political control over his most responsible lieutenants, how, Washington complained, could he be held responsible for the army's failures?[73]

The manner in which the Continental Army was raised added to Washington's command problems. Each state was asked to muster an annual quota of men for the army. In return for raising these troops, however, each state insisted on keeping its units intact (e.g. the New Jersey "line") rather than allowing their recruits to be dispersed throughout the Continental Army as needed. Moreover, the states insisted on the right to appoint all of the officers for their lines, just as they did for their own militia. Thus Washington was faced with achieving military success with an army that was three armies in one: Continental troops recruited directly by Congress or by Continental officers, troops raised and organized by the state governments as separate units under Continental command, and state militia subject to perfunctory recall by their states. As Washington commented to one of his old colleagues, "If in all cases, ours was *one* Army, or *thirteen* Armies allied for the common defence, there would be no difficulty in solving your question [about the appointment of generals]; but we are occasionally both, and I should not be much out if I was to say that we are sometimes *neither* but a compound of *both.*"[74]

Republicanism on a Large Scale

Washington's unique vantage point during the War for Independence (he was, after all, the *only* commander-in-chief) provided him with an opportunity to assess, firsthand, confederation politics. No other American of his time—not Adams, not Jefferson, not Franklin—witnessed the birth of thirteen infant republics and a national Congress from a perspective remotely like Washington's. As commander-in-chief he was subject to the authority of a curious array of departments, committees, secretaries, and boards at the national level, while simultaneously having to assuage the local concerns of thirteen very independent, very different constitutional republics. As the eight years of his commission dragged on, much of this constitutional infancy must have seemed to Washington as painful and as troublesome as a breech birth.

Washington emerged in 1783 still very much the republican, but his republicanism had taken on deeper hues as a result of his wartime experiences. He was still the Virginia gentleman, but his willingness to consider a republic on a national scale forced him to jettison much of the oppositionist Country ideology that had characterized his early political career in Virginia. He was still a political and social conservative, but the war had convinced him that conservatism was best served by a national government sufficiently energetic to instill its special brand of public virtue on the widest scale possible. He still harbored a vision of a continental America stretching to the Mississippi, but he now believed that only a national government could safeguard the interests of the West from Europe and the predations of the Eastern states.

In short, the war had caused Washington to rethink his notions of what a constitutional republic should look like. Reluctantly at first, then with increasing vehemence, Washington began to see a *national* political system—a stronger union of some sort, though he still lacked a specific point of reference—as the only salvation for America's political, economic, and military troubles. Washington was certainly not the first American nationalist, but he became the first great national symbol of the nationalist cause.

To get to that point required him to radically rethink the nature of public virtue. Like most republicans, Washington believed that there could be only one true public interest. The common welfare had to be something more than just the result of an open competition between numerous interests within the community. Such a competition, he thought, would surely give sway to private interests rather than the genuine common interest. Moreover, harmony, not conflict, was essential to a virtuous community. This understanding explains why most republicans believed that good government could emerge only in a small republic—large, diverse populations would inevitably diverge over the question of what was in the public interest and would succumb, whatever the formal constitutional arrangements, to powerful partisan interests.

Such partisanship and division were anathema to a good republican. So it was with Washington early in the war. After his early, impolitic criticisms of New England soldiers, Washington tried to create a truly national army organized around the common goal of defeating the British and protecting the liberties of all Americans. But partisan bickering among the officers, especially disputes over the relative contributions of various states' regiments, interfered with that goal. To one brigadier he wrote, "How strange it is that Men, engaged in the same Important Service, should be eternally bickering, instead of giving mutual aid! Officers cannot act upon proper principles, who suffer trifles to interpose to create distrust and jealousy. All our actions should be regulated by one Uniform plan, and that Plan should have one object in view, to wit, the good of the Service."[75] This same notion informed his analysis of national politics. For Washington there was a clear public interest held in common by all patriotic Americans—winning the war. There was no room for ambiguity or legitimate differences of opinion on this goal. All else that was of value to the community—constitutional government, liberty, republicanism, prosperity—depended on winning the war. To Washington it was inconceivable that there could be any dissent to the idea that military victory was genuinely in the public interest.

To Washington, then, virtue was wedded to one's willingness to sacrifice private interest in service to the public interest. Once the public interest was determined, a desire for fame should lead honorable men only to unanimity and unity of purpose. "If we would pursue a right System of policy, in my Opinion, there should be none of these distinctions. We should all be considered, Congress, Army, &c. as one people, embarked in one Cause, in one interest; acting on the same principle and to the same End."[76]

It came as a rude shock when Washington found that many politicians in state and national government could not agree on what was genuinely in the public interest. He was particularly upset with the behavior of the state governments, many of which could not fully embrace any notion of the public interest that emanated from Congress or the army. Their particular view of republicanism taught them to be wary of centralism (a traditional enemy of true republicanism) masquerading as public virtue. Thus, it was more than narrow self-interest and petty partisanship that led many state governments to withhold wholehearted support from Congress and the army. For many Pennsylvanians and Marylanders and Rhode Islanders there was more to the public interest than winning the war. State citizens also shared a common interest in preserving their local republics against the centralizing impulses of Congress and the Continental Army. These "small scale" republicans feared an American "court" as much as a distant Parliament. Each was an instrument for undermining liberty and independence. Winning the war, though clearly in the common interest of all the states, should not come at the expense of devaluing state governments and state constitutions.

Washington tried to assuage these fears as much as possible. As noted above, he deferred to state authority even when it was inconvenient. He wrote nearly as frequently to state governors, taking them into his confidence and asking for their advice, as he did to Congress. Even when he most desperately importuned the states for support, he never conditioned those pleas with military threats. In the end, his efforts were to no avail. No matter how much Washington cajoled, no matter how much he demonstrated the army's trustworthiness, an unbridgeable gulf separated Washington's understanding of the common interest from that of the "small scale" republicans.

When he realized that this local support would never materialize in the way he envisioned, Washington began to take a more active role in the promulgation of a new version of republicanism. Beginning in the winter of 1779–1780 Washington used his political influence on behalf of three goals inherently incompatible with the older, "small scale" republicanism. First, he argued that the Congress should be granted greater powers to act on matters of general interest to the confederacy. Second, he maintained that in those matters of general interest the power and authority of the national government should be supreme over any state interests. Finally, in order to more effectively meet these new responsibilities, Congress should establish a strong executive branch, preferably with individual executives capable of accepting and exercising political responsibility.

There is a spirited debate among historians as to whether the Revolution established national sovereignty or the sovereignty of the several states.[77] For the most part, Washington tried to distance himself from that issue, which was debated by his contemporaries as well. But starvation and mutiny among his troops and the prospect of military disaster forced him off the fence. When a nationalist faction arose within Congress and many of the states in 1780, especially among veterans of the war, Washington abandoned his carefully constructed policy of deference to the states and indicated his unequivocal support for the nationalists.[78] He laid out his principle objections to "politics as usual" in a long letter to a former member of Congress:

> In a word, our measures are not under the influence and direction of one council, but thirteen, each of which is actuated by local views and politics, without considering the fatal consequences of not complying with plans which the united wisdom of America in its representative capacity have digested, or the unhappy tendency of delay, mutilation, or alteration. I do not scruple to add, and I give it decisively as my opinion, that unless the States will content themselves with a full, and well chosen representation in Congress, and vest that body with absolute powers in all matters relative to the great purposes of war, and of general concern . . . we are

attempting an impossibility, and very soon shall become (if it is not already the case) a many headed Monster, a heterogenious Mass, that never will or can, steer to the same point. The contest among the different States *now*, is not which shall do most for the common cause, but which shall do least.[79]

This letter is one of Washington's most bitter; other parts of it are even more strident and accusatory. But it lays out the parameters of his nationalist thinking. His criticisms of confederation politics were both structural and ideological. He was outraged at the timidity of Congress and by its practice of merely recommending measures to the states. Rather than a Congress with authority to match its responsibilities Washington saw a system in which "each State undertakes to determine, 1st. whether they will comply or not 2d. In what manner they will do it, &ca. 3dly. in what time."[80] Blame for this political timidity was placed entirely at the doorstep of the states. Their local views, jealousy of the national government, unjustified fear of the army, and self-interest combined to make them the greatest obstacle to attaining the unity necessary for winning the war. Washington usually spoke in rather broad terms on the subject of expanded congressional powers, calling for Congress to act in matters of "general concern." Beyond a suggestion that Congress be granted the authority to lay taxes, borrow money, and provide for the army, he offered few specific recommendations as to what those powers ought to be. In truth, though, he was more interested in vesting Congress with greater enforcement (executive) powers than in expanding the scope of its legislative powers.

Structural reforms would fail, though, if they were not presented as part of a broader appeal for national unity. Washington still believed that republican governments, regardless of form, could survive only if they were virtuous. Congress was much to blame for the army's difficulties, but Washington became less inclined to criticize that body as the war lengthened. Many of its members had at least *tried* to supply the army and support the great national patriotic cause. But the states, in Washington's eyes, had lost their nerve. Increasingly protective of localist, parochial notions of the public good, they undermined the common interest of all Americans in winning the war. Part of Washington's despair was grounded in a creeping fear that virtue was fighting a losing battle against self-interest and that republican government was impossible after all. Therefore, Washington spoke about arousing the talented, honorable men of America—men of acknowledged virtue—to save the republican spirit from the hydra of parochial factionalism. Congress needed more comprehensive powers, but without virtuous men at every level of government the great experiment was doomed to failure.

The second plank of Washington's constitutional reform program called for sharp constraints on the powers of the state governments. He did not propose to abolish the states (a position that only a few extreme nationalists were prepared to consider) and conceded their primacy in managing local affairs and maintaining public order. Moreover, part of his rationale for increasing the powers of the national government was that without more comprehensive central direction to the country's affairs each of the thirteen states, and the liberties they so jealously championed, would succumb separately to British military and economic pressure.[81] Only a national government with supremacy over the states in all areas of general interest could hope to bring the war to a successful conclusion. Congress, "after hearing the interests and views of the several States fairly discussed and explained by their respective representatives, must dictate, not merely recommend, and leave it to the states afterwards to do as they please, which . . . is in many cases, to do nothing at all."[82] Washington's federal model allowed for state interests to be represented only in Congress. Once Congress, composed as it was of delegations from each state, had determined the common national interest, further opposition or noncompliance by any state would be impermissible. The principle of democratic centralism would forbid any additional checks upon national authority from thence forward. State power would have to give way entirely in such matters.

Finally, Washington insisted that any expanded congressional powers could only be made effective by vigorous, responsible executive leadership. The antimonarchist, anticentralist, anticorruption sentiments held by many revolutionary legislators were slow to yield to Washington's claims. The history of Congress's efforts to manage the business of war demonstrates that the idea of a plural executive operating under the close supervision of a jealous legislature died especially hard. Congress initially supervised the army and its provisioning as a committee of the whole. When that proved unwieldy Congress established a committee of five of its members, the Board of War. Later still, the board was recast to allow members from outside Congress—men presumably with administrative skills. None of these arrangements met with much success or the commander-in-chief's approval. Even when Congress was able to raise the necessary supplies the distribution system was so disorganized that the provisions rarely reached the army expeditiously.

Washington campaigned for single executives—men vested with the kind of responsibility and authority to "act with dispatch and energy."[83] As early as 1775 Washington had lobbied for a clearer line of executive responsibility. Notes for a letter to Congress reveal that he had planned to "express gratitude for the readiness which the Congress and different committees have shown to make every thing as convenient and agreeable as possible, but point out the inconvenience of depending upon a number of men and different channels through which these supplies are to be furnished and the necessity of appointing a Commissary General for these purposes."[84] When his nationalist allies in Congress finally adopted a plan to allocate executive power to individual ministers Washington was ecstatic—an enthusiasm that was tempered somewhat by Congress's subsequent wrangling over the selection of the ministers. In his own mind, the value of energy in the executive branch was proven by the military campaign of 1781 when British military confidence was mortally wounded at Yorktown. Washington attributed much of the success of that campaign to Robert Morris, Congress's superintendent of finance. By raising the money necessary to supply the army and by taking personal responsibility for its effective distribution Morris confirmed Washington's confidence in a strong executive.

The Political Experience of War

The war did not create the political character of George Washington. Much of Washington the Virginia rebel of 1774 was still recognizable in Washington the triumphant commander-in-chief of 1783. But the war did compel him to rethink many of his assumptions about the prospects of republican government. While his optimism about an American empire of virtue and justice had been unreserved in 1774, his experiences in the war made him increasingly skeptical that such an empire was natural or inevitable. Believing in republicanism was one thing;

raising it up in an increasingly chaotic, even revolutionary, America was quite another matter.

Several themes emerge from a close reading of Washington's wartime correspondence. First, he came to believe that no community could long rely solely on the virtue and public spiritedness of its ordinary citizens. Self-interest and factionalism would corrode public virtue if it was not invigorated by the leadership and public example of the better sort of men. In addition, a system of laws based on sound republican principles had to be vigorously enforced at all levels of government. Otherwise, citizens would come to see a real advantage in pursuing their own self-interest. Second, there were common interests (e.g., independence, economic prosperity, security against foreign intrigues) shared by all Americans that transcended the interests of smaller communities and states. Because these common interests benefitted the whole, they had a higher claim to authority than other, more local, public interests. Third, powers sufficient for attaining the general interests of all Americans had to be attached to a national government. Such a government (and Washington was still unsure of its precise form and structure) not only had to have plenary powers to deal with those common national interests, but its executive had to have enough authority to guarantee compliance with its measures. National supremacy thus had to be the rule in all areas affecting the common interest. Fourth, agencies of the national government had to be made permanent. The army surely would be one of those permanent institutions, but Washington anticipated that other national agencies would require the same continuity. Ministries for foreign affairs, finance, and war were essential, and he hinted at the possibility of a national bank, an agency for managing the western lands, and even a national university.

The war also reinforced a lesson learned in his Virginia years. Successful generals must immerse themselves in politics as much as in battlefield tactics. He had tried to remain aloof from American partisan politics early in the war, often seeking to project an image of the republican hero standing above the fray, motivated only by a sense of personal honor and public virtue. He feared, because of the ideological predisposition of most Americans against standing armies and placemen, that any political influence he might attempt to exercise could well backfire, undermining the war effort and destroying his own carefully constructed public persona. But to raise his army, keep it supplied, and earn the cooperation of Congress and the states Washington came to recognize that such a posture was untenable. Washington thus became an increasingly active and influential political player. He wrote candid, behind-the-scenes letters to Congressmen and state leaders (a practice he had avoided the first year or two of the war when he was playing the nonpartisan) whom he believed might influence political events. Political allies communicated with him regularly, keeping him informed of the political scene and soliciting his views on various plans and proposals. He surrounded himself with aides such as Alexander Hamilton, John Laurens, and Joseph Reed who were chosen deliberately for their political skills rather than their military experience.

After 1781, with military victory imminent, Washington turned his attention more and more to the political problems of an independent United States. He was full of political ideas—ideas he deemed vital to the success of the constitutional order. But the overwhelming demands of commander-in-chief had prevented him from embarking on the sort of careful reflection that would enable him to place these ideas within the sort of "system" that he so much admired. Sentiments, no matter how deeply felt, did not make a coherent political theory. Ironically, his impending retirement, which he often envisioned as a return to the simple life of a farmer, would immerse him ever more deeply in American political life and provide him the time to more fully contemplate his vision for an American empire.

3 / The Restive Correspondent

The year 1781 ended well for Washington and for the revolutionary cause. Nathanael Greene's southern campaign had been enormously successful and had restored American morale in the Carolinas. Washington's own reputation had been restored by the successful Franco-American operation in Virginia. Finally, after six frustrating years Washington could lay claim to the personal military honor he had longed for—the defeat of a sizable British army on the battlefield. Moreover, Yorktown had vindicated Washington's grand strategy for the war. He had argued long and hard, and not always successfully, that the war could be concluded only by defeating British forces in the field—a goal he believed was attainable only by the use of professional (Continental) troops under his consolidated command. Washington had insisted that if his strategy were followed and the British army, or important elements of it, were defeated, Britain would quickly sue for peace. Indeed, with the ignominious surrender of Cornwallis and his army peace rumors swept the country.

We can only speculate about Washington's thoughts upon receiving Cornwallis's surrender proposal. Perhaps he imagined a quick end to a war that only a few months earlier had seemed incapable of resolution. Perhaps he anticipated a return to the life of the country gentleman at Mount Vernon—a retirement that surely would carry with it the reputation and public honors that he had so ardently pursued. Perhaps he looked forward to a quiet life as a revered public figure in a nation governed wisely and justly by the noblest of republican principles. Perhaps. But Washington remained curiously subdued amid the groundswell of enthusiasm over the news from Yorktown. Cornwallis's surrender was ''an interesting event that may be productive of much good if properly improved.''[1] But he would go no further.

Although Yorktown signaled the end of the military crisis, Washington remained wary, noting that the British still retained a potent military presence on the continent. But Cornwallis's capture had embarrassed the British command structure and had emboldened parliamentary factions that wanted peace with the Americans. Washington and Congress were informed by Guy Carleton, the new British commander-in-chief in North America, that no further offensives would be initiated, and although Washington still suspected British mischief, the war was effectively over.

For others, Yorktown would come to symbolize the final triumph of American dedication and patriotic ardor. For Washington it meant only the onset of the "great crisis." Most of Washington's energies for the previous six years had been focused on winning the military war for independence. He had conducted himself in a manner befitting a republican general dedicated to preserving republican institutions. But important as his conduct was to his self-image, it had little effect on the development of American political practices during the war. The states were busily writing, revising, and implementing new constitutions without any particular help from Washington. Only a few months earlier Congress had at last ratified a constitution for the United States, the Articles of Confederation, again without the benefit of Washington's opinions.

As peace negotiations neared their conclusion in 1783 the exhausted Washington wrote to his brother about his wish to unburden himself of all further public responsibilities: "This event will put a period not only to my Military Service, but also to my public life; as the remainder of my natural one shall be spent in that kind of repose which a man enjoys that is free from the load of public cares."[2] While he probably anticipated basking in a postwar aura of fame and adulation, he also seems genuinely to have wanted to bring his public life to a close. But his impending resignation from the army served only to elevate his awareness of things political—and he did not like what he saw.

Washington's letters throughout the early and middle 1780s resonate with a dark pessimism about the future of the republican experiment. Whenever he acted as a representative of the American cause, as in his addresses to his troops and his letters to foreigners, he felt obliged to present a uniformly optimistic picture. In his farewell address to the Continental Army he enthused that "the enlarged prospects of happiness, opened by the confirmation of our independence and sovereignty, almost exceeds the power of description."[3] But his private correspondence reveals an assessment of America's prospects decidedly less sanguine. Events were bringing "our politics . . . to the brink of a precipice; a step or two farther must plunge us into a Sea of Troubles."[4] Similar expressions of foreboding appear persistently in Washington's personal letters. To the trusted Henry Knox he wrote: "Our affairs, generally, seem really, to be approaching some awful crisis."[5] Washington must have recalled the ideals of the Fairfax Resolves—sister states standing together for self-government and the restoration of constitutional principles—and wondered whether the "awful crisis" of the confederation period was not every bit as threatening as that presented by the corrupt ministries of 1774.

In short, the Revolution was not working out as Washington had expected. As a farmer, he well understood the notion of the "false spring," in which premature warmth brings crops and trees to bloom only to have them withered by an unexpected blast of cold. The republic, or at least his conception of a republic, seemed to be under assault from the frigid blasts of self-interest, localism, class-based politics, and licentiousness. If the promised fruits of republicanism were to be harvested Washington would have to invest more of his energies in its care and nurture. Thus, rather than quiet retirement, Washington found himself expanding his extensive network of correspondents: governors and former governors, congressmen and former congressmen, officers and aides from his army days, men of influence at every level, even sympathetic Europeans. Old friends such as George Mason and Patrick Henry tried out their thoughts on Washington, but so too did new correspondents such as James Madison, Alexander Hamilton, and Gouverneur Morris, each an ally from the nationalist movement earlier in the decade.

This whirlwind of letter writing compelled Washington to reflect more carefully on the lessons of his experiences. As a result his constitutional vision emerged from this "critical period" more coherent than ever before. As that vision coalesced he became increasingly critical of the existing constitutional order. Sentiments and values that had previously been expressed in rather general terms were now translated into a specific policy agenda. Finally, Washington attempted to actively influence political developments during the confederation period, using his vast network of associates to play the role of an *eminence grise*, preferring to distance himself from any active involvement in political events but offering aid and comfort to those who shared his constitutional agenda.

Five letters, or sets of letters, from this period serve as the clearest exposition of Washington's reaction to the "crisis of the 1780s" and his emerging constitutional agenda on the eve of the Philadelphia Convention. First, his 1783 Circular Letter to the States provides us with his most thorough assessment of political difficulties in the union and offers, albeit still in rather general terms, some of his suggestions for constitutional reform. Second, his letters on behalf of the Potomac Canal illustrate two key components of his constitutional vision: his support for western expansion and its importance for establishing a *national* constitutional order and his conception of the nexus between commercialism, interest, and republican government. Third, in his correspondence with his nephew, Bushrod Washington, the older Washington explains the importance of constitutional government and the dangers of factionalism and populistic democracy. Fourth, his letters regarding Shays's Rebellion and other "difficulties," while revealing little new in Washington's politics, explain his increased willingness to consider actions more forceful and dramatic than mere letter writing and evidence a growing confidence in his own vision. Finally, his correspondence with Madison, Mason, Knox, Edmund Randolph, and others from late in 1786 until his decision in 1787 to serve as a delegate in Philadelphia suggests that he was prepared to be more than a neutral bystander at the convention. Indeed, as with the Fairfax Resolves more than a decade earlier, we will later see that Washington's contributions to the final authorship of an important constitutional document, in this case the Virginia Plan that set the tone for the Philadelphia Convention, were more substantial than previously thought.

The Oracle of Newburgh

By 1783 peace with Britain was assured. Had he seen his republican duties as merely military Washington might have been expected to retire to Virginia secure in the knowledge that his own reputation was now unassailable. But political events in Congress and in the states troubled him deeply. A few years earlier he had supported the nationalist faction in their drive to strengthen the efficiency and energy of Congress. But the collapse of Robert Morris's finance plan and anticipation of the expected removal of British troops from the United States encouraged the states to quickly retrieve many of their old privileges. National affairs appeared to Washington to be slipping once again into the black ooze of state-based politics—a politics of self-interest, fear, and parochialism. Supporters of state power recounted the now-standard republican liturgy about the importance of liberty and locally controlled government. But Washington's experience had convinced him that however alluring this small-scale republicanism was in theory, in practice it could only bring about the collapse of the great American republican experiment.

His impending retirement offered Washington a unique opportunity to influence the course of national politics. He had injected himself into that sphere only sporadically during the war, usually limiting his political activity to letters encouraging his supporters to keep up the good fight. But his unrivaled status as the first genuine national hero combined with his position as a disinterested observer to give him great political leverage.[6] It was not a moment he was prepared to let pass. So in June of 1783, after several weeks of careful thought and writing, Washington submitted his last, his longest, and his most provocative Circular Letter to the States from his headquarters in Newburgh, New York.[7] It marked the retiring general not only as a man with a clear political vision, but as a man who, despite his protestations to the contrary, was likely to play a prominent role in shaping the postwar political order.

The letter began inauspiciously enough. The announcement of his impending retirement was followed by warm congratulations to all who had participated in the success of the Revolution. But Washington soon abandoned this conventional valedictory and signaled the real purpose of his message.

The Citizens of America . . . are . . . possessed of absolute freedom and Independency; They are, from this period, to be considered as Actors on a most conspicuous Theatre, which seems to be peculiarly designated by Providence for the display of human greatness and felicity . . . Heaven has crowned all its other blessings, by giving a fairer oppertunity for political happiness, than any other Nation has ever been favored with.[8]

Two further themes then emerged. First, there was no shortage of political liberty in America. American freedom was not the object of some hoped-for future; it was already the envy of the world. Second, this expansive liberty, in combination with the bounties of education, commerce, and experience in self-government, offered Americans an opportunity to demonstrate that constitutional government under republican principles was truly attainable. Washington then shifted his tone. Liberty alone would not be enough to bring about the republican millennium. Critical choices had to be made, choices that would determine whether America "will be respectable and prosperous, or contemptable and miserable as a Nation."[9]

Clearly for Washington, one critical choice preceded and shaped all others: Should the United States be a nation among nations, or merely a loose confederation for mutual convenience and support? Many of the republican thinkers of the day, including the Country ideologues so influential in Washington's early career, opted for the latter arrangement. To them, liberty was inversely related to the power of central governments. The more distant the rulers were from the ruled (or, to use republican terminology, the more distant representatives were from their constituent citizens), the less sensitive the rulers would be to the rights and liberties of the ruled. The corruption of republican principles was inevitable without a vigilant citizenry willing to exercise a jealous regard for their personal liberties. Distant, centralized regimes made such vigilance all the more difficult and, thus, only accelerated the degenerative process.

Washington was aware of these feelings (he had, after all, shared many of those sentiments before his wartime service); yet he was convinced by his revolutionary experiences that these feelings were, at best, misguided and, at worst, dangerously wrong. The "present crisis" could be avoided if, and only if, a "national character" could be established. Without saying so directly, Washington's remarks implied that those who insisted that liberty and virtue could only be maintained in small-scale republics, like the existing thirteen states, were operating in a world bounded by libraries, philosophical societies, and the after-dinner talk of comfortable gentlemen. That world bore no resemblance to the one that Washington had come to know. In his view independence had been won only through the concerted efforts of a national union exemplified by Congress and the Continental Army. Now, independence could be preserved in an uncertain world only by resorting to the same agency—a strong national union. His indictment of postwar politics was pointed: "This may be the ill-fated moment for relaxing the powers of the Union, annihilating the cement of the Confederation, and exposing us to become the sport of European politics, which may play one State against another to prevent their growing importance, and to serve their own interested purposes."[10]

Washington's paradoxical, yet remarkably prescient, position was that the rights and liberties of the government and people of Virginia or New York or Rhode Island could *only* be preserved in the context of a strong national union. His diagnosis was that the very parochialism and spirit of liberty that many thought essential to the preservation of those freedoms was actually a lethal virus within the American body politic. The separate states, no matter how rich or well governed, were no match for the predatory actions of an unrepublican Europe. He explained this worldview in grim terms: "Without an entire conformity to the Spirit of the Union, we cannot exist as an Independent Power. . . . It is only in our united Character as an Empire, that our Independence is acknowledged, that our power can be regarded, or our Credit supported among Foreign Nations." No amount of republican feeling or love of liberty could compensate for the lack of an effective national government. If the states continued to behave as thirteen local republics, he warned, they would soon find themselves "in a state of Nature." Citizens would soon discover that their passion for liberty had degenerated into little more than self-indulgent licentiousness. *This*, not the adoption of a strong national government, was the path to tyranny and arbitrary power. No temporary association for limited purposes would suffice. The Confederation was just such an association; but even though it was carefully constituted and drew, on occasion, the service of some of the best men in America, it was simply not up to the task. The union had to be made more permanent if independence were to be assured and republican liberty preserved.[11]

If the constitutional superstructure of American politics was insufficient to support a permanent union, then what did Washington propose? First of all, he offered a series of specific reforms intended to create "an indissoluble Union of the States under one Federal Head."[12] Most of these reforms were more a matter of firm adherence to preexisting constitutional principles than a call for radical change. For example, he called on the states to immediately delegate greater legislative "prerogatives" to Congress. Yet from the context of his remarks it is clear that he meant that the states should respect the *existing* powers of Congress under the Confederation. Congress had ample legislative powers. What it lacked was a commitment from the states to refrain from using the banner of liberty as a mask for preserving local prerogatives instead of the genuine interests of all Americans. Washington further maintained that it was in the states' own interest that "there should be lodged somewhere, a Supreme power to regulate and govern the general concerns" of the republic, making clear at the same time that Congress was the logical place to entrust that "Supreme power." He also insisted that legislative authority would come to naught without adequate enforcement of national laws. Washington proposed no change in the executive arrangements of the Confederation, but he tried to impress on the states the importance of accepting the responsibilities of partnership in a real union: "There must be a faithfull and pointed compliance on the part of every State, with the late proposals and demands of Congress, or the most fatal consequences will ensue."[13] Without diligent compliance by every state, no amount of congressional legislation could carry the day.

None of this was particularly new. Washington had remonstrated against state malfeasance and nonfeasance for much of the war. What particularly irked the retiring general was that, much to his amazement, cooperation among the states seemed to be declining to levels even lower than he had witnessed during the war. He was so distressed by this lack of cooperation that he suggested that anyone who opposed the union or proposed measures to dissipate its strength be treated as a traitor to the patriotic cause. He did not pursue this most extreme measure any further, but it is an indication that he was not about to concede any ground to the proponents of states' rights. He wrote, as much in frustration as in anger, that unless the states showed a greater willingness to be governed by the provisions of the national Congress, "it will be a subject of much regret, that so much blood and treasure have been lavished for no purpose, that so many sufferings have been encountered without a compensation, and that so many sacrifices have been made in vain."[14] Long before Webster and Lincoln, Washington was committed to the notion that "united we stand, divided we fall."

Washington then encouraged the states to join with Congress in supporting two particular measures that would assure the honor of "the national character." He had endorsed each proposal on numerous occasions during the war. But by reiterating them now, Washington was trying to impress on the states that these policies were not just militarily expedient (the war, after all, was now over) but were essential to the creation of a national character grounded in public virtue.

Washington first called on the states to show their "Sacred regard to Public Justice."[15] Public justice in this instance meant the payment of revolutionary debts, especially those owed to the officers and soldiers of the army. Washington's arguments read like the brief of an unseasoned lawyer. No consistent principle animated his advocacy; he moved back and forth between practical, constitutional, and moral arguments without rooting his claims exclusively in any of the three. But the overall effect was compelling.

His two practical arguments were rather simple. First, free government in America (and he most probably meant here, republican government) could only endure if citizens trusted their government. If Congress's word to creditors could not be trusted, could *any* national government in the future, however revised, hope to attract the loyalty and patriotism necessary for long-term stability? Important things must be done right, at the start, or republican government would find its reservoir of public confidence perilously low.

Second, in *private* life honorable men were obliged to fulfill their contracts even when the performance of those contracts was inconvenient or painful. Washington believed that *public* governments should be held to that same standard. Property rights in general would be jeopardized if governments could blithely ignore them when they wished. Thus, he argued that national forfeiture should be seen as having the same effect on the trustworthiness of government as private bankruptcy on the trustworthiness of individuals. Who would be willing to invest in useful, but potentially risky, national projects under those circumstances?

His constitutional argument was equally straightforward. The debts had been incurred in the common defense of the nation. They had been legally authorized by Congress under its constitutional authority.

Therefore, the states were obliged to take whatever measures were necessary, including the laying of taxes, to retire the debts. But even here, his appeal included references to private honor and public virtue—claims that were more moral than constitutional: "Let us then as a Nation be just, let us fulfil the public Contracts, which Congress had undoubtedly a right to make for the purpose of carrying on the war, with the same good faith we suppose ourselves bound to perform our private engagements."[16]

He had long held that a contract, *any* contract, was a sacred bond, a moral pact, between the parties. Failure to fully live up to one's contractual obligations was dishonorable, and we should recall that dishonor was counted among the gravest of sins in a society constructed along republican principles.[17] His respect for contracts was also a sign of his deeply rooted social conservatism. Human nature, particularly as evidenced in the lower classes, was something not to be trusted. The law, though, by example and by coercion could be made to encourage appropriate behavior. Reflecting several years earlier on the business dealings of the unfortunate Jacky Custis, he had remarked: "I see so many instances of the rascallity of Mankind, that I am . . . convinced that the only way to make men honest, is to prevent their being otherwise, by tying them firmly to the accomplishment of their contracts."[18] Washington was not prepared to accept the notion that an American empire could be constructed on such "rascallity" in government. Republican governments should be paragons of public virtue, not slaves to the baser instincts of human behavior. Not satisfied with an appeal to public virtue, Washington also questioned the *private* virtue of those opposed to honoring the public debt. (Indeed, it again illustrates Washington's repeated appeals to private virtues, such as honor, frugality, and liberality, as the standards by which to measure public virtues. The two were, for him, virtually undifferentiated.) Where his most precious principles were involved George Washington was quite capable of shaming his opponents in the most florid terms:

Where is the man to be found, who wishes to remain indebted, for the defense of his own person and property, to the exertions, the bravery, and the blood of others, without making one generous effort to repay the debt of honor and of gratitude? In what part of the Continent shall we find any Man, or body of Men, who would not blush to stand up and propose measures, purposely calculated to rob the Soldier of his Stipend, and the Public Creditor of his due?[19]

The picture he painted of the plight of disabled veterans was especially poignant and was intended to make opponents of full funding squirm uncomfortably: "Nothing could be a more melancholy and distressing sight, than to behold those who have shed their blood or lost their limbs in the service of their Country, without a shelter, without a friend, and without the means of obtaining any of the necessaries or comforts of Life; compelled to beg their daily bread from door to door!"[20] How could a national character be built on such a foundation of dishonor? We might be inclined to say that it was a bit of a cheat for Washington to place the claims of all creditors, most of whom were neither homeless, friendless, penniless, or limbless, on a moral par with the sacrifices of disabled war veterans. But Washington was not being hypocritical. He genuinely believed that *all* public debts were equally valid and that republican governments could have no part in faithlessness.

His next specific policy recommendation was even more quixotic. Noting that the "defence of the republic" required a "proper Peace Establishment," Washington recommended that "the Militia of the Union" be "placed upon a regular and respectable footing." He must have known the response this proposal would generate, therefore he did not press the far more centralist notion of a professional Continental Army that he had advocated earlier in the war. This time he only recommended that there be a common organization among all the state militia (no doubt intended to alleviate many of the disputes over rank and command that Washington had faced during the war) and that all militia be armed and supplied in a standardized way.[21] Presumably, these policies would emanate from Congress.

Even this watered down proposal was ignored. Many other Americans had their political attitudes shaped by the war; and what they had learned was often quite different from what Washington had learned. The mutinies of 1781, the march of the Pennsylvania Line on Philadelphia, the numerous instances of looting and foraging, and the putative officers' revolt at Newburgh had reinforced many Americans' traditional antipathy toward centralized military establishments. They trusted Washington; but one did not have to be a state particularist to share their apprehensions about a nationally directed militia.

All of these proposals were part of a larger indictment of the great obstacle to union—the jealousies of individual states. He knew that the union would stand or fall on "the system of Policy the States shall adopt at this moment."[22] It was the states that stood accused—accused of denying important powers to Congress, failing to keep good faith with the nation's creditors, promoting liberty to the point of licentiousness, placing themselves "in opposition to the aggregate Wisdom of the Continent."[23] The states had to be made to see that their collective interest was best represented in Congress and that failure to support Congress was an assault on the national union that protected and nourished them all. Thus Washington continued to envision a republic on a national scale that would protect the liberties of the people and promote the common good far more effectively than could the states individually.

His proposed remedies combined constitutional reforms, specific policy recommendations, and a plea for a changed political climate. In this sense Washington's experiences during the war had compelled him to see politics as a deeper, more complex phenomenon than the simpler politics of deference in which he had been raised. Perhaps most significantly, the Circular Letter revealed that Washington had grasped the distinction between a constitution and constitutionalism. A structurally flawed constitution was not the only problem. The crisis of the 1780s was equally attributable to a lack of commitment by the states (or, to be more precise, certain self-interested factions within the states) to the principles of constitutionalism. Constitutions were not self-enforcing. Constitutions, especially republican constitutions, required "the prevalence of that pacific and friendly disposition, among the People of the United States, which will induce them to forget their local prejudices and policies, to make those mutual concessions which are requisite to the general prosperity, and in some instances, to sacrifice their individual advantages to the interest of the Community."[24] Washington's Circular Letter suggested that the climate for constitutionalism at the national level was still imperfectly formed. Until Americans could be convinced of the advantages of a national constitution, a process made more difficult by the actions of the small-scale republicans, the great promises of the Revolution would remain unfulfilled.

The West—Keystone of a Continental Empire

In the fall of 1784 the retired general embarked on the last of his many trips westward. The ostensible purpose of the journey was to tend to his trans-Allegheny lands. But the real reason for the expedition was to explore several possible routes for a canal-and-road system that would connect the Potomac River with the Ohio River and the vast riches of the West.

A Potomac canal had long fascinated Washington. As early as 1754 he had written after a journey up the Potomac that the waterway offered the ''more convenient least expensive and I may further say by much the most expeditious way to the [western] Country.''[25] As a Virginia legislator, he worked with fellow enthusiasts in Maryland to bring the two states together to construct a canal on the Potomac. There were ''immense advantages which Maryland and Virginia might derive by making Potomack the Channel of Commerce between Great Britain and that immense Territory Tract of Country which is unfolding to our view.''[26] The Ohio lands were a great prize. Other states were already exploring canals and turnpikes to bring commerce to and from the West through their borders and to their own seaports, so there was more than a little urgency to Washington's cause. Finally, in 1772 Washington successfully sponsored legislation in the Virginia House of Burgesses to join with Maryland in improving navigation on the river.[27]

The war deferred any further consideration of this grand plan, yet his interest in the West remained prominent in his thoughts. This is evidenced by a letter to James Duane written not long after Washington's retirement in which he laid out an extensive plan for the settlement of the western territories.[28] As we shall see, the development of the western lands was an essential element of his vision of large-scale republicanism for postwar America. Yet he was silent about any such projects in the Circular Letter, arguably his most comprehensive prescription for constitutional nationalism. There was, however, good reason for its omission. Washington was well aware that his support for the Potomac Canal and for westward expansion would not be perceived as disinterested by actors in other states. Those perceptions would be well founded and Washington knew it, admitting that he was "not so disinterested in this matter" as he would have liked.[29] He owned about fifty-eight thousand acres of land in the Ohio Basin. If a sure and certain means of transportation were established between the Ohio and the Atlantic to supplant the longer, more perilous journey down the Mississippi, then the value of these lands would appreciate considerably. Washington would be able to command top dollar in rents as well as being able to attract the "right kind" of tenants. In addition, if the Potomac became the principal route from West to East then Alexandria would surely become one of the leading commercial centers in the nation—an outcome that could not but have improved his own economic interests. Thus, had Washington suggested that Congress be given the power to take a more prominent part in westward expansion and to legislate the sorts of internal improvements that the Potomac Canal represented he would have undermined the rest of his message. An important source of Washington's influence in political affairs was his image as a disinterested figure, as one who stood to gain little personally by his political efforts. Washington wisely recognized that on matters related to the West he was rightly seen as self-interested and as an advocate for the parochial interests of Virginia. (Other states, after all, had their own plans for the territories.)

Although he refrained from mentioning such matters in the Circular Letter, Washington did not concede that there was any conflict between his personal interests and the common national interest. In fact, he insisted that much of his enthusiasm for the project was because it was a vital ingredient in his vision for a republic drawn on a "large scale." Once again, a portion of his argument was couched in the language of national security. The United States was still a small nation, clinging ever so tenuously to a narrow strip of land along the Atlantic seaboard. Enemies, real and imagined, were everywhere. While many of his fellow Americans saw the principal military threat as coming from Britain and the continent, Washington was convinced that the western frontier presented even more danger—and not from Europeans or Indians, but from people who were nominally Americans! These western settlers lived lives fraught with physical danger and economic hardship. Washington grasped the political implications of this precarious existence. These settlers stood "upon a pivot; the touch of a feather, would turn them any way."[30] With British interests to the north and Spanish and French interests to the south and west, western immigrants would look to whichever benefactor could make their lives less dangerous or more prosperous. If passage to New Orleans or Montreal were made easier than passage to the ports of the American states, then these frontier dwellers would soon convert those economic attachments to political loyalties and be drawn into the orbit of Spain or Britain. In short, the United States needed to cement the West firmly into the union for its own protection or the frontier would rapidly become no more attached to the United States than "the Country of California."

The Potomac Canal would join the West to the East in a great American empire. At first, commerce would be the bond. But commerce was only a means to a more important end. He hoped his plans for a canal would succeed

> *more on account of its political importance* [my emphasis] than the commercial advantages which would result from it, altho' the latter is an immense object: for if this Country, which will settle faster than any other ever did (and chiefly by foreigners who can have no particular predilection for *us*), cannot by an easy communication be drawn this way, but are suffered to form commercial intercourses (which lead we know to others) with the Spaniards on their right and rear, or the British on their left, they will become a distinct people from us, have different views, different interests, and instead of adding strength to the Union, may in case of a rupture with either of those powers, be a formidable and dangerous neighbour.[31]

Carefully supervised by Congress, westward expansion could be used to promote nationalism. Two kinds of settlers would be especially useful in making the West a bastion of nationalist fervor. Washington recommended, first of all, that Congress be given sole authority to distribute the western bounty lands promised to the former soldiers of the Continental Army. The frontier could not "be so advantageously settled by any other Class of men, as by the disbanded Officers and Soldiers of the Army." They would "connect our governments with the frontiers, extend our Settlements progressively, and plant a brave, a hardy and respectable Race of People, as our advanced post . . . [and] would give security to our frontiers."[32] Settlement by the army had political advantages as well. These were men who had already pledged their allegiance to the *national* government once. If they now received land from that same government it would cement their national loyalty even further. These "new Americans" would serve as an effective buffer against the expansion of state interests at the expense of the nation.

But soldiers alone would not provide sufficient numbers to fill the vast expanses of the frontier. Therefore, Washington continually urged Congress to invite the right sort of European settlers. Those who exhibited the appropriate republican virtues were especially desirable. These included the "oppressed and persecuted of all Nations and Religions" (presumably they would care a great deal about liberty), those of "moderate property," and those with a determination "to be sober, industrious, and virtuous members of society."[33]

To make all of this work—the canal, westward expansion, provision for bounty lands, immigration policy—Washington believed that it was essential that Congress have plenary authority to administer the western lands. The states could not be permitted to have anything at all to do with the matter. For one thing, administration of the western lands for the common national interest would remove one source of perpetual jealousy among the states. More than once during the war disputes about which states had claim to which western lands had strained the comity of the union. Second, a system of national administration would establish some order in the settlement process. Washington believed in "progressive" settlement. Lands on the near frontier could be sold and settled immediately. But lands further west should only be opened up when the first tier of lands was sufficiently "filled up." If the states separately opened up all their western lands, or if they prevented Congress from placing any limits on the extent of settlement, it "would open a more extensive field for Land jobbers and Speculators. Weaken our frontiers, exclude law, good government, and taxation to a late period, and injure the union very essentially in many respects."[34] Washington wanted "useful citizens" endowed with a sense of obligation to the national government. To that end he urged Congress to obtain title to all of these disputed lands and then sell them to individual settlers at a fixed, moderate price. (Free land would encourage idlers and speculators. A fair price would attract hardworking farmers.) The revenues would enhance the national treasury; settlement would be directed westward in an orderly, progressive manner; and a growing body of citizen-farmers dedicated to republican principles and the value of a strong union would result.

Washington's views on commerce and trade were cut from the same cloth as his expansionist policies. Like many classical republicans he genuinely despised speculation and the "avidity . . . among our people to make money." He conceded to his friends that the "spirit of commerce," though capable of much energy and enterprise, was not without disadvantages, especially as a proper basis for a republican social order in which some sense of the common good and disinterestedness was essential. Yet he also recognized that "from Trade our Citizens *will not* be restrained, and therefore it behooves us to place it in the most convenient channels, under proper regulation, freed *as much as possible*, from those vices which luxury, the consequence of wealth and power, naturally introduce."[35]

Like liberty, then, the spirit of commerce was a public virtue *only* if directed toward the common interest: "To promote industry and economy, and to encourage manufactures, is certainly consistent with that sound policy which ought to actuate every State"—and the suitable instrument to direct that policy was an energetic national government.[36] But the jealousies among the states were a threat both to "that sound policy" and to the new nation's independence. Washington was especially fearful of the impact of Great Britain's trade policies on the union. He envisioned Britain's great mercantile behemoth using these internecine economic rivalries to pit one state against another, thus subverting the still-fragile American economic "union." Unless a central government with more expansive powers to regulate national commerce emerged, Britain would probably regain by the purse what it had surrendered on the battlefield—American dependence. Two years before the Philadelphia Convention, Washington wrote: "The resolutions . . . vesting Congress with powers to regulate the Commerce of the Union, have I hope been acceded to. If the States individually were to attempt this, an abortion, or a many headed Monster would be the issue. . . . If we are afraid to trust one another under qualified powers there is an end of the Union."[37]

Washington's plans for a great Potomac Canal were not, then, just the idle tinkerings of a self-interested Virginia planter. They were part of a comprehensive vision for establishing a national republic linked by a shared interest in commercial activities and aspiring to republican principles. A canal to the West would encourage settlements in the American interior. These settlements, in turn, would serve as a protection for previously vulnerable borders. To assure the loyalty of these new Americans their economic connections to the old states would have to be promoted. For this, a strong national government with the power to regulate *all* forms of commerce, domestic or foreign, was necessary. Once granted these powers, the national government could encourage commerce among all the states, old as well as new, East as well as West. As these interstate commercial ties proliferated and prospered, loyalty to the national government would increase and the particular interests of the states would be rejected in favor of a new, more enlightened common interest.

This scheme may lack the sophistication and fiscal gymnastics of Hamilton's Report on Manufactures, but it reveals that Washington had already grasped the interconnectedness of political and economic policy and that each could be deliberately shaped to serve his vision of a national republic. Virtue was not innate even to a liberty-loving people. But if the people's interests could be tied to the success of large scale republicanism, then self-interest could yet be made to serve virtue's purposes.

The Case of the Naughty Nephew

In the fall of 1786 an interesting correspondence proceeded between Washington and his nephew, Bushrod Washington. The elder Washington had taken a paternal interest in the fortunes of the young man, at one point personally recommending him for study with one of the great American lawyers of the day, James Wilson.[38] It seems clear that Bushrod shared his uncle's interest in public affairs as well as his conclusion that the nation was in the midst of a great political crisis. Their correspondence suggests that there was little that divided the two men on matters of ideology or policy. Thus, this particular exchange is especially noteworthy because the older Washington patiently, but firmly, indicated that Bushrod was going in a direction that the general disapproved of.

Bushrod had written that he had lately been involved in organizing local (Virginia) Patriotic Societies. These societies of "sensible and respectable gentlemen" were established "to inquire into the state of public affairs; to consider in what the true happiness of the people consists, and what are the evils which . . . molest us; the means of attaining the former, and escaping the latter; to inquire into the conduct of those who represent us, and to give them our sentiments upon those laws, which ought to be or are already made." After a general statement of the societies' ends, most of which alluded to traditional republican values, Bushrod concluded with the news that there would soon be a meeting "to instruct our delegates what they ought to do, the next to inquire what they have done."[39] Fully expecting a "well done" for his efforts, Bushrod eagerly asked what Washington thought of all this.

Much to his surprise (as evidenced by a subsequent letter in which he rather defensively attempted to clarify the society's role and his own part in it) Bushrod found himself being lectured by his uncle and told that if it was the older man's approbation that was wanted, it would not be forthcoming.[40] Washington expressed his particular fears about two aspects of the Society, each of which tells us much about the depth and sophistication of Washington's ideas about republican government on the eve of the Constitutional Convention.

Washington noted first that "I have seen as much evil as good result from such Societies as you describe the Constitution of yours to be; they are a kind of imperium in imperio, and as often clog as facilitate public measures." Could Bushrod not see the danger in a segment of the community nominating itself to speak for the public interest, especially when representatives had been specially chosen to make that determination? Might not a few designing members of the society "direct the measures of it to private views of their own?"[41] This was not the first time that Washington had railed against the "spirit of party" and its despised companion, factionalism, nor would it be the last.[42] In his personal pantheon of political evils, parties and factionalism ranked with paper money and the machinations of European politics as the greatest threats to the adolescent American republic. In his view, factionalism could have *no* legitimate role in a republican form of government.

What accounts for Washington's deeply felt opposition to political parties? Why the antipathy toward factionalism? How could he have been so profoundly fearful of political elements that we today assume are intrinsic to liberal constitutions? The answer is twofold. First, the tenets of republican ideology as Washington received it and understood it viewed party spirit and factionalism as an evil so dire that it could tear asunder any republican constitution and undermine the quest for the good society. Second, Washington's recent ordeal as commander-in-chief had given him a firsthand look at the effects of factionalism. He needed no fancily argued treatise to instruct him on how factionalism could obstruct great public achievements. He could see daily confirmation of what his ideology predisposed him to believe. For Washington, theory and experience once again validated each other.

Washington's classical republicanism had as its central precept, its *modus vivendi*, the promotion of virtue and the identification and elevation of virtuous men. This virtue could only be attained by pursuing that which was truly in the public interest or common welfare. Fame was accorded to those men who sacrificed their self-interest in service to the commonwealth. But this vision implied that there was something called the public interest to which virtuous men could unanimously subscribe. The idea that there could be equally valid, but different, notions of the public interest was utter nonsense to Washington—a heresy upon good republican precepts. Harmony, not conflict; unity, not diversity, characterized his classical republican vision of society. Factions, because they represented interests of the particular rather than of the general, were an obstacle to virtue. Indeed, organizations like the Patriotic Society could be considered unpatriotic to the extent that they prevented the nation from achieving harmony and unity.

But Washington's feelings did not derive from ideology alone. Experience had confirmed those sentiments. Here again, the most immediate, most relevant, most galvanizing experience had come from his service in the Continental Army. If he had any doubts about the undesirability of faction before 1775, the war quickly hardened his views. Successful prosecution of the war required one thing above all else—unity. Any wavering or hesitation in the commitment to the great national goal of independence only prolonged the military struggle and increased its cost in both economic and personal terms. In this context it is no wonder that his wartime letters are filled with fears of factionalism and divisiveness among Americans.

One source of faction was obvious—the Loyalists (abetted in Washington's mind by those whose caution caused them to remain as uncommitted in the struggle as the contending armies would permit them). He was suspicious of their "diabolical acts and schemes" intended to "raise distrust, dissensions and divisions among us."[43] Washington was reluctant to execute Loyalists or confiscate their property. He was too much the social conservative for that. But on several occasions he did attempt to relocate them, segregate them, and even compel them to identify themselves so that their ability to influence or subvert the revolutionary cause could be minimized.

A more troublesome source of faction, however, was not in the enemy camp, but in his own. It was during the war that Washington had developed his political antipathy toward the states. He suffered from their repeated interference with the prerogatives of Congress and of his own national command. They seemed to him capable of supporting the national interest only when it coincided with local needs. The problem was not with the confederational structure *per se*. When Washington spoke about strengthening the federal union it was still in the context of a union of states. He was, after all, still a Virginian. (His efforts on behalf of the Potomac Canal project were understood by all as being particularly beneficial to his home state.) He did not believe in a unitary national government. But he *was* convinced that the political leaders in many of the states were utterly incapable of acting in the common national interest. Writing on the possibility of amendments to the Articles of Confederation that would strengthen the hand of Congress in national affairs, Washington commented acidly "that there is more wickedness than ignorance in the conduct of the States, or in other words, in the conduct of those who have too much influence in the government of them; and until the curtain is withdrawn, and the private views and selfish principles upon which these men act, are exposed to public notice, I have little hope of amendment without another convulsion."[44]

To George Washington, Bushrod's Patriotic Societies appeared as one more source of disharmony in a union that he believed was disintegrating rapidly. Bushrod's rejoinder to Washington indicated that the purposes of the society were virtually identical to the general's. They, too, were concerned with advancing the public interest, restoring republican virtues to an increasingly corrupt system, and promoting the national union. But Washington continued to hold back. There was something about the permanency of the society and its posturing as the spokesman for the public's interest that continued to trouble him. His hatred of factions was so strong that he found it difficult to endorse even an organization that embraced the Washingtonian vision!

The Patriotic Societies bothered Washington on another level. They maintained that representatives were "the servants of the electors." Moreover, on broad notions of the national interest and public good "the people are the best judges of . . . their own interests." Therefore, the societies proposed to instruct their elected representatives on issues of the day.[45] Bushrod and his friends were arguing on behalf of a "delegate" theory of representation. A delegate's responsibility is to stand as a mirror to his constituents, reflecting their wants and interests as accurately as possible. In this sense, the representative merely *re-presents* the views of those who elected him.

George Washington could not accept this definition of representative government. The genuine public interest could not be merely the reflection of the aggregated self-interests of thousands of constituents. This sang too much like the siren of democratic government, and Washington would have none of it. He still believed in government by a disinterested elite—men of property and independence, presumably with sufficient wisdom and experience to serve their constituents' true interests by acting for the common good. The structures of a republican form of government and the prospect of regular elections were devices sufficient to guarantee the responsibility of elected representatives. Washington was especially miffed at the short leashes (and the "instructions" of the Patriotic Societies would, of course, be yet another tether) that erstwhile republicans would place around the necks of delegates to Congress: "To me it appears much wiser and more politic, to choose able and honest representatives and leave them in all national questions to determine from the evidence of reason, and the facts which shall be adduced, when internal and external information is given to them in a collective state."[46] Congress, then, should be a deliberative body with a corporate, rather than individual, responsibility to the people. This idea, he thought, still provided ample checks on the representatives by those who elected them.

Men, chosen as the Delegates in Congress . . . cannot officially be dangerous; they depend upon the breath, nay, they are so much the creatures of the people, under the present constitution, that they can have no views (which could possibly be carried into execution) nor any interests, distinct from those of their constituents. My political creed therefore is, to be wise in the choice of Delegates, support them like Gentlemen while they are our representatives, give them competent powers for all federal purposes, support them in the due exercise thereof, and lastly, to compel them to close attendance in Congress during their delegation.[47]

We don't know that Washington ever read Edmund Burke's discussion of the role of parliamentary representatives. But Washington's thoughts on representation, both with regard to the responsibility of the individual legislator and to the function of the body as a whole, were virtually identical to Burke's famous defense of the "trustee" principle.[48] Ironically though, Bushrod Washington sensed far better than his uncle the profound change that republican thought was undergoing on matters such as representation and consent of the governed.[49] George Washington was certainly not alone in clinging to this old republican orthodoxy; but his views would soon be tested in the crucible of the presidency. This would not be the last he would hear from organizations like the Patriotic Society.

From Massachusetts to Philadelphia

For a man whose roots were so undeniably Virginian, it is striking how often Washington's career was shaped by events in that most un-Virginian of states, Massachusetts.[50] His early military career was frustrated in part by the decisions of the colonial supremo in Boston, Lord Loudoun. His most significant early appearance on the stage of national politics was as an advocate for the Fairfax Resolves—resolutions dedicated to uniting all Americans against British high-handedness in Boston. His first great victory as American commander-in-chief was the successful siege of British troops in Boston. Now, in the fall of 1786, events in Massachusetts were once again to shape Washington's political career.

Much of America was in an economic recession in 1786. As in most recessions its effects were borne more heavily by some Americans than others. In western Massachusetts economic hardship combined with long-standing political resentments to induce an armed rebellion against state authority led by former revolutionary officer, Daniel Shays. News of the insurrection caused Washington's barometer on national affairs to fall precipitously, triggering some of his most pessimistic reflections on the future prospects for republican government. The rebellion did not alter his political views. Indeed, as we shall see, Shays's Rebellion only confirmed his earlier jeremiads about impending disaster and his portents of ''some awful crisis.'' But his correspondence concerning the events in Massachusetts is significant because it coincides with his deliberations about whether to step onto the public stage again as an active participant in national political affairs. Although he had been content until that winter of 1786–87 to play the part of Cincinnatus, maintaining an interest in politics but preferring to exercise his influence quietly and largely out of the public eye, his restiveness over the state of public affairs became so acute that he decided to accept Virginia's offer to be a delegate to the upcoming convention at Philadelphia—a course of action fraught with the risk of permanent damage to his hard-won public status.

The story of Shays's Rebellion has been better told elsewhere,[51] but a brief review of the insurrection and, especially, its causes will help to place Washington's response into some context. The recession of 1786 had led to a decline in land values and agricultural prices for most American farmers. What made this hardship more painful in Massachusetts, though, were the policies of the state government. Dominated by the eastern cities whose welfare was tied more to trade and credit than was that of the interior, the General Court (Massachusetts's state legislature) enacted hard-money laws that required most debts to be paid in specie. In addition, the General Court imposed heavy taxes intended in part to redeem the war debts not only of the state, but also of Congress. The vigorous enforcement of these taxes and the perception that county courts were becoming exclusive instruments of the largely eastern creditor class exacerbated long-standing political divisions. Poverty and apathy had caused the western towns to be grossly underrepresented in the General Court.[52] Thus, the hard-money policies of the legislature were seen by many westerners as a declaration of war by the eastern mercantilists on virtuous, liberty-loving farmers. Local courts and the "eastern lawyers" that infested them were objects of particular derision.

The rebellion that emerged was largely unorganized. Mobs and threats of mobs sprang up in many towns, but little suggests that a concerted organization was behind them, certainly nothing as coordinated or as covert as the revolutionary Committees of Correspondence. A small band of ersatz "minutemen," led by Daniel Shays, began to drill in earnest, though for what purpose no one really knows. These spontaneous challenges to organized government evoked mortal fear among conservatives in the state who were sufficiently frightened by events to help the governor raise an army commanded by Benjamin Lincoln. This state "militia" scattered the rebellion in a series of minor skirmishes; and by early 1787 the whole thing was over.

The significance of the rebellion was not in what it was, but in what people *thought* it was. Washington, in particular, remained from start to finish singularly ignorant of the circumstances surrounding the rebellion: "For God's sake tell me what is the cause of these commotions."[53] The one person who served as Washington's primary source of information on the "commotions," Henry Knox, exaggerated the whole episode from start to finish. At one point he informed Washington that the rebels were a dangerous army of upwards of twelve-thousand well-armed men—this at a time when Knox surely knew otherwise (Shays's "army" was actually yet to organize and would never number more than about two thousand). Knox also hinted that the rebels were "levelers," dedicated to an egalitarian redistribution of property and political power.

Washington remained baffled by the motives of the rebels. His letters asked again and again whether they had legitimate grievances. If they did, Washington wondered why the government did not rectify them. Perhaps the state did not have the resources to deal with the problem immediately, but surely it could at least tell the people what it intended to do. If, on the other hand, the disturbances were the result of an excess of liberty ("licentiousness"), then why did the state not use its power and authority to put an immediate stop to them? A third hypothesis was that the whole insurrection was the work of a British conspiracy. Initially, this explanation appealed most to Washington. After all, he had maintained for some time that the self-interest and parochialism of the state governments would make them easy prey to manipulation by the British. But Knox's letters convinced him that the rebellion was purely domestic.

All three explanations, though, were grounded in a common perception—the great American experiment in self-government was in grave peril.

> What, gracious God, is man! that there should be such inconsistency and perfidiousness in his conduct? It is but the other day, that we were shedding our blood to obtain the Constitutions under which we now live: Constitutions of our own choice and making; and now we are unsheathing the sword to overturn them. The thing is so unaccountable, that I hardly know how to realize it, or to persuade myself that I am not under the illusion of a dream.[54]

Still, such a profound despair about American affairs was nothing new for Washington. In spite of all of his hopes for self-government in America, Washington retained a deep, occasionally even fatalistic, pessimism about achieving the republican dream. From 1780 on, it is almost impossible to find a period in his letters when he is not decrying the onset of some great crisis that threatens the very foundations of the constitutional order. Sometimes the villain is the perfidy of the British, sometimes the self-interestedness of the state governments, sometimes the lack of virtue in the American people, and sometimes the lassitude of Congress; but in every case the diagnosis is the same—republican self-government, like the virtuous citizenry that it requires, is so fragile that it demands constant nurturing, or else the noble experiment would fail not only in America, but in the Old World, too.

Thus, the significance of Shays's Rebellion is not that it transformed George Washington into a nationalist, or a conservative, or a republican, or an advocate of energy in government. He was all of those things before 1786. What changed was his determination to play a part in "saving" the experiment. When the rebellion was in its early stages his response was the same rather equivocal position he had maintained since the close of the war: the Articles of Confederation, as the embodiment of the federal constitutional system, should be supported fully by all of the member states, but amendments for its improvement should be considered. He was as yet unclear as to what the insurgents were up to.

If they were interested in constitutional reform, then perhaps they could yet be dealt with. But if they intended to harm the good order of the community, then "employ the force of government against them at once." Under no circumstances should a constitution established by the people be made hostage to the demands of an armed mob; nothing could make republican government "more contemptible" in the eyes of the world. "Let the reins of government then be braced and held with a steady hand, and every violation of the Constitution be reprehended: if defective, let it be amended, but not suffered to be trampled upon whilst it has an existence."[55]

When Washington learned that the rebellion had been dispersed he was greatly relieved and congratulated his Massachusetts friends on the success of the supporters of the state's constitutional government. But before the episode was closed he had already received notice of a call to a new convention in Philadelphia charged with the authority to consider amendments to the constitution (the Articles of Confederation). He also knew that there was an active campaign to sponsor him as a delegate to the convention. For several months he debated with himself and with his closest Virginia friends whether to go to Philadelphia.[56] In the end he accepted the charge. But the acceptance came months after the rebellion had ended. How then could the rebellion have had any influence on his decision?

The key to answering that question can be found in the republican idea of decay. Republican constitutions were usually founded in a spirit of unity and common purpose. Constitution making was a human undertaking of extraordinary moment; the disinterestedness that was needed for such an effort required a degree of public virtue found only on rare occasions. Once a constitution was established, the more normal forces generated by self-interest would begin chipping away at its finely balanced properties. Eventually, the constitution would either become the captive of a particular faction within the society who would use the power of government self-interestedly to suppress the liberties of the people or, even worse, would make government so ineffectual and lacking in respect that anarchy would ensue.[57]

Any constitution, but especially one grounded in the spirit of republicanism, faced the prospect of decay. Only regular renewal—a resort to first principles—could preserve the constitution. But if public virtue were to descend too far down the slippery slope of corruption, factionalism, and self-interest, then it would be best to simply have done with it. At a time when the outcome of Shays's Rebellion was still in doubt Washington confided to Henry Lee that "Influence is no Government. Let us have one by which our lives, liberties and properties will be secured; or let us know the worst at once."[58] The rebellion was symptomatic of a failure of constitutional nerve that was rapidly spreading throughout the union. Conflict was nothing new to American politics, but in the six months before the Philadelphia Convention Washington seems to have come to the conclusion that social and political gangrene was poisoning the constitutional tissue faster than it could be excised: "Fire, where there is inflamable matter, very rarely stops."

Even as Shays's Rebellion was disintegrating, new conflagrations were flaring up. Washington's neighboring state of Maryland was being torn asunder over the issue of paper money, and he saw the frightening visage of the paper-money junto in almost every state. Virginia had so far rejected most of these inflationary measures, but Washington lacked confidence that even his own state could long remain immune to the cancer of public disorder that seemed to metastasize with every letter he received.

We know now that this crisis was greatly exaggerated. Washington's correspondents were not a cross section of America in 1786. Many of them were social conservatives, former Revolutionary War generals and political allies, fellow nationalists, and men of property—men who held many political values in common with Washington. He relied on these correspondents as his eyes on national affairs. They kept Washington remarkably well informed on the events of the day, but they also shaded his perception of those events with their own biases. In a few cases, Henry Knox's accounts of Shays's Rebellion being the most extreme example, they even resorted to outright fabrication. Given his pessimistic nature and his tendency to view bad political news as the product of unseen conspiracies, it is no wonder that Washington had come to the conclusion that these events signaled the final crisis of the constitution. The rapidly spreading decay had to be reversed or the constitution would be irrevocably lost, and with it would go Washington's hopes for the "noble experiment."

Shays's Rebellion did not alter George Washington's political sentiments one iota. It confirmed many of his worst fears, but it did not create those fears. It did not, as some have supposed, convince him to abandon his support for the Articles. But the rebellion, taken together with a constant fusillade of news in the winter of 1786–87 about internal and external threats to the constitution, did convince Washington that some sort of drastic remedial action was necessary if republican self-government in America was to be preserved. It was in this context that he finally agreed, reluctantly, to accept appointment as a delegate to the convention in Philadelphia.

Republican hagiography demanded that its heroes always be willing to defend the republic against corruption and decay. As much to confirm his own virtue as to attain any specific reforms, Washington determined to end his public "retirement." To his old friend Lafayette he wrote that he had decided to attend a convention called by Congress "to revise and correct the defects" of the Articles. "What may be the result of this meeting is hardly within the scan of human wisdom to predict. It is considered however as the *last essay to support the present form* [my emphasis]."[59] If the effort failed, he would "know the worst at once."

4 / The Framer as Partisan

The process of founding the American Constitution neither began nor ended in Philadelphia in the summer of 1787. Important elements of our constitutional tradition, such as a commitment to the rule of law, a concern for liberty, and even the centrality of constitutional instruments themselves, were firmly in place before the call for a convention went out. Other important constitutional understandings, some deriving from custom and others implemented by formal amendment, emerged well after the federal Constitution was written and approved. Judicial review, executive dominance in matters of war and peace, an expansive federal responsibility for the economic well-being of the nation, and a commitment to political equality are all elements of our modern Constitution that transcend the text of the Constitution as first ratified.

Most significantly, an ethic of constitutionalism was already deeply ingrained in American political culture before the Philadelphia Convention.[1] One can point to the fact that all of the newly independent states established constitutional regimes as evidence that this ethic had put down permanent roots. No state could rightfully lay claim to popular legitimacy until it had constituted itself through a written compact of some kind. Thus, we ought not become overwhelmed by the mystique of 1787—the myth that the Founding Fathers somehow "created" the American constitutional tradition.

Yet while there seems little doubt that the tapestry depicting *any* American postrevolutionary political culture would have been deeply colored by a commitment to constitutionalism, there is equally little doubt that the particular hues of the yarn and the distinct patterns of the weave might have been different had there been no federal Constitution. A fascinating intellectual parlor game can be constructed from a consideration of the "what ifs" of history. What if the South had won the Civil War? What if Hitler's invasion of Britain had been successful? What if the British had met the constitutional demands of the American colonists? What if Alexander Hamilton (or John Hancock or John Adams) had been the first president? All of these "what if" propositions would make for interesting historical fiction. But for the serious scholar, these scenarios are ultimately unsatisfying. Real events are difficult enough to interpret without introducing nonevents into the calculus. Yet while we cannot know what our constitutional tradition would have looked like if the events of 1787–88 had not transpired, it requires no preposterous leap of imagination to suggest that it would have been different. In that sense, we ought not understate the significance of the Constitution of 1787.

George Washington's contributions to the writing of the Constitution are difficult to assess. Isolating the contributions of any single individual to a corporate project like the Constitutional Convention is always problematic. But Washington's imprint is there nonetheless. It can be found in Washington's encouragement of James Madison's plans for the convention that culminated in the submission of the Virginia Plan. It can be found in the symbolic significance of Washington's very attendance at Philadelphia, lending the enterprise a political legitimacy that it might otherwise have lacked. It can be found in his unstinting partisanship on behalf of the federalist cause—support that many of his contemporaries believed was critical to the success of the ratification struggle. And finally, it can be found in Washington's willingness to accept the presidency, a step that placed a final imprimatur on the new Constitution, encouraging even its opponents to give the new arrangements critical breathing space.

To Philadelphia or Not to Philadelphia

Washington received with great enthusiasm the call for a convention to consider amendments to the Articles of Confederation. After all, he had since 1780 counted himself among those who wanted a stronger national government; he had called for amendments to the Articles of Confederation in his Circular Letter to the States in the summer of 1783. The proposed convention now offered "an occasion so interesting to the wellbeing of the Confederacy" that Washington was initially tempted to suspend his retirement from public life in order to attend.[2] When Virginia quickly extended an offer to Washington to head that state's delegation to Philadelphia, the stage was set for his triumphal reentry into public life as the savior of the republic.

Nevertheless, he hesitated. For almost six months Washington played the reluctant bridegroom. He informed his correspondents that he supported the call for a convention and had great hopes for its work but that his own participation could not be relied upon. Still, he refused to give an outright no. Letters arrived almost daily from his friends in every part of the union imploring him to come to Philadelphia. Never saying no, never saying yes, Washington maintained his options until the last minute. Only when he left Mount Vernon on May 9, 1787, did his suitors know that Washington's commitment was final.

Washington was reluctant to go for two reasons. First, the Society of the Cincinnati, a fraternity of Revolutionary War officers, was convening in Philadelphia at about the same time. As president of the society in the previous year he had found himself in the eye of a storm. Critics of the Cincinnati, ever fearful of standing armies and whiffing the aroma of aristocracy, had complained about several aspects of the society. Washington had consulted several of these critics, principally Thomas Jefferson, and had urged the society to make several alterations in its constitution to meet their objections. While he retained a strong attachment to these former officers, the affair had been distasteful and had done much to confirm his decision to remain aloof from public affairs. As a result he had declined the society's invitation to attend its convention. His initial enthusiasm for the call for a convention to revise the Articles of Confederation waned considerably when he realized what his attendance would mean. He would be snubbing his old friends whose invitation he had declined and, perhaps even more importantly to a man of Washington's sentiments, he would be raising questions about his personal honor: "Under these circumstances it will readily be perceived that I could not appear at the same time and place . . . without giving offense."[3] The possibility for genuine insult was certainly there, yet Henry Knox, one of Washington's most trusted confidants and the formative force behind the Cincinnati, assured him that going to Philadelphia would not lower his esteem in the eyes of the officers. Indeed, they would view it as more evidence of his service to the nation.

Yet Washington still wavered, a reluctance that can be better explained by a second, less noble, reason. What, after all, had been the result of every prior effort at constitutional reform? Had not his own plea for more energetic measures in 1783 been uniformly ignored? Had not the recent Annapolis Convention been so poorly attended (in Washington's view yet another sign of the self-interest and perfidy of the states) that it had dissolved without resolving any of the issues for which it had been convened?[4] Washington was never a great political philosopher, but experience had made him an exceptionally good reader of the political winds. He knew that his reputation was his only real source of political influence, especially outside of Virginia. He also understood that expending his reputation on behalf of failed enterprises could only diminish his ability to affect the course of political events. To paraphrase Richard Neustadt's famous work on the American presidency, nothing predicts future success as well as past successes, and nothing predicts future failure as well as past failures.[5] Washington understood this principle and clearly wanted to distance himself from the Philadelphia effort until he was more confident of its chances for success. The crises of 1786–87 were escalating to an ominous level, but it was still unclear whether the forces representing energy in government, a strong national union, and social stability were yet strong enough to have their way. The "thinking part of the people of this Country" supported the call for a convention.[6] But was that enough? As he put the problem to Knox, one of the reasons against his attendance was "an apprehension that all the States will not appear; and that some of them, being unwillingly drawn into the measure, will send their Delegates so fettered as to embarrass, and perhaps render nugatory the whole proceedings. In either of these circumstances . . . I should not like to be a sharer in this business."[7]

In sum, Washington never doubted the propriety of a convention to consider constitutional reforms. His support for the effort was enthusiastic from the outset. He also understood that his own reputation cast on the side of the reformers would aid the effort immensely. What he seemed unwilling to do was to commit that enormous, but not irreducible, reputation to the cause before he had some sense that his own efforts would be decisive. Biographers debate whether Washington's indecisiveness was morally defensible given the stakes involved. But when he became convinced that the Virginia delegation, at least, was committed to nothing less than a complete reexamination of the principles of union, he hesitated no more. Once committed, Washington added his considerable influence to the side of those who were prepared to risk the most. And that is no small thing.

Virginia's Plan

On May 29, 1787, after the delegates had spent several days debating matters of procedure and protocol, Edmund Randolph, governor of Virginia, arose to address "the main business" of the convention. He discussed the seriousness of the crisis facing American affairs and indicated some of the specific defects of government under the Articles of Confederation. He then offered fifteen resolutions for consideration, the first of which "Resolved that the Articles of Confederation ought to be so corrected & enlarged as to accomplish the objects proposed by their institution; namely, 'common defence, security of liberty and general welfare.' "[8] The rest of the Virginia Plan, however, was committed to a project far more ambitious than merely correcting and enlarging the Articles.[9] It sought, instead, to subvert the old constitution and substitute an entirely different notion of government—one that to the ears of one of its most perceptive critics, Robert Yates of New York, "meant a strong *consolidated* union, in which the idea of states should be nearly annihilated."[10]

Three-and-a-half months later a new federal Constitution was submitted to the states for their approval. The finished product bore little resemblance to the Virginia Plan submitted by Randolph. The outline of governmental structure proposed by the plan was still discernible, but many of its most distinguishing features (e.g., nullification of state laws, a national legislature based solely on state population or wealth, provision for a council of revision, an executive accountable to Congress) had vanished. Why then do we continue to pay such homage to the Virginia Plan and to James Madison, whose acclamation as the Father of the Constitution is based in large part on his role as principal author of the plan? How could the plan have been so important to the founding process when so few of its words found their way into the Constitution?

What makes the submission of the Virginia Plan such a pivotal moment in the Philadelphia Convention and thus in the development of our particular constitutional tradition is vested in a fundamental truth in politics: timing counts. Scholars and politicians have long understood that control of the agenda usually leads to control of the substantive outcomes. The Virginia Plan set the convention on a course in which a new constitution, not mere revision or reform, was the agenda. As this agenda played out, the federal Constitution emerged rather differently in its details from the one envisioned in the Virginia Plan. But the decision to even consider a new constitution was set in motion by the plan. What if the convention had become bogged down in the kind of bickering over specific amendments to the Articles that had plagued Congress for several years? What if Hamilton's more audacious plan had been introduced first? We don't know. What we do know is that the agenda-setting Virginia Plan moved the delegates down a path from which they did not waver after Randolph's presentation—the creation of a new constitution, more nationalist than anything contemplated under the Articles.[11]

Washington's own plans and aspirations for the convention—the elusive "intentions" of this framer—cannot be discerned from any one document. His political ideas had always been more concerned with the purposes of government; he had spoken only occasionally about particular procedural or structural aspects of government. Constitutional arrangements were not unimportant to Washington (he was convinced, for example, that the Articles of Confederation were seriously flawed), but instead of specific constitutional reforms he concerned himself more with advocating certain policy ends, such as a strong national defense establishment, payment of the war debt, the promotion of foreign and domestic commercial linkages, western expansion, hard currency, and a general strengthening of the union.

Even when his decision to attend the convention was imminent, Washington cloaked his constitutional vision in generalities. A letter to James Madison shortly before he departed for Philadelphia comes closest to revealing Washington's hopes, or intentions, for the convention. He confessed to Madison, first, that he would be disappointed if the national government did not emerge with more powers ("energy") at the end of the day. Second, he would be equally disappointed if the national legislature "still wants . . . that secrecy and dispatch (either from the nonattendance, or the local views of its members) which is characteristick of good Government." In short, he envisioned a legislative body fully capable of making *national* policy. A Congress that served as an assemblage of local ambassadors would no longer do. Third, any system for selecting national legislators should enable them to *be* national legislators. Congress must exercise its powers "with a firm and steady hand, instead of frittering them back to the Individual States where the members in place of viewing themselves in their National character, are too apt to be looking." His final observation revealed the despair induced by Shays's Rebellion, the failure of the Annapolis Convention, the weakness of Congress (and the states) in the face of European intrusions into American affairs, the rage for paper money, and other events of 1786–87. Washington wondered whether public virtue, the foundation of any truly republican society, had declined so far that perhaps his faith in the noble experiment had been misplaced all along. Republicanism depended on a shared notion of what was in the public interest. Without that consensus, force (or at least greatly centralized power) might be the only remedy for saving the union. "I have my doubts whether any system without the means of coercion in the Sovereign, will enforce Obedience to the Ordinances of a Genl. Government; without which, every thing else fails." But even here Washington's recommendations lacked specificity. Coercion was necessary, "But the kind of coercion you may ask? This indeed will require thought."[12]

Thought was certainly necessary. Washington prided himself on his ability to reflect deliberately and not succumb to unenlightened passion. But this same letter also signaled Madison that Washington had jettisoned his earlier fear that the convention might end in failure. Despite the risks, Washington was now prepared to move beyond the point of recommending half-measures. He admitted to Madison that he was anxious "that the convention may adopt no temporizing expedient, but probe the defects of the Constitution to the bottom, and *provide radical cures* [my emphasis]; whether they are agreed to or not; a conduct like this, will stamp wisdom and dignity on the proceedings, and be looked to as a luminary, which sooner or later will shed its influence."[13]

Madison had already come to the conclusion that the Articles of Confederation provided too fragile a scaffold on which to construct constitutional reforms and was preparing some proposals for a new constitution.[14] Washington's letter emboldened Madison even further.

Perhaps his proposals could be endorsed by the entire Virginia delegation, adding the weight of Washington's enormous reputation to his
own ideas? In words that virtually mirrored Washington's, Madison assured the general that his call for radical reforms was right on the mark:
"Temporising applications will dishonor the Councils which propose
them, and may foment the internal malignity of the disease, at the
same time they produce an ostensible palliation of it. Radical attempts,
although unsuccessful, will at least justify the authors of them." Having assured Washington that the two Virginians were of one mind on
this point Madison then sought to enlist Washington's support, in-
forming him that he (Madison) had "formed in my mind *some* outlines
of a new system" and that he was taking "the liberty of submitting
them without apology, to your eye."[15] Madison's outline was nothing
less than an exposition of the principles soon to animate the Virginia
Plan.

The Virginia delegates were among the first to arrive in Philadelphia.
In his diary Washington wrote of his continuing concern about the
prospect of another Annapolis. May 14:"This being the day appointed
for the meeting of the convention . . . it was found that two States only
were represented." May 16: still "only two states represented." May 19:
A day after New York's delegation arrived, "No more states represented."[16] Despite these worries Washington met almost daily with the
other Virginia delegates to review strategy and to revise Madison's recommendations in hopes that they might be the instrument by which
Virginia could seize control of the convention. Virginia was, after all,
the largest state in both land and population; some care was needed to
assure that any new system would give "that great state a rightful place
in the councils of the republic."[17] The product of those deliberations
was the Virginia Plan.

No notes of those meetings exist, so it is difficult to assess Washington's contributions to the plan. One account suggests that Washington
was the dominant force within the delegation and that Madison, even
granting his authorship of most of the plan's principal provisions, was a
"brain truster" in service to Washington and the other senior members
of the delegation.[18] This assessment goes too far. Madison's leadership
in presenting the ideas of the plan to his colleagues is indisputable. But
it is useful to remember that Madison's notions did not spring *ex ni-
hilo*. Washington and many other critics of confederational politics had

been voicing similar ideas for some time. Washington had, for example, previously urged consideration of some method of truly *national* representation (resolves 3, 4, and 5). He had pleaded since the days of the Revolution for the establishment of a coercive power in the national government (resolve 6). As commander-in-chief he often called on Congress to establish executives with clear responsibility and authority to implement the nation's laws, especially with regard to supplying the army (resolve 7). His antipathy toward the particularism of the states was well-known, and he certainly would have supported almost any provisions that prevented the states from obstructing great national purposes (resolves 6, 8, and 14). Thus, when Randolph arose to address the convention he truly spoke for Washington as well as for Virginia.

The Silent Delegate from Virginia

The Virginia Plan was the first substantive proposal before the convention, but it was not the first order of business. The delegates recognized that they would have to agree on rules and procedures for the convention before proceeding to the concerns that had brought them to Philadelphia. A presiding officer had to be chosen. Washington was the obvious choice, and the delegates quickly moved to place him in the chair. The delegates could not know exactly what would transpire in the convention. But they surely sensed that their recommendations, whether mild or radical, had little chance of success unless the delegates could lay claim to some measure of legitimacy; they needed to portray their work as a genuine legacy of the Revolution. Americans of 1787 were inclined toward a view of events that was more than a bit conspiratorial. If the convention could be portrayed by suspicious opponents as a self-interested, or even worse, unpatriotic, rump gathering, then its recommendations would be quickly dismissed. But with George Washington presiding, any criticisms of the convention's patriotic credentials would be deflected.

Apart from this symbolic function, though, what role did Washington play in the work of the convention? Can he be counted among the most important framers? At first glance the answer seems obvious. Washington believed that his position as the convention's presiding officer obliged him to direct the proceedings without expressing his own views. Only once, at the very end of the convention, did Washington speak on a matter of constitutional substance. The delegates were about to approve the enrolled version of the Constitution when Nathaniel Gorham, a delegate from Massachusetts, moved that the number of representatives not exceed one for every thirty thousand persons, instead of forty thousand persons as the draft Constitution stipulated. According to Madison's account Washington rose and said

> that although his situation had hitherto restrained him from offering his sentiments on questions . . . yet he could not forbear expressing his wish that the alteration proposed might take place. It was much to be desired that the objections to the plan recommended might be as few as possible—The smallness of the proportion of Representatives had been considered by many members of the convention, an insufficient security for the rights & interests of the people. He acknowledged that it had always appeared to himself among the exceptionable parts of the plan; and late as the present moment was for admitting amendments, he thought this of so much consequence that it would give much satisfaction to see it adopted.[19]

Madison notes that there was no opposition to Gorham's motion and that it was immediately agreed upon unanimously, apparently without even a recorded vote. The unanimity is a bit surprising. The size of congressional districts had been debated earlier in the convention. The draft of the Constitution at that time had stipulated that each state would be allocated one representative for every forty thousand persons. Madison feared that with immigration and the addition of new states this rigid formula would soon make the House of Representatives too large to act as a deliberative body. Therefore, he and Roger Sherman proposed that the phrase be amended so that apportionment would be assigned by a rate *not exceeding* one for every forty thousand persons. The motion was approved without dissent.[20] In other words, on the one earlier occasion when the convention had considered the question of the size of legislative districts it had replaced a rule that guaranteed one representative to every forty thousand persons with one that stipulated that the *minimum* size of districts would be forty thousand persons—a choice that clearly favored energy and legislative effectiveness over representation. It was a time when the large-scale republicans who favored an invigorated national government dominated the convention's agenda.

Washington's support for lowering the threshold for representation is curious for two reasons. First, Washington was firmly in the camp of the large-scale republicans before, during, and after the convention. Yet Gorham's motion not only revived a notion more dear to the small-scale republicans than to men of Washington's ilk, it reopened a question on which the nationalists had earlier prevailed without much opposition. Second, the whole matter of the size of legislative districts was, frankly, not very important in the grand scheme of things. It did not affect the structure, purpose, or powers of the federal plan of government that was about to go forth to the states. It was an interesting detail, to be sure; but it was still only a detail.

Yet Washington took this one occasion to speak before the convention and in so doing persuaded the earlier winning coalition to concede a point they had already obtained.[21] Washington's reason for reducing the minimum size of congressional districts reveals the pragmatic side of his constitutional thinking. The sentiments of most Americans in 1787 were, broadly speaking, republican. But one of the most important distinctions between small-scale republicans and large-scale republicans was the former's concern for adequate representation. Representatives had to be close to the people; they had to truly reflect the values and interests of the community in which they lived. Indeed, small-scale republicans believed that the representative and his constituents should be so much in harmony that the representative would perceive the protection of the people's rights and liberties as the protection of his own. To this end, there should be many representatives (to avoid domination of the assembly by a few), and they should be close to the people (in other words, they should be chosen from small, homogeneous districts).[22] Washington, Madison, and other large-scale republicans understood that ratification of the new Constitution would require the support, or at least the quiescence, of some of these small-scale republicans. Washington correctly anticipated that the representation question, if not shaped well, might confirm the fears of many of the Constitution's potential opponents.[23] Washington thought it wise to moderate the apportionment formula in order to focus the ratification debate on issues more advantageous to the federalists.

If, however, this were Washington's sole contribution to the founding, some might wonder why his portrait hangs in the gallery of constitutional demigods. How could a delegate who took such a minuscule role in the debates and who spoke not at all on the great issues of the convention be characterized in nearly every interpretive history of the Constitutional Convention as one of the most important Founders? This, however, is the wrong question. It equates one's level of oratory with one's effectiveness; it suggests that political influence can only be evidenced by overt public activity.

First, the contributions of Washington-as-symbol would have been indispensable even had he not taken an active role in the convention's deliberations. We often fall into raptures about the careful architecture of the Constitution or about how the delegates manifested the highest form of reason and deliberation or about the elevated quality of the convention's debates or about the collective intelligence of the Founders. However much these encomiums are deserved, it is paradoxically true that for much of America the work of the Constitution was judged on an entirely irrational, personalistic criterion—George Washington was for it. In this sense, it might be argued that Washington's greatest founding contribution was in his decision to attend the convention. By lending to the project his unparalleled public reputation and status as revolutionary hero he provided a reservoir of public sympathy that the federalists were able to tap effectively in the ratification struggle.[24]

But Washington was no mere symbol; he was an active participant in the work of the convention. Harkening back to his diligent service as commander-in-chief, he was one of a handful of delegates who attended every session of the convention. He despaired that the wrangling and periodic deadlocks at the convention would cause the delegates to disperse without finishing their work, a result that would cause him far more personal humiliation than it would the rest of the delegates. But he never abandoned the project.[25]

Although Washington as presiding officer chose not to participate in the great debates of the convention, he remained a member of the Virginia delegation and very likely *voted* on every substantive issue before the convention. Indeed, on those many occasions when the convention deliberated as a committee of the whole house Washington stepped down from the chair and sat with his fellow Virginians. But at no time did he surrender his vote as a delegate. We know this despite the fact that Madison recorded the roll calls by states, not by individuals. On a few occasions when the sentiments within the Virginia delegation were not unanimous Madison reveals how those individuals voted. In almost every instance, Washington is shown to have cast a vote. Why Madison goes to these lengths in explaining the votes of Virginia's delegates is uncertain. He offers no such individual polling for any of the other state delegations. Some have suggested that Madison was attempting to show to a later generation that Washington and Madison were on the same side of many of the more controversial issues at the convention.[26] Whatever Madison's motives were, his notes are powerful evidence that Washington actively participated in the work of the convention.

What did Washington vote for? That is a more elusive question. Since Madison only recorded a few of Washington's individual votes, we cannot know for certain where he stood on the hundreds of other motions and proposals. But it is reasonable to assume that he probably voted with his fellow Virginians in most of those cases. Thus, Virginia's vote is probably a fair reflection of Washington's constitutional agenda. And where did Virginia stand? She consistently supported a national government with substantially extended powers, a national legislature and executive chosen directly or indirectly by the principle of proportionality (a typical large-state position), substantial limitations on the powers of the states to restrict or interfere in national concerns, a strong executive with virtual independence from the states, and she opposed an enlargement of the powers of the Senate (again, a large-state position). Virginia, then, supported the broad notion of large-scale republicanism but also voted so as to enhance Virginia's relative influence within that national republic.[27] There is nothing in this agenda inconsistent with ideas that Washington had advocated months and even years before the convention, so it is likely that he lent consistent support to the delegation's positions.

But Washington's votes on several specific questions, including a few in which he was on the losing side, *are* known. Those votes provide a more specific frame of reference for assessing Washington's constitutional intentions. Aside from his aforementioned support for smaller legislative districts, Washington's known positions at the convention can be grouped into two areas of concern: first, his consistent support for a strong, independent, and energetic executive, and second, his commitment, with one significant exception, to an expansion of powers for the national government.

Washington was justifiably uncomfortable with discussions of the executive power. His political instincts were almost always on the mark, and he surely knew that his presence at the convention affected the way the other delegates, aware that Washington would probably be offered the mantle of national leadership, perceived the structure and powers of the national executive. Some hint of this feeling can be seen on the first day in which the matter of the executive branch was considered. James Wilson moved that the executive consist of a single person, and Charles Pinckney seconded the motion. Madison then reports that "a considerable pause" ensued in which no delegate appeared willing to speak to the motion. Washington, as chair, was forced to ask the delegates if they wished to vote on the motion—a suggestion intended to elicit debate on this important matter. Again, silence. John Rutledge finally offered some thoughts on the subject, but only after he had "animadverted on the shyness of gentlemen on this and other subjects."[28] One can only speculate on the cause for this initial reticence since the delegates were rarely without strong feelings on other important questions. The most likely answer is that the delegates did not wish to offend Washington and had some difficulty at first in separating the man from the office. But Washington's reluctance to engage in these debates apparently assured the delegates that he intended to distance himself from the discussions. After those first awkward moments, the executive debates proceeded vigorously.

But Washington's silence did not signal his lack of interest in the subject. His sentiments toward executive authority appear at least three times. On James Wilson's motion recommending a single executive, Washington predictably voted "yes."[29] His revolutionary experience had soured him on executive power administered by committee. Only the singular energies of Robert Morris had enabled the army to win its decisive victory at Yorktown. At most other times, the executive arrangements under the Confederation had amply demonstrated their inadequacy to Washington. He did not wish to see the new Constitution travel down this rutted road again.

When executive branch matters were taken up again six weeks later Washington again confirmed his sentiments in favor of a strong executive. This time the issue was executive independence. At this point in the debates the executive was to be selected by the national legislature for a renewable term of seven years. James McClurg of Virginia moved to have the executive serve "during good behavior." McClurg's resolution, supported by Madison, was intended to unfetter the executive from control by the legislative branch. A president's tenure in office could only be terminated as a result of actions so clearly detrimental to the national interest as to trigger the extraordinary majorities stipulated in the impeachment clause. They argued that the principle of separation of powers insisted that simple majorities within the legislature, subject as they might be to quickly shifting coalitions, could not be permitted to hold the executive hostage to its will. If reeligibility were contingent upon such tenuous arrangements no executive could ever perform his constitutional responsibilities without the specter of legislative disapproval and removal. Another Virginian, George Mason, spoke, and presumably voted, against the motion. Since Virginia voted to support the motion (the convention disapproved it) Washington almost certainly must have voted in favor of it. Such a view would be consistent with his "strong executive" sentiments, especially if Farrand is correct in suggesting that the motion was less concerned with proposing an elected monarch than with signaling a broader concern for executive independence.[30] Washington would have been justifiably nervous about supporting the former but would have been quite comfortable with the latter principle.

On July 26 the convention considered the now much-amended part of the Virginia Plan regarding the executive. It approved the resolution and committed it to a Committee of Detail for further fine-tuning. Washington, however, voted against the resolution, a position that at first glance might seem curious. Again, we have no discussion in the record that explains his position. But one provision in the resolution would have given him pause. The resolution called for the executive to be ineligible for a second term. Washington's views on rotation in office were well known and reflected his conservative republican beliefs. Some republicans believed that the power of political office was so inherently corrupting that all elected officeholders should serve short terms with no reeligibility. This provision would hold true especially for the national executive whose power of appointment might allow him to accrue an inordinate influence over public affairs if unchecked by a term limitation. It was the old Country fear of the Court—a fear

Washington no longer shared. The president would be an American, not some far-distant potentate. The Constitution provided for ample checks on his power. All that a term limitation would accomplish, Washington complained to Lafayette, was to preclude "ourselves from the services of any man, who on some great emergency shall be deemed universally, most capable of serving the Public." The electoral college virtually assured that any president would be a man of great virtue and reputation. To then deliberately undermine the ability of the people to keep such a man in office seemed to Washington to assume such a depravity in men as to make republican government a hopeless quest.[31] Again, Washington preferred energy in government over arrangements intended to limit the opportunity for corruption.

Finally, as the convention neared final agreement on the new Constitution, Hugh Williamson of North Carolina proposed that the legislative majority needed to override a presidential veto be reduced from three-fourths to two-thirds of Congress. A few delegates saw the matter as one in which seven senators (conceivably from only four states) could, with the cooperation of the president, thwart the will of the people. Others, and we must count Washington among this group, saw the resolution as an attempt to limit the independence and authority of the executive. The electoral college already ensured that the president would be a person worthy of the nation's highest confidence. Additional limits on the president's ability to protect the public interest from temporary majoritarian impulses would undermine the principle virtue of a republican presidency—an executive capable of guarding the people's liberties against "democratical" forces. Washington (with Madison) voted against the motion, but it carried nonetheless.

These few votes place Washington firmly in the "strong executive" camp at the convention.[32] His other votes reveal an almost equally fervent support for a strong national legislature with powers fully consonant with energetic government. On June 8 the delegates considered a motion "that the National Legislature should have authority to negative all Laws which they should judge to be improper."[33] The Virginia Plan had stipulated that the national legislature could only negative those state laws that were deemed inconsistent with the federal constitution. Thus the effect of the motion was to restore the negative power to the scale first envisioned by James Madison, whose preference was for a "negative in all cases whatsoever." Discussions among the Virginia delegates before the convention apparently modified Madison's original proposal in favor of the less expansive version that appeared in the plan, though for what reasons we cannot say for sure.[34] Virginia voted in favor of the motion, with Madison, Wythe, and McClurg marked "aye" and Mason and Randolph opposed; but the motion failed in the convention. (Indeed, the negative on state laws would eventually be removed entirely.)

Madison notes, curiously, that Washington was "not consulted" on this vote. At first glance this seems odd, for Washington was one of the most diligent participants in the work of the convention. Yet Madison's account should not really be so surprising. Even in these early days of the convention it was clear that Washington would probably take a prominent part in the new government, most likely as chief executive. Washington seems not to have wanted to admit it; retirement still seemed preferable to the hurly-burly of national politics. But his abstention here is once again a mark of his political sense. Washington would certainly have supported the motion on its merits. He had long held little regard for many of the state legislatures and had spoken often of having a Congress empowered to legislate in all areas that affected the national interest. As a defensive mechanism, he surely would have supported a motion that prevented the states from intruding into Congress's plenary authority. Had he opposed the motion, his vote would have divided the Virginia delegation 3–3; thus we can presume that Washington supported the stronger negative. But since Madison did not need his vote, Washington wisely refrained from expressing his true sentiments. As a matter of principle, he strongly supported any measure that would prevent the states from passing "illiberal" legislation: paper-money bills, stay laws, limits on trade, and the like. As a matter of practical politics, he probably recognized that such an adamantly antistate stance might later threaten his ability to generate confidence in the national executive.

Another illustration of Washington's support for a strong, independent general government was his consistent support of taxing powers. The lack of such a steady source of revenue had often been the crux of General Washington's entreaties to Congress and the states during the Revolution. So long as it was dependent on the states for funds and had no means to enforce compliance with its requisitions, Congress was a government in name only. He had consistently urged the states to permit Congress to lay taxes directly upon the people. He was especially enamored of the impost (a duty on imports). He believed it was a voluntary tax capable of enabling Congress to do "much good, justice, and propriety."[35] Because the impost required the consent of all thirteen states, any one state could prevent its enactment. By 1786, after five years of compromise and cajoling, the impost had been ratified by twelve states—even by the usually obstinate Rhode Island. But the thirteenth state, New York, approved it with such conditions that Congress finally gave up.[36] The failure of the impost, as much as Shays's Rebellion or any other event of 1786–87, hardened Washington's attitude toward the Articles of Confederation. The episode reaffirmed what Washington had known (and experienced) for almost ten years—the states would never give Congress the support that an honorable nation needed.

The nationalists at the convention believed that independent taxing authority went hand in hand with energetic government. But there was less consensus on the kinds of direct taxation that would be appropriate. On August 21 Madison moved that exports could not be taxed "unless by consent of two thirds of the Legislature." This amendment was a change from the absolute prohibition against such taxes that the convention had already approved. Supporters believed that the two-thirds provision would offer a sufficient safeguard against abuse. The issue was one of a number of measures where the state delegations divided roughly along the Mason-Dixon line. Southern states were opposed, believing that export taxes would penalize their substantial trade with Europe in agricultural commodities. Washington and Madison supported the motion, believing that such limitations might cut off the national government from an important source of revenue. Import duties, export duties, and the sale of lands were the only obvious direct sources of revenue. Remove one pedestal and the national government's independence might be irreparably weakened. Washington was a busy, though none-too-successful, exporter, as were many of his Virginia neighbors. But in a matter such as this, localism had no place in his thinking. How could the export trade or even his own state long remain healthy in a weak union? Without a strong national government the European leviathan would soon seize the very economic liberties that many of the delegates sought to protect. Clear as this truth was to

Washington, he could not convince even his Virginia delegation, and they voted with five other states to defeat the motion.

On August 13, the convention considered (for what seemed like the umpteenth time!) whether money bills should originate exclusively in the House of Representatives. The request was not extraordinary. It was a right under the ancient British constitution that only the people's representatives could authorize taxes. Many colonial assemblies jealously maintained that right against the usurpations of the royal governors, and nearly every state constitution continued this tradition in some form or another. Yet some delegates insisted that in a bicameral legislature with both chambers responsible to the people, the British analogy was not apt. Strict adherence to such a rule would only clog the machinery of government. Moreover, without equal authority in such business the Senate would fail to attract the "better sort of men." Madison comments that Washington opposed giving the House this exclusive role regarding money bills, a position that was hardly surprising given his sentiments in favor of high-toned government. But Madison notes that the matter was not a high priority with Washington and that he was willing to concede the point in order to mollify other delegates whose votes might be needed later. Ironically, the convention defeated the proposal (in other words, supporting Washington's *real* sentiments) this time, but later revived it.[37]

There was at least one other issue, though, on which Washington was averse to yielding *any* ground. He had long reserved a special kind of animus toward paper money. Charles Beard argued that Washington's hatred of paper money was a result of his personal economic circumstances. Beard pointed out that much of his wealth was tied up in landholdings whose value was principally in the rents and mortgages that Washington could collect. If debtors could pay those obligations in depreciated currency at, say, forty cents on the dollar, then Washington would find himself at a disadvantage.[38] (Keep in mind, however, that much of this land came to Washington either through marriage or by bounty. In either case, he had not paid for it in specie.) Others insist that Washington's economic status was more complicated.[39] As is true with most "farmers," Washington was often in debt for his seed, forage, equipment, and even his taxes. Under those conditions Washington would have been as delighted as any other debtor to pay off in paper.

In sum, Washington's interests cannot be exclusively classified as either debtor-oriented or creditor-oriented.

It is just possible that Washington opposed paper money as a matter of principle. Recall, for example, Washington's adamant insistence on Americans paying their lawful debts to the British at a time when his self-interest would have been better served by "stiffing" them. Washington was both a conservative and a Virginia "gentleman." As such, he believed that a contract was a bond of personal honor. To pay off a debt in devalued currency, even when such payment was legal tender, was to devalue one's personal reputation as well. He could occasionally joke about the issue, as when he urged Madison to write him regularly even though Washington admitted that he might not always have the time to reply: "I shall become your debtor, and possibly like others in similar circumstances (when the debt is burthensome) may feel a disposition . . . to pay you off in depreciated paper, which being a legal tender . . . you cannot refuse. You will receive the nominal value, and that you know quiets the conscience, and makes all things easy, with the debtor."[40] But he could also be brutally serious, at one point authorizing his manager to look for ways to evict tenants who "have taken advantage of me by paying paper money when Six pence on a shilling would pay a pound."[41]

Like most conservatives Washington tended to project private virtues (and vices) onto the public arena. If deception, opportunism, and dishonorable conduct were departures from private virtue, so also were they corruptions of public virtue. And no republic worthy of the name could long survive if it provided ordinary citizens with the wherewithal (paper money) to undermine private virtue. Washington saw paper money as a cancer, a political virus capable of sweeping all before it: "Paper money has had the effect in your State that it will ever have, to ruin commerce, oppress the honest, and open a door to every species of fraud and injustice."[42]

As a political economist, George Washington was rather unsophisticated in his thinking and drew much from vestiges of his old Country ideology. Beyond his concern for public virtue, his specific objections to paper money were threefold. First, it disadvantaged the "productive" classes—those in society who generated the wealth that benefitted all. "Depreciation keeps pace with the quantity of the emission, and articles, for which it is exchanged, rise in a greater ratio than the sinking value of the money. Wherein, then, is the farmer, the planter, the artisan benefitted? The debtor may be, because as I have observed, he gives the shadow in lieu of the substance; and in proportion to his gain, the creditor or the body politic suffer."[43] Paper money favored consumption over production, profligacy over frugality, and short-term gain over long-term prosperity. Such policies did not, in Washington's view, favor the genuine public interest.

His second objection to paper money was in the way he thought it promoted speculation. "An evil equally great is, the door it immediately opens for speculation, by which the least designing, and perhaps most valuable, part of the community are preyed upon by the more knowing and crafty speculators."[44] Washington was especially sensitive about the evils of speculation. During the Revolution he railed against the actions of speculators, middlemen, and stock jobbers, all of whom he accused of war profiteering. Such men added nothing to the wealth or productive capacity of the community; indeed, they drained off resources in a way that jeopardized the freedom of all Americans. Some of this feeling was no doubt the traditional Virginia planter's distrust of banking and cities. But the war had made Washington's hatred of speculation even more pronounced. If speculators were for paper money, then that was all the more reason for him to oppose it.

Finally, paper money introduced the very sort of social divisions that Washington believed were incompatible with true republicanism. By pitting debtor against creditor and class against class, the paper-money question destabilized society and jeopardized the sense of common purpose essential for the survival of republicanism.

As Washington arrived in Philadelphia, the paper-money cancer had already metastasized into the political bloodstream of Maryland, Massachusetts, Rhode Island (where Washington later referred to its adherents as the "paper money junto"[45]), and even of Virginia. Thus it should come as no surprise that when, on August 13, the convention considered whether to strike the clause that granted Congress authority to "emit bills on the credit of the United States" Virginia (and presumably Washington) voted in favor of the motion.[46] This was the only vote Washington cast that would have restricted the power of the new national government. Thus, we cannot say that his nationalistic fervor knew no bounds.

The Intentions (and Successes) of a Framer

On September 17, 1787, almost four months after the Convention had been called to order, Benjamin Franklin rose to implore the delegates to consider their own fallibility and join in signing the finished document as a sign of their collective efforts. George Mason, Edmund Randolph, and Elbridge Gerry declined, each for his own reasons. But the remainder agreed to affix their signatures to the document.[47] The immediate business of *proposing* a new Constitution was at an end.

How important was George Washington to the shaping of that new Constitution? How successful was he in imprinting his own constitutional agenda onto the final product? The first of those questions is the more problematic. It is always difficult to sort out the specific contributions that any one individual makes to a collegial enterprise. That effort is especially difficult when the historical record is as incomplete as it is for the convention. Moreover, Washington's visible participation in the work of the convention was slight—just nine discernible votes and one substantive suggestion on the last day of the convention. Add to this the fact that on those nine votes he was on the *losing* side six times, hardly the record of an influential framer.

The second question calls for a different sort of assessment. Rather than asking what Washington's influence was relative to other delegates (a question that we have seen poses insurmountable measurement problems), it asks how completely Washington accomplished his own constitutional agenda. This view of political influence seeks to assess one's influence principally by measuring how well one achieves one's own goals.[48] Players who consistently "win" in the political process (that is, those who achieve their goals) are deemed powerful. Whether those same players were the exclusive agency of their successes is largely irrelevant. By this approach Washington's effectiveness at the convention can be best determined by asking how closely its results conformed with his preconvention agenda. If Washington emerged with lots of "wins" and relatively few "losses," his effectiveness would be difficult to dispute.

Washington did not believe that the final work of the convention embodied a complete triumph of his constitutional aspirations. To Edmund Randolph, fellow Virginia delegate to the convention but a nonsigner of the Constitution, he conceded that there were "some things in the new form, I will readily acknowledge, which never did, and I am persuaded never will, obtain my *cordial* approbation." Yet, in his attempt to win over the wavering Randolph he further noted that "in the aggregate, it is the best Constitution that can be obtained at this Epocha."[49]

Washington had good reason to support the Constitution. It contained much that *did* meet with his cordial approbation. Washington had recommended many constitutional reforms in the previous half-dozen years—some specific, some more general. A review of these themes suggests why Washington became one of the Constitution's most resolute advocates in the struggle for ratification.

One cluster of themes prominent in Washington's preconvention agenda was concerned with establishing a stronger, more energetic central government with powers sufficient to address and resolve what he believed were grave national problems. He had been particularly critical of the states and their propensity to interfere with the great goals of the union. To Washington's disappointment, the convention refused to grant to Congress the power to nullify state legislation. That decision was hardly surprising given the political realities confronting the delegates. The final document would have to be submitted to the states for their approval. Such a provision would probably have "nullified" any hopes of ratification.

But other provisions pleased him. The states were specifically prohibited from interfering with many of the most important functions of the national government (Art. I, Sec. 10). Both the president, through his authority to "take care that the laws be faithfully executed" (Art. II, Sec. 3), and the judiciary, through its authority to hear all cases involving federal questions (Art. III, Sec. 2), were given substantial power to enforce national law, even against the states if necessary. The Supremacy Clause (Art. VI) made it clear that federal laws and federal treaties were superior to state laws.

The new Constitution also granted exclusivity to the national government in military matters and foreign relations, an issue of central concern to Washington since his service as commander-in-chief. True, Congress under the Articles of Confederation held similar responsibility, but it was responsibility without authority. The new structure of the Constitution provided an arsenal of powers fully capable of preempting any state interference in such matters.

The Philadelphia Convention had also gone substantially beyond the Articles in providing constitutional authority for the national commercial republic that Washington had envisioned. Congress's power over interstate and international commerce appeared to be plenary (Art. I, Sec. 8). More to the point, the states were prohibited from having any say in this business other than through their representatives in Congress (Art. I, Sec. 10). Washington must have been especially pleased that the Constitution had given to Congress exclusive power to "make all needful rules and regulations respecting the territory or other property belonging to the United States" (Art. IV, Sec. 3)—a power absolutely indispensable to Washington's plans for progressive settlement of the West. He had hoped, too, that the new government would have the vision, the will, and the power to undertake grand projects in the national interest, such as his trans-Appalachian canal. The ability to establish this infrastructure was essential to his notions of using the national government as the instrument for linking the West to the East. The Constitution did endow Congress with the power "to establish post roads," but the plain words of the document fell short of the expansive national power Washington had envisioned. The "necessary and proper" clause would eventually provide the requisite constitutional legitimacy for just such efforts, but in 1787 this question remained ambiguous. Perhaps Washington was satisfied that at least such projects were not included among the specific prohibitions against national power (Art. I, Sec. 9).

Much of the remainder of Washington's pre-convention agenda found its way into the Constitution. The guaranty clause (Art IV, Sec. 4), made effective by the president's newly established power to nationalize the state militias, went a long way toward relieving his anxieties over the domestic crises of the 1780s. The source of many of those anxieties—the illiberal and unjust actions by the legislatures of several states—was addressed in two ways. First, the national government would be insulated against these forces by its thoroughly republican structure and its substantial checks on legislative tyranny. Second, the guaranty clause implied that national power could be invoked to suppress the "democratical" (and therefore un-republican) impulses that Washington saw taking hold in some of the states, principally Rhode Island.

He was probably also pleased with the way the Constitution dealt with the question of republican representation. Like all good republicans, Washington perceived public consent as the keystone of any form of government. But he had expressed his dismay over the quality of national representation under the Articles. Republican theory required that the "better sort of men" be induced to serve their country *and* that such representatives be relatively free from immediate popular control in order to pursue the common interest as their reason, experience, and virtue dictated. This new Constitution seemed to strike an equitable balance between direct (House of Representatives) and indirect (Senate, presidency, judiciary) representation. The varied selection processes offered methods that assured about as much "filtration of talent" as a republican people were likely to tolerate. Longer terms for these more indirectly chosen officers would serve as a damper on the presumably less educated, less propertied, less disinterested, and, perhaps, less virtuous House. Washington may have been a bit disappointed by the convention's decision to provide salaries for federal officials. Washington's concept of civic duty, drawing upon the ideals of the Roman republic and of the Virginia gentry within which he was raised, made him scornful of the notion of pay for public service. But since the larger scheme of representation was both republican and conservative, he was quite happy about the convention's work.

Finally, for Washington the new Constitution promised to arrest the rising tide of fiscal irresponsibility and immorality. States were now forbidden entirely from coining money, emitting bills of credit, or allowing anything other than gold or silver as legal tender (Art. I, Sec. 10). This was a strong antidote, indeed, for the paper-money disease. Washington was unable to convince the delegates to place a similar restriction on the fiscal activities of the federal government, but with independent taxing powers that now operated directly on the people and that could not be interfered with by the states, there was now every likelihood that the federal government would have access to the sorts of revenue that would make such "soft money" policies unnecessary. The new government also assumed the debts of the old confederacy (Art. VI); but with ample taxing authority of its own, Congress would no longer have to make unmanly supplications to the states for money. Justice and honor could finally be done to the oft-deferred revolutionary promissories. Washington's personal pledge to his soldiers could now be redeemed. In addition, the contract clause (Art. I, Sec. 10), enforced by the national supremacy principle, would preserve the sanctity of private business dealings and prevent attempts by debtors to alleviate their obligations through state legislative action. The Constitution affirmed that "honesty [was] the soundest policy" and assured that all those who had expressed their faith in the Revolution would finally get their due.[50]

So, then, how successful *was* Washington at the convention? From this accounting we can confidently conclude that he was very successful. The Constitution addressed nearly every major concern that he had raised in the previous six or seven years and did so in ways that fit well with his avowed goals. George Washington was certainly not the only delegate to emerge with a close congruence between his pre-convention agenda and the finished constitutional product. Indeed, some delegates may have been even more successful than Washington in that respect. But it was clearly a document that greatly encouraged Washington. In contemplating the initial prospects of the convention he had insisted, "Let us raise a standard to which the wise and honest can repair."[51] In retrospect, his equivocation to Randolph may have only been intended to bring the governor "on board"; Randolph's support was thought to be critical to ratification in Virginia. It is clear that the new Constitution was, for Washington, just such a standard.

A Partisan Founder

The extent of Washington's enthusiasm for the new Constitution can be seen in his willingness to enlist in the federalist cause.[52] Philadelphia had been only the first step in redeeming the Union; the work would not be finished until ratification by each of the states. Until then, the crisis that inspired Washington to travel to Philadelphia would remain as threatening as ever.

Initially, Washington seemed prepared to occupy his usual position above the partisan fray, writing Lafayette on the day after the convention's adjournment that he would not campaign either for or against the Constitution.[53] After all, he perceived quite correctly that a good portion of his public reputation was attributable to his image as a nonpartisan Patriot. But by the time he had returned to Mount Vernon he had apparently concluded that he (and the Constitution) stood to lose more if the ratification effort failed than if he came down foursquare on the side of the federalists. He wrote letters to some of the leading Virginia political figures (Patrick Henry, Benjamin Harrison, Edmund Randolph, and Thomas Nelson) hoping to persuade them of the Constitution's benefits.[54] (With the exception of Randolph these individualized appeals did not win any converts.) He then encouraged federalists to write essays in public gazettes—to appeal to public opinion in any way possible—and later encouraged the dissemination of tracts by James Wilson and, of course, the great essays by Madison, Hamilton, and Jay that are known to us now as the *Federalist Papers*.[55] He even allowed Madison to use the claim that "George Washington supports the Constitution" whenever Madison deemed that it might be useful to the cause.[56] That he would delegate custodianship of his public reputation to anyone, even a trusted friend and federalist, indicates Washington's commitment to the new Constitution. For almost a year Washington kept up a steady stream of correspondence with federalists throughout the nation, offering his moral support, rejoicing over the ratification effort's successes, worrying about its potential defeats, and in a few instances counseling federalists about specific strategies for ratification.[57]

For one who warned against the "baneful effects of the spirit of party" for most of his public life, Washington was remarkably partisan during the ratification struggle. His commitment to classical republican theory explains both his strong aversion to partisanship and, paradoxically, his willingness to engage in partisan behavior on behalf of the Constitution. He believed that a virtuous republic was one that valued harmony, order, and a common sense of purpose. A virtuous republic could have but one true constitution, one true expression of the public interest, one true protector of the liberties of the people. But constitutions could be corrupted by self-interest—an impulse so powerful that men of virtue had to be constantly on the alert to protect the republic against such corruption and depravity. So long as reason and virtue and frugality prevailed in society, the republic might continue. But once passion, guile, demagoguery, and self-interest began to dominate public discourse the decline and fall of the republic was inevitable. Classical republicans, therefore, tended to view political debate not as an arena in which different interests openly competed for the right to define public policy (the "pluralist" view that today dominates American political practice), but rather as a struggle between right and wrong, between good republicans and those who would tear down the republic to serve their own narrow interests. To these men the notion of a loyal opposition or of continuous party competition was sheer nonsense. A republic could only be rooted in one notion of the common good. Anything else was corruption.

Washington saw the federalists as the genuine republicans in this affair, and his descriptions of their qualities were heavily larded with phrases intended to situate them as the true defenders of republicanism. The Constitution's supporters were men of "abilities and property."[58] They were the "zealous advocates for and patriotic sufferers in the acquisition of American Independence"; only the federalists could lay claim to the title of "true patriots."[59] He portrayed the federalist effort from beginning to end as predicated upon a commitment to prudence and reason. Federalists merely wished to present the case for the Constitution to the people. Since Washington believed that the weight of reason was all on the federalist side, the people, when properly informed, would see the merits of the new Constitution and decide rightly.[60]

In contrast to this portrayal of federalists as the authentic vessels of republican virtues, the antifederalists were cast as enemies of the people and of the republic. Conspiracy theory was a common way of viewing one's opponents in this age. Republican eschatology predicted that the corruption of the constitution would almost always come from within and that the enemies of the republic would seek to shield their self-interest behind the mask of public virtue. Washington was thus unwilling to concede *any* ground to the antifederalists; conspirators had nothing to commend them. Even before the Constitutional Convention had completed its business Washington had predicted that the sort of men likely to oppose any new constitution would be either demagogues, state particularists, or "interested characters."[61] Further, they probably would not engage in a fair and open public debate using principles of common reason; they would, instead, act as a conspiratorial cabal: "Whilst many *ostensible* reasons are assigned to prevent the adoption of [the Constitution], the real ones are concealed behind the Curtain, because they are not of a nature to appear in open day."[62] Washington's letters contain the sorts of venomous criticisms that he had previously reserved only for Tories. Antifederalists were men driven by motives of "disappointment, passion and resentment." They were, on the one hand, "persons of too little importance to endanger the general welfare of the Union"; yet, on the other hand, they were capable of introducing "anarchy and confusion" into public affairs. They were "apparently unprincipled men" capable only of "unfair conduct"— conduct largely directed at appealing to "the ignorant" and inflaming the "passions" of the people. They were demagogues dedicated to a campaign of lies and misrepresentation.[63] This was strong stuff. But Washington was not alone in using this sort of language. The antifederalists were just as fervently convinced that *they* were the true guardians of republicanism and that federalism was the devil incarnate—the great corrupter of public virtue. Both federalists and antifederalists, like most Americans of the eighteenth century, were imprisoned by a conspiratorial worldview that compelled them to portray each other in such partisan terms.[64]

Even after the Constitution had been ratified Washington could not bring himself to completely trust those who had been antifederalists. He suspected that they still maintained an active, covert conspiracy against the new Constitution and would do whatever they could to undermine its effective operation. He had hoped that a new spirit of reason and moderation would inform postratification political discussions. Early signs from Massachusetts gave him some cause for optimism; the antifederalists had conceded defeat in an honorable way and had announced themselves willing to support and participate in the new government. But he soon came to believe that this posture of moderation was a ploy and that the antifederalists were working in concert (a "junto" as Washington put it) to elect their own partisans as officials in the new government.[65]

Washington was no less a committed partisan himself and showed it in his activities surrounding the elections of 1788. He confided that he wanted only the "most disinterested, able, and virtuous men" in the new government and that "much will depend upon having disinterested and respectable characters in both Houses."[66] But when one looks more closely at precisely who these "disinterested" individuals were, it becomes clear that they were supposed to resemble Washington and his fellow federalists.

Washington warned his allies throughout the states that they had to be constantly on guard against antifederalist machinations. He was particularly worried about events in Virginia. Virginians, he thought, were warm supporters of the Constitution, estimating at one point that seven in ten were sympathetic to the cause. But he feared that inattention by the federalists to the business at hand might surrender this hard-won advantage. Evidence soon confirmed Washington's fears: Madison had been denied a seat in the Senate. Washington now saw visions of a sinister conspiracy, with Patrick Henry's hand pulling the strings of the unrepentant antifederalists. He implored federalists to stand for election, arguing that if they declined, the Constitution would be robbed of its dignity.[67] He applauded every federalist victory as a triumph of "patriotism, instead of faction."[68]

Washington, of course, had another reason for his vigorous federalist partisanship in the 1788 elections. It was evident by the summer of that year that Washington would be the first president under the new Constitution. To those who were pushing his candidacy he had written that he had performed his full measure of duty for his country and that he wished to retire once again from public life. The ritual of reluctant acceptance was now rather familiar.[69] But he must have known, perhaps even as early as the Philadelphia Convention the previous summer, that his willingness to accept the presidency was essential to the federalist endgame. Knowing that his own public reputation, the success or failure of his own administration, and the viability of his own constitutional vision were at stake, he wanted to be sure that the new government would be amply peopled with those who shared that vision. There would be much rough weather before the new ship of state sailed into safe harbor. It would be better to traverse those waters in the company of friends.

5 / The Framer as Interpreter

When George Washington arrived in New York in 1789 to take his oath of office, no one doubted that he was the president of a newly reconstituted United States. There remained much doubt, however, as to what, precisely, this new presidency *was*. A few properties of the presidency seemed clear (for the time being): the qualifications for the office, the mode of selection, and the length of the presidential term. Ambiguity reigned, however, when the political character of the presidency was considered. As Ralph Ketcham has aptly put it, "Far from everything being settled, virtually nothing was."[1] The cryptic words of Article II, "The executive Power shall be vested in a President of the United States," offered little guidance to the first occupant of the office. What should be the relationship between the president and the other branches of the federal government: the Senate, the House, and the Judiciary? Between the president and the states? Between the president and the people of the United States? Between the president and the world community? Even more broadly, what were the president's responsibilities to the Constitution itself?

In the Declaration of Independence, Thomas Jefferson had written confidently about the existence of "self-evident truths." But the Constitution, with its emphasis on the distribution and application of political power rather than on the rhetorical flagellation of a king, contained few such truths. The skeleton of a constitutional government was present, but it was without sinew and lacked clear definition. Perhaps the best indicator of the new Constitution's lack of clarity was the degree to which the Founders themselves, the men who had written the document in Philadelphia or discussed it in state ratifying conventions, disagreed over its interpretation. For Washington, then, the project of the first presidency was not so much defined by the desire to fulfill a personal policy agenda as it was by the need to clarify the powers of the office and the role of the person who occupied it.

Washington was aware of the ambiguity of the constitutional text; he was also aware of his potential as an authoritative explicator of that text. He shared with many others of the founding generation the view that a constitution draws its life not merely from the words of the written document, but also from the deeds and understandings of those responsible for acting under its commands.[2] Founding was a continuous and open process in which customs, practices, and institutions unmentioned in the Constitution would add specific meaning to the outline of 1787. In a letter to several of his advisers in the spring of 1789, Washington noted, ''Many things which appear of little importance in themselves and at the beginning, may have great and durable consequences from their having been established at the commencement of a new General government.''[3]

The veneration of the Constitution that characterizes much contemporary American political thinking (and that has been promoted to occasionally absurd lengths in the ''good feelings'' generated by the current Bicentennial period) can deflect us from the tangible anxieties of Washington and his contemporaries. For them the survival of the new Constitution and its federal government was anything but sure. The Articles of Confederation had already been cast aside as a failure. Several states were also in the midst of constitutional crises whose outcomes were unsure. The republican experiment was still in jeopardy, and hard choices would have to be made to ensure its survival.

Washington clearly understood that he was in a unique position to affect those choices and, thus, the meaning of the Constitution for future generations. He was, after all, the *first* president. As patently obvious as that statement is, we ought not underestimate its significance. The constitutional slate was uniquely clean for Washington as it never could be again for any of his successors. If we imagine our constitutional tradition as a great river we can easily see the important advantage that being first confers. The first rivulets from the constitutional spring can be made to flow in almost any direction. Those interested in moving the course of the stream can steer it as easily one way as another, for there is little weight behind the water. But later, as the stream continues it gathers more water, deepening the original channel. Those wishing to change the flow further downstream find that it requires extraordinary efforts to counter the weight that the river now carries.

Put another way, many contemporary constitutional practices can be said to derive from "the persistence of original forms."[4] Certainly not all of the "forms" proffered by Washington have become part of our constitutional tradition. Subsequent presidents, for example, have not felt obliged to take their authority as commander-in-chief as literally as Washington did. None have followed the example of his conduct in the Whiskey Rebellion, when he took to horse to lead the nation's troops in the field. While Washington or Eisenhower or Grant might have fit the part, visions of the corpulent Taft or tiny, anemic-looking Madison at the head of an army are sufficient to justify the principle of delegation employed by later presidents.[5] But there are many other examples of how Washington's choices set our constitutional tradition onto a course easily recognizable today. Some might be tempted to minimize the significance of these choices. "Washington was only doing what the Constitution required," some might say. "What else *could* he have done?" But our familiarity with these forms, our confidence that these choices surely were the only sensible ones, mask the fact that many of these choices were matters of great debate during Washington's presidency and that other choices less familiar to us might have just as easily become our "original forms."

Washington came to this enterprise with an array of political resources unmatched by any president since. As the commanding general of the victorious Continental Army he emerged without challenge as the one authentic *national* hero of the Revolution. His journey six years earlier from New Jersey to Annapolis to relinquish his revolutionary command to Congress had become a "victory tour." Towns large and small along the route outdid each other in their efforts to honor the retiring general. Many of the celebrations were wildly spontaneous. Now, in 1789, the people once again turned out to cheer the new president as he journeyed from Mount Vernon to New York. No other American could lay a similar claim to the affections of the people; not Jefferson, not Hamilton, not Franklin, nor any other of his contemporaries could rival his reputation. George Washington inspired the nearest thing to a "cult of personality" that this nation has ever witnessed.[6]

This immense reservoir of popular adulation was supplemented at the outset of his administration with a level of political support unmatched since. First, his selection by the electoral college was unanimous.[7] The electors represented the "better sort of men" that Washington hoped would provide leadership for the new republic. Their confidence in him meant that Washington began his tenure with a political base of support that embraced the elite and the ordinary alike. In addition, the new Congress, while not partisan in the sense that it would become later in his administration, was dominated by men whom Washington perceived as political allies. Throughout much of 1788 he was concerned that the "federal party" would not obtain control of the new government. But his fears melted away with the summer and fall elections as he learned of the victory of more and more "friends of the Constitution"—friends who he was confident shared his constitutional vision.

There can be little question that the new president did have a constitutional vision. He shared with many others of the founding generation a commitment to classical republican principles. His singular experience as commander-in-chief in the Revolutionary War had induced him to reshape those ideals on a larger scale. Now he was uniquely situated to make manifest that constitutional vision. As he remarked to James Madison, "As the first of everything, in *our situation* will serve to establish a Precedent, it is devoutly wished on my part, that these precedents may be fixed on true principles."[8] Founding was an unfinished project in which Washington intended to play a significant role, defined by his own sense of the "true principles" of the Constitution.

Constitutional Order and the Rule of Law

Not the least important of the constitutional norms endorsed by the new president was his commitment to the rule of law itself. Republicans were addicted to constitution making. For the founding generation it was not enough to declare one's love of liberty; one also had to demonstrate a capacity for exercising that liberty by establishing effective instruments of self-government: constitutions. Indeed, republicans put great stock in their professed willingness to abide by laws of their own making. Liberty without a regard for the public interest was licentiousness. Order without respect for liberty under law was tyranny. Republicanism with its concern for ordered liberty and the promotion of public virtue saw constitution making as a genuine "founding" act. Constitutions defined a people, stated their public aspirations, preserved their natural liberties, and created institutions of self-government to protect them from foreign intrigues and from their own worst passions. Republican citizens were not mere subjects. Subjects obeyed the law because the government (the king) had more guns or because medieval rituals of fealty commanded obedience. Citizens, on the other hand, were covenanted one to another by the laws established in the common interest by governments of their own making. In addition, citizens obeyed the law because it served their mutual interest in maintaining order and stability within their own communities. Perhaps most significantly, in republican communities the law was binding on all. The law was not just an obligation of subjects to obey an unfettered monarch whose own actions were to be judged by different criteria (usually of his own making). Republican law bound lawmakers and citizens equally.

This, of course, was an idealized republic. As self-confident as the founding generation is sometimes made to appear, we can easily forget just how uncertain it was about this whole business of republican government. In his first Inaugural Address Washington had noted that "the destiny of the Republican model of Government" was staked "on the experiment entrusted to the hands of the American people."[9] In 1789 the viability of constitutional self-government was still in question. Most of the states had established constitutional governments during the Revolution.[10] But this by no means had settled the issue. Several states were already suffering convulsions that raised substantial doubts as to whether government without a monarch could ever establish a stable political society within which peace and prosperity could grow. One need only remember Washington's anxieties over the "commotions" of 1786 in New England: "They exhibit a melancholy proof of what our transatlantic foe [Britain] has predicted . . . that mankind when left to themselves are unfit for their own government. I am mortified beyond expression when I view the clouds that have spread over the brightest morn that ever dawned upon any Country."[11] Washington was not at all sure that republican governments, with the mere wave of the constitutional wand, could exhibit the "efficiency" and "energy" that republican ideology self-confidently proclaimed. Even as he prepared to accept the presidency his doubts persisted. "I see nothing but clouds and darkness before me."[12] Some of those clouds had lifted for Washington with the success of the Constitutional Convention, the Constitution's ratification, and the election of many good federalists in 1788. But the development of the new constitutional government still presented the president with formidable problems.

Washington's most immediate concern was best encapsulated by James Madison in his famous Federalist Paper No. 51: "If men were angels, no government would be necessary. If angels were to govern men, neither external nor internal controls on government would be necessary. In framing a government which is to be administered by men over men, the great difficulty lies in this: you must first enable the government to control the governed; and in the next place oblige it to control itself."[13]

As commander-in-chief of the Continental Army, Washington had been both frustrated and angered by the lack of authority given to the Congress. The national government, the government that ought to have been the best expression of the American people, lacked "dignity," "honor," and "energy" not only among the courts of Europe, but also among its own citizens. Thus Washington, as the first president, set out to ensure that the new constitutional government would project ample dignity, honor, and energy. He did so in two ways. First, he took every opportunity, both in symbol and substance, to assert the Constitution as the supreme law of the land and the national government as the custodian of its true meaning. Citizens and, especially, the states would have to be brought around to accepting the primacy of federal law. He would have no part in the sort of obstructionism and disrespect toward the national government that he had witnessed for eight years in the army. Second, as a deliberate tactic to induce greater confidence in and loyalty to the Constitution, Washington chose on several occasions to *deny* the power of the national government, or more particularly his own power as president. In almost every instance his clearly stated reason was that the constitution (the law) compelled him to do so. Washington's strategy was, in his own mind, simple common sense. People would only attach themselves to a government and obey its Constitution if they could be convinced that officers of that government were bound by the same constitution. Formal checks and balances of the kind described in *The Federalist* only solved Madison's "if men were angels'' problem *when, and only when*, legal limits on power were taken seriously by those endowed with that power.

Washington versus the States

As *The Federalist* suggested, not only was the national government to be limited and balanced within itself, it was also to be limited by the reservation of a substantial reservoir of power to the states that protected them (and their citizens) from abuse or usurpation by the national government. Many have argued that federalism, or at least the redefinition of the concept of federalism that emerged from the Constitutional Convention, remains the one original American contribution to the world of political ideas.

Ironically, Washington came to New York believing that there was very little genius in federalism. From his experiences in the Revolutionary War he determined that state sovereignty was not the bastion of liberty and the font of republican virtue that its advocates so dearly maintained. The states, in his mind, had demonstrated only that they could serve as the breeding grounds for the tendentiousness and petty jealousies that continued to imperil the union. As a large-scale republican he firmly believed that liberty and republican self-government could only prevail in an unfriendly world through the aegis of a national agency.

But how did this deep suspicion of state power affect Washington the president? And did his choices affect the ways in which we have come to understand the role of the president today? From the first days of his administration it is clear that Washington had a constitutional agenda predicated in large part upon establishing a national government (and a presidency) independent of and superior to the power of the states. Achieving this end required a bit of creative interpretation by the president. The Constitution did not clearly define the role of the chief executive. Was he to be simply an administrator—a kind of exalted clerk? Or a ceremonial head of state to give the new government legitimacy in the eyes of foreign kings and princes? Or a Solon-like giver of law in the national interest? Or the protector of the Constitution? To some extent presidents have become all of these, but the roles to which George Washington devoted most of his energies were those of national symbol and head of state. In choosing to emphasize these roles he hoped to impress the American people with the importance of establishing an identity with the national government, and to equally impress the state governments with the primacy of national authority.

One of the earliest opportunities for demonstrating this primacy arose in the context of a matter that would strike us as unremarkably ordinary. Thanksgiving proclamations were a well entrenched custom by 1789. Such proclamations, as well as requests for days of fasting or prayer, had been common during the war. However, when the new Congress in its first session requested a national day of thanksgiving it provoked a debate about the proper constitutional relationship between the nation, the states, and the people. Washington saw it as an opportunity to invoke his own sense of the new Constitution. During the war Washington communicated important information or requests to the states through circulars (a common letter transmitted to each state governor or legislature separately). It was a cumbersome process, but he had little choice. His legal position was as an agent of the states acting collectively through their delegates in Congress. He had no authority to speak directly to American citizens. He could not request aid, make appeals to patriotism, call for volunteers, or ask for a day of prayer and thanksgiving unless solicited by state officials.

When the first Congress routinely resolved to commemorate a day of national thanksgiving some states' rights advocates assumed that the request would be transmitted to the state executives for their implementation just as had been done previously—a clear attempt to revive at least the *forms* of the Confederation. Washington would have none of this. He saw the episode as an opportunity to establish a direct link between the national government and the American people through the office of the presidency. Taking his lead from the words of the Preamble ("We the people . . .") he determined that there would be no intermediaries between the president and American citizens everywhere. Not only was his proclamation directed to the people of the United States, but it asked a special blessing for the national government and the Constitution, but not the states![14]

Washington also asserted that whenever national power and interests were at issue, the president and the state governors were not equals. Two examples will suffice to make the point—one, straightforward; the other, absurd. During the notorious Citizen Genet affair, Washington was anxious to avoid any incidents that might compromise his policy of neutrality. Genet, the French ambassador to the United States, had been working actively to enlist American supporters in the French cause and to pull the United States, with or without the sanction of its elected government, into an alliance against Great Britain. One of his schemes was to outfit captured British merchantmen in American ports as French privateers. Washington worried about the British reaction. Would they view this as a provocative act? After all, providing a safe haven for one belligerent against another is hardly consistent with neutrality.

The issue came to a head with the *Little Sarah* affair. The *Little Sarah* was a British merchant ship captured off the Virginia Capes and sailed by its French captors to Philadelphia. Word came to Washington that French seamen were arming the ship with cannon, presumably to convert her into a privateer. Today, it might seem a simple enough thing for the president to put a stop to. But in 1793 the situation was different. The small federal army was garrisoned almost exclusively on the western frontier to fight Indians. The navy consisted of a few desultory revenue cutters—hardly the sort of force to strike fear into the great naval powers of France and Britain. In short, the president had no permanent establishment either for obtaining information or acting on it. He was forced to rely on the state governments for much of his intelligence and law enforcement. Even though the *Little Sarah* (now rechristened the *Petite Democrate*) was anchored virtually in sight of the national capital, Washington had to ask Governor Thomas Mifflin to provide him with information on the ship's activities and with sufficient harbor police to prevent any untoward happenings. This business had an unsatisfactory end. Washington's cautious posture eventually permitted the *Petite Democrate* to embark unopposed (though the ominous presence of a large French fleet in the West Indies probably precluded any other response). Yet Governor Mifflin, an old political foe from Washington's revolutionary days, had complied with the president's requests with considerable diligence, providing almost daily information. This was a matter of foreign policy, an area in which the federal government's authority was constitutionally supreme. Mifflin never once questioned Washington's authority to subordinate a state governor on a matter of this sort.[15]

The second incident is interesting not merely as a constitutional precedent but also as an example of the sort of nonsense that often happens when two enormously vain men clash over a matter of protocol. During his trip through the northern states in the winter of his first presidential year, Washington expressed an interest in dining with the governor of Massachusetts—no less a personage than John Hancock. Washington understood that Hancock first would call upon the president at his lodgings; the two would then repair to Hancock's home for dinner. When Hancock declined to visit the president, claiming ill health, Washington canceled the dinner engagement. It appeared to Washington that the Governor was making a statement about their respective standing under the Constitution—that a president first ought to pay his respects to a Governor because of the preeminent status of the states within the Union. Washington suspected that Hancock's complaint of ill health was a none-too-subtle ploy intended to force Washington to pay the first courtesy call. He dashed off a note to Hancock: "The President of the United States presents his best respects to the Governor, and has the honor to inform him that he shall be at home 'till 2 o'clock. The President of the United States need not express the pleasure it will give him to see the Governor; but at the same time, he most earnestly begs that the Governor will not hazard his health on the occasion."[16] Hancock conceded the field and, according to Woodrow Wilson's account, arrived at Washington's lodgings "swathed . . . in flannels and borne upon men's shoulders up the stairs."[17] Less charitable observers claim that it was merely Hancock's way of saving face. Silly? Perhaps. But Washington had made his point.

Interestingly, the Hancock protocol escapade arose in the context of an event intended to solidify the role of president as symbol of national authority and unity. Remembering the reluctance of some states to accept the primacy of the Continental Congress in national affairs, Washington planned a campaign to appeal directly to the American citizenry. Like a monarch surveying his realm (and often accompanied with the sort of pomp and circumstance reserved for royalty), Washington made it a point to travel to every state in the Union within a few years of his inauguration. In the fall of 1790 he toured the New England states. This was the trip that occasioned the Hancock visit. Later in 1790 he made a separate trip to Rhode Island shortly after that state had at last ratified the Constitution and officially entered the Union. He did so even though he had long reviled that state's noxious "paper-money junto" and radically egalitarian politics. In 1791 he completed the cycle with a tour of the southern states.[18] On every trip and in virtually every town the great hero was welcomed with enthusiastic, patriotic celebrations.

These presidential tours illustrate an important paradox of Washington's presidency. In legal-constitutional regimes public officials derive their respect and authority from the office they hold. As private citizens they may still wield great influence over public affairs, but they have *authority* only when acting under the color of law. The reverse was true for the first president. Washington quite simply was revered and respected far more than the as yet untested Constitution. Washington's public credibility was unassailable; such was not the case for the Constitution. By "showing the flag" (which, in a sense, was himself) the president intended to win the hearts and minds of ordinary Americans. Washington's clear purpose was to use his personal charisma to endow the presidency with much of its authority. That transference was the singular mission of the tours. For many Americans the Constitution was legitimated because Washington supported it. Thus, the presidency was also respected because Americans everywhere could see the great man filling the office.

All of this was but a prelude to what Washington believed must surely come. Sooner or later, the authority of the federal government (and the presidency) would be directly challenged—a challenge that would test whether the new government could act with "dignity" and "energy." In March of 1791 Congress, at the urging of Secretary of the Treasury Alexander Hamilton, passed a series of fiscal measures that included an excise tax on "spirituous liquors." There were a few grumblings that the measure would not be popular. Excise taxes, after all, had been the object of much revulsion in colonial times. Some congressmen feared that the appeal of taxation even *with* representation would quickly diminish, as would public support for the Constitution. But all recognized that the assumption of the war debt required taxation. The excise was only a small part of the revenue package, and most congressmen concluded that it was not unreasonable.

The whiskey tax fell almost exclusively on westerners who often relied on their distilleries for cash income.[19] Few were surprised when active opposition to the tax emerged in Pennsylvania, Kentucky, western Virginia, and the Carolinas in the summer of 1792. Washington could not permit the law to be so publicly flouted. Images of Shays's Rebellion were still fresh. When "occurrences of a nature so repugnant to order and good Government" happen "and lenient and temporizing means have been used, and serve only to increase the disorder; longer forbearance would become unjustifiable remissness, and a neglect of that duty which is enjoined on the President."[20] Compare these thoughts to his assessment of Shays's Rebellion: "Know precisely what the insurgents aim at. If they have *real* grievances, redress them if possible; . . . If they have not, employ the force of government against them at once. If this is inadequate, *all* will be convinced that the superstructure is bad."[21] So Washington moved cautiously. He issued a proclamation declaring the opposition proceedings "subversive of good order, contrary to the duty that every citizen owes to his country, and to the laws, and of a nature dangerous to the very being of a government." He cited his constitutional duty "to take care that the laws be faithfully executed" as justification for insisting that order be restored and lawbreakers brought to justice. But he mobilized no army (he confessed that unleashing a *federal* army would confirm the worst fears of the anti–standing army faction: "There would be a cry at once, 'The Cat is let out;' we see now for what purpose an Army was raised") and made no threat of specific executive action.[22]

At this point he still sought to employ moral suasion and popular appeals. He charged "all Courts, Magistrates and Officers" to uphold the law, leaving only a veiled reference to more direct actions if these pleas went unanswered. Most significantly, the president presumed that among these "Magistrates" were the governors of the affected states. Washington sent each of them a copy of the proclamation and included an additional message stating that "I feel an entire confidence that the weight and influence of the Executive of [each state] will be chearfully exerted in every proper way, to further the objects of this measure, and to promote on every occasion, a due obedience to the Constitutional Laws of the Union." Where enforcement of the laws of the federal government was concerned, Washington firmly believed that governors were constitutionally subordinate to the president.[23]

It was not the first time that Washington had asserted this kind of authority over state governors. For three consecutive years beginning in 1790 Washington had requested several states to send militia for a campaign against frontier Indians. The governors had gladly complied. After all, it was their territory that was affected, and the president's plan meant that the federal government would pay for the expedition. But the expedition was to be commanded by a federally appointed officer; once mobilized, the state militias ceased to be under the jurisdiction of the governors. Organized as state units they were nonetheless the president's men exclusively.[24]

In these three instances—the *Little Sarah* affair, the first Whiskey Proclamation, and the Indian expeditions—Washington was laying the foundation for national supremacy and a strong presidency. He grounded his actions in each case upon the Constitution, principally the "commander-in-chief" clause and the provision authorizing the chief executive to "see that the laws be faithfully executed." Most importantly, he interpreted each of these provisions as a *personal* responsibility. As we shall see later, he often preferred to employ a consultative style in his presidency. But responsibility under the Constitution for actions of the chief executive was not collective; it was his alone. This also meant that the obligations of citizens and state officials under the laws of the Constitution were also due to him alone.

Corn Liquor and a Nationalist Constitution

The significance of these early precedents was manifested when opposition to the excise tax reemerged in 1794. The first protests had been quieted in large part by Congress's willingness to amend the excise bill, removing some of the most objectionable enforcement provisions. Washington's proclamation probably had some influence as well (many of the oppositionists were war veterans still loyal to their old commander), but little more than that can be claimed. But Hamilton's renewed determination to aggressively collect the tax and prosecute resisters rekindled the embers of protest. Whether Hamilton intended to foment a rebellion, he certainly got one.[25]

Reports filtered back to Philadelphia that tax collectors were being threatened and beaten, courts closed, and the homes of "revenuers" burned. Some of these reports, coming as they did from Hamilton's agents, were exaggerated. But to Washington the events signaled a crisis in federal authority: "If the Laws are to be so trampled upon, with impunity, and a minority (a small one too) is to dictate to the majority there is an end put, at one stroke, to republican government; and nothing but anarchy and confusion is to be expected thereafter."[26] Order or anarchy: for Washington this was the critical test of republican government. Either citizens could live peacefully and prosperously under laws of their own making, or they could not. He could conceive of no middle ground.

Washington did not doubt that he had the constitutional authority to suppress the rebellion. But he resisted pressure from more hawkish Federalists like Hamilton and Knox to call out the militia immediately in a massive show of force. To the president this would be putting the constitutional cart before the political horse. He recalled the humiliation of the Congress during the war when proclamation after proclamation, each of them constitutionally grounded, had been ignored by the states. Whatever came out of the rebellion would be an important precedent, but a precedent of what?

Governor Mifflin of Pennsylvania was a Jeffersonian. Could he be relied upon to answer a call for the use of his state's militia? When, in Shakespeare's *Henry IV, Part One*, Owen Glendower boasts, "I can call spirits from the vasty deep," the skeptical Hotspur replies, "Why, so can I, or so can any man; but will they come when you do call for them?"[27] Washington shared Hotspur's skepticism. This was, after all, no popular crusade against Indians. This would be a call for Americans to take up arms against Americans—in Mifflin's case, of Pennsylvanians against Pennsylvanians. Washington feared more than just a rebellion by mountain farmers, he feared a complete breakdown in the authority of the federal government vis-à-vis the states. If Pennsylvania refused to recognize the constitutional authority of the president could the Union long survive? Washington endorsed Edmund Randolph's view that massive force exercised without a solid base of popular support "would heap curses upon the government" because republican government must ultimately rest on "the affection of the people."[28] So Washington refrained, at first, from calling for troops.

Instead, he chose to employ a complex strategy that involved, first, offering amnesty to those elements within the rebellion that might be induced to declare their loyalty to the federal government. The West was still the key to Washington's grand vision of an American empire. If he wished to "attach" the interests of westerners to those of the federal government he would have to take care not to permanently alienate them. Brutal suppression, even to uphold the Constitution, would perhaps irrevocably shatter any hope of bringing the West into the federal orbit. Westerners would look for new patrons, perhaps Spain or France or even England.

The second part of his strategy was to mobilize popular support for the government's cause by encouraging Americans to see the conflict as Washington saw it, as one between constitutional government and violent anarchy. In particular, Washington was careful to find out which states *would* answer a call-up of militia. He could count on Virginia. His old friend Henry Lee was now governor. Besides, Washington was still a Virginian. Virginians could be relied upon to defend the president's honor against Pennsylvanians! But what of the other states, Pennsylvania in particular? A war between the states would be no less damaging to the constitutional union than a war between the federal government and one of its states.

Washington's double game seems to have had its desired effect. The offer of amnesty to those who would swear loyalty to the federal government drew away many of the erstwhile rebels. This defection isolated the most militant of the rebels and allowed the administration to portray them as a treasonous opposition dedicated to violent "insurrection" against constitutional government.[29] When Washington finally determined that only force would compel the submission of these "diehards," he was able to link the administration's actions with the revolutionary cause—still a potent symbol for most Americans. He characterized the government's purpose as "nothing less than to consolidate and to preserve the blessings of that Revolution which at much expense of blood and treasure constituted us a free and independent Nation."[30] His proclamation asked the militias of four states (New Jersey, Maryland, Virginia, *and* Pennsylvania) to defend the Constitution against the rebels, a call that was met with an oversubscription of troops. These were state troops, but they were commanded by federal officers for the purpose of enforcing federal law against citizens of a member state. The military power of the states was now harnessed to the federal plowhorse.

Managed differently, the Whiskey Rebellion might have led to the establishment of a very different sort of Constitution than the one envisioned by Washington—perhaps a union looking much more like the old Confederation than a nationalist republic. The successful government action against the rebels by no means settled the relative status of the states and the federal government. It would take a Civil War to do that (and, perhaps, not even then would the issue be resolved). But Washington's effective invocation of presidential power on behalf of the federal government began to direct the stream of constitutional tradition down a course that certified the presidency as the unchallenged symbol and representative of national power.

The President as Constitutional Literalist

One might presume from the previous discussion that Washington was a committed "strong presidency" man, dedicated to bringing to the office all of the "energy" and "dignity" that would make the United States respectable in the eyes of the world. By this standard the president would assume leadership for national politics, propose public policy and guide it through to its final effective implementation, and vigorously enforce compliance with the national law. This assessment is but partly true, and it would seriously misstate Washington's constitutional philosophy to read his presidency in this light.

The delegates at the Philadelphia Convention had agreed almost unanimously that the great political problem they faced was how to provide for a government of sufficient power and authority to deal with matters of national concern. Washington and others understood that a strong, unified executive was essential to the achievement of that vision. A government (even one where public policy remained largely a legislative prerogative) was no government at all if it did not have the power to enforce its laws through an "energetic" executive. In this limited sense Washington *was* a strong president. The fragmentation and weakness of the Union was the one factor that had compelled his attendance at Philadelphia. As president he was not likely to undermine the great purpose for which he believed the Constitution had been ratified. Thus, he took every opportunity to use his office to assert federal dominance over the states in matters constitutionally entrusted to the national government. When he asked for compliance from governors or ordinary citizens he made sure that he asked it in the name of the Constitution of the United States, and when he finally resorted to coercion to quell the Whiskey Rebellion he once again insisted that he was acting on the basis of the law of the land, not merely appealing to some mysterious, ancient prerogative.

But when we step back from the issue of federal-state relations, the portrait of Washington as a strong president becomes less sharply drawn—a portrait in water colors rather than oil. Some have suggested that Washington used the Constitution more as a rule book than as a broad guideline for the use of power. Indeed, there are numerous examples of Washington denying his own authority in a matter under dispute because of a particularly literal approach to reading the Constitution.

The case of the "unappointed" justice is illustrative of Washington's great sensitivity to the specific wording of the Constitution. In 1793 Washington nominated William Paterson of New Jersey to sit as an associate justice on the Supreme Court. Well-qualified to serve, Paterson had been attorney general of New Jersey, a delegate to the Philadelphia Convention, and a member of the United States Senate, where he was an important player in the creation of the Judiciary Act of 1789 (the authorizing legislation for the judicial branch). But Paterson's service in the Senate soon posed a constitutional problem. A provision of the Constitution (Art. I, Sec. 6) stated that "no Senator . . . shall during the Time for which he was elected, be appointed to any civil Office under the Authority of the United States, which shall have been created . . . during such time." Paterson had recently resigned from the Senate to accept the chancellorship of New Jersey, but "the time for which he was elected" had not expired. Moreover, he had helped write the Judiciary Act, which had created the associate justiceships of the Supreme Court. (The Constitution had created only the Supreme Court, leaving to Congress the authority to establish the Court's size.) When Washington learned of this he immediately rescinded Paterson's nomination: "It has since occurred that he was a member of the Senate when the Law creating that Office was passed, and that the time for which he was elected is not yet expired. I think it my duty therefore, to declare that I deem the nomination to have been null by the Constitution."[31]

This decision must have been painful for Washington. Not only was Paterson a good choice, he was willing to serve. Washington had already suffered enough embarrassments in trying to staff the Supreme Court. He was turned down far more often than not—in one instance a confirmed nominee had second thoughts and decided not to show up— and found it difficult throughout his two terms to keep a full complement of six persons empaneled on the Court.[32] Fortunately, Paterson's Senate term was due to expire in four days when the new Congress assembled. Washington then resubmitted Paterson's nomination, and it was quickly approved by the Senate.[33]

In the context of the modern presidency Washington's behavior strikes us as slightly naive, perhaps even inept. Why publicly declare your nominee constitutionally invalid when the new Senate was not likely to meet until after Paterson's term had expired anyway? Why go out of the way to raise questions about your constitutional authority, particularly when you had written and spoken for many years on behalf of a strong executive? The answer to this enigma is twofold. First, Washington took the Constitution seriously. One factor separating republican governments from tyrannical ones was a commitment from the governors, no less than the governed, to be bound by law. Self-government was defined as much by self-discipline and self-denial as it was by the expression of popular rule. This posture was nothing new for Washington. His opposition to British colonial policy had been based on constitutional objections. During the war he had felt bound by ill-considered policies of Congress and the states because they were properly the law. Even in his personal affairs, Washington, though ever capable of using the law to his own advantage, conceded that the law ruled. In one of his many tenant-landlord disputes he objected that the jury was being summoned well before the date set for hearing the suit. This he thought quite unfair as it left the jurors exposed to the influence of local characters favorable to the tenants, while Washington, living many miles away and unable to attend the trial, would be at a disadvantage. Nevertheless, he conceded that ''if it is an event to be regretted, it is equally unavoidable, as it is constitutional.''[34] This commitment to the notion of rule of law often led him to narrow, literalist readings of the Constitution.

But his reasons for exercising such deference to the constitutional text were as purposeful as they were principled. An appropriate (and highly visible) deference to the Constitution and to the other branches of the federal government was actually part of a strategy for establishing a strong presidency. This was, after all, a new form of government that had been established only after heated, often recriminatory, debates in the state ratifying conventions. Its opponents were still wary and suspicious. Only twelve years earlier many Americans had declared independence from "the present King of Great Britain" because of a "history of repeated injuries and usurpations, all having in direct object the establishment of an absolute tyranny." Even the Country ideology in which Washington had received his early political education was deeply suspicious of the corruption of Kings (executives) and their ever-present placemen. Governmental arrangements, even those with Washington at the helm, that resurrected notions of an energetic executive would not be observed merely because they carried with them the trappings of constitutionality. Sons and daughters of the Revolution would need more assurance than that no new American monarchy was being contemplated.

Washington believed that the public and the Congress needed to be shown that the president could be trusted. If the first president chose to run roughshod over the Constitution for his own political ends, then the antifederalists and their fears about monarchical tendencies in the new government would be proved right and a bitter conflict over the Constitution's legitimacy would probably ensue. If, however, the confidence of the public and of congress in the chief executive were to increase—if they could be assured that the president could be relied upon to safeguard the Constitution and not use it for his personal aggrandizement—then Washington and, more importantly, future presidents would find it easier to assert a more directive role in national policy making. As Garry Wills has noted, part of the Cincinnatus myth of Roman legend is that power must first be denied before it can be *freely* exercised.[35] Washington was a president concerned with constitutional limits; but he was in no sense a weak president.

The Deferential Presidency and
the Case of the Unopened Packet

Consider the question of the president as legislative leader—a role expected of modern presidents. Washington's reading of the Constitution informed him that, at least in internal matters of national concern, the power to make law for the federal government resided with Congress. The text was explicit for Washington on this point ("all legislative powers herein granted shall be vested in a Congress"), therefore he was quite deferential to Congress's prerogatives. His formal addresses to

Congress rarely set out his policy agenda in a fashion that we would recognize today. In his first annual address to Congress, for example, he mentioned not a single specific legislative proposal. He did note that "many interesting objects . . . will engage your attention." For example, he suggested that Congress ought to legislate in such matters as the "proper establishment of the troops," "uniformity in the currency," a "uniform rule of nationalization," "the advancement of agriculture, commerce, and manufacture," and "the promotion of science and literature."[36] Beyond these broad generalities, most of them little more than restatements of Congress's powers enumerated in Article I, Washington offered no specific recommendations or legislative "package." He continued this pattern in all of his subsequent annual addresses to Congress.[37]

Some have interpreted this reticence as an indication that Washington was a president without a clear substantive vision who therefore forfeited the opportunity to exercise decisive policy leadership for the new nation. But such an indictment misses the real thrust of Washington's presidency: the establishment of a viable republican constitutional government. Washington never lacked a vision of American politics. In the years before his election as president, he had written again and again about policies he believed essential to the health of the nation. He pleaded for an end to paper money, the full funding of the national debt as a matter of "public justice" and "national honor," broad powers to regulate and promote national commerce and manufactures, a system of roads and canals to connect the western interior to the eastern states, a liberal policy of immigration, the use of imposts as a source of federal revenue, and the establishment of a national university. A glance at the fragmentary excerpts of his original, but undelivered, first inaugural address makes clear that this was still his domestic political agenda in 1789.[38]

Yet the record confirms that Washington did not take an active role in "politicking" for his preferences, though his Federalist supporters within and outside the administration surely acted as his surrogates. Even during his second term, when partisanship escalated to a point where he no longer could rely on his accommodational leadership style, he still refused to involve himself directly in the legislative process or to interfere with what he saw as the rightful (constitutional) prerogatives of Congress. Lawmaking was the business of Congress, and he consistently refused to interject himself into their turf. To one European, apparently amazed by Washington's seeming lack of authority, he insisted that

> however convinced I am of the great advantages to be derived to the Community [from legislation to improve agricultural methods] in my public capacity, I know not whether I can with propriety do any thing more at present than what I have already done. I have brought the subject in my speech, at the opening of the present Session of Congress, before the national Legislature. It rests with them to decide what measures ought afterwards to be adopted for promoting the success of the great objects, which I have recommended to their attention.[39]

Washington here concedes that he is no policy leader. The weight of his office and his enormous personal influence would not be brought to bear even in support of policies that he supported.

But to interpret this detachment from the hurly-burly of politics as a sign of presidential weakness is to overlook Washington's larger constitutional agenda. His primary purpose was to establish the integrity of the presidency as the trustworthy and vigilant guardian of the people's Constitution. One must remember that in 1789 the Supreme Court was a lightly regarded body whose functions were as yet undefined. Today, it may be true that "the Constitution is what the judges say it is."[40] But during Washington's administration, judicial review, with its ability to make of the Court the definitive interpreter of the meaning of the Constitution, was still far in the future.

Washington most often used the term "Chief Magistrate" when referring to his own presidency. The choice of that title was deliberate. His notion of a strong presidency was not predicated on the success of a particular set of personal policy preferences. Rather, he envisioned that presidential strength was measured by his ability to control the meaning and application of the Constitution for the people, the states, and the other branches of the federal government. Constitutionally, he could argue that this power derived from his authority "to take care that the laws [and what was the Constitution but the *supreme law* of the land?] be faithfully executed." But the claim would be credible only if Washington could show ample evidence of his willingness to be bound by the text of the Constitution, even, *and especially*, when the matter at hand affected the nominal power of the presidency.

This willingness to defer to the authority of Congress as a matter of constitutional principle is best illustrated by the slightly ludicrous case of the unopened packet. In December 1790, Washington received a packet from the National Assembly of France, then in the throes of its own revolution. It was addressed to "The president and Members of the American Congress." The packet had been delivered to the president, and he was the first party addressed in the salutation. Thus Washington could have opened it without controversy. (Indeed, had Washington not raised the question there is every likelihood that Congress would have taken no notice of the business.) Yet Washington chose to submit the matter to the Senate for their advice: should he open it, or should Congress? The Senate decided that the president should break the seal, examine the contents, and report back to Congress if the message warranted. "An executive who took pains of this sort to respect the authority of the legislative branch was not," Douglas Freeman commented, "likely to have a clash."[41] Yet by willingly conceding his prerogative to Congress in this matter he acquired something more permanent in return—a reservoir of political trust that he could draw from in the future when matters more essential to establishing a strong presidency were at issue.

The Old Precedent: Irresponsible Executives

Washington believed that the powers of government ought to be as cooperative and unified as possible. Mixed government and shared responsibility were the best means for achieving good policy. The implementation of policy, on the other hand, ought to be as centralized as possible. Enforcement responsibility ought to reside within a single person who, in turn, should be granted powers sufficient to meet that responsibility.

This was, perhaps, his most bitter lesson of the Revolutionary War. The Continental Congress struggled throughout the war to find an effective way to supervise and provision the army. At first, Congress acted as a committee of the whole. When that proved ineffective they established a committee of five members of Congress to serve as the ar-

my's "executive" head. In 1777 they made another change, this time retaining the idea of a five-member board, but selecting the members
from outside of Congress. At several points during the war they empowered some of their colleagues to serve as "committees-at-camp," going
to Washington's headquarters to oversee and expedite administration of
the war effort. In each of these instances, though, Congress insisted on
retaining executive power for itself.

Washington was impressed only by the utter ineffectiveness of these
approaches. The states were the principal bogeymen impeding his prosecution of the war, but his regard for Congress's methods of administration was not much higher. Even when Congress succeeded in raising
the necessary supplies the distribution system was so fragmented that
rarely did the provisions reach the army where or when they were
needed.

Washington lobbied throughout the war for single executives—men
who could take responsibility for specific enterprises. In his notes for a
letter to Congress in the summer of 1775 he planned to "express gratitude for the readiness which the Congress and different committees
have shown to make every thing as convenient and agreeable as possible, but point out the inconvenience of depending upon a number of
men and different channels through which these supplies are to be furnished and the necessity of appointing a Commissary General for these
purposes."[42] Congress met Washington's request in this case, but it was
not until 1781, only months before Yorktown, that Congress finally
abandoned plural executives in favor of individual secretaries for war,
marine, foreign affairs, and finance.[43] Robert Morris's success in supplying the army in those crucial months only reinforced Washington's bias
in favor of strong, independent executive leadership.

The war taught Washington another lesson: those burdened with political responsibilities should also have sufficient authority to meet
those responsibilities. General Washington often lacked that authority—with consequences that, in his mind, seriously compromised the
war effort. For one, Washington never had the unity of command that a
commander-in-chief ought to have. The eastern, middle, and southern
armies were all under his direct control. But the northern army was another matter. From the war's outset the northern army command was
an object of conflict among New York interests and factions within
Congress. Philip Schuyler, one of the most powerful figures in New

York politics, successfully lobbied for command of the northern army. Although nominally under Washington's authority, Schuyler behaved more like an equal than a subordinate—a consequence of his independent political base. In time, Schuyler relinquished the command, but rather than consolidating command under Washington, Congress continued to exercise direct control over the northern army.[44] This army won several important engagements in the war, most notably the Battle of Saratoga, but Washington was frustrated by his inability to effectively coordinate the northern army with the rest of his troops. On many occasions he was compelled to plead with the northern commander to provide troops and supplies or to join with him in combined operations. Never was he in a situation where he could *command* the northern army.

Washington had accepted the post of commander-in-chief of the Continental Army believing that responsibility for the success or failure of the war was conferred on him alone. This was surely not true. Congress and the state governments were still constitutionally responsible for the war. Nevertheless, Washington bemoaned this bifurcation of command, believing that it jeopardized his chances for success. His reputation (no small concern for a classical republican) would be the victim of failure. He complained that ''I see the impossibility of serving with reputation, or doing any essential service to the cause by continuing in command and yet I am told that if I quit the command inevitable ruin will follow from the distraction that will ensue. . . . I am fully persuaded that under such a system of management as has been adopted, I cannot have the least chance for reputation.''[45]

Washington's unity of command was further weakened by his inability to obtain complete control over the appointment of his field generals. He fought a losing battle with Congress over the merit principle—in his view the only criterion for the selection of officers (but, additionally, the only criterion that would give the commander-in-chief control over the appointment process). Because most of his generals carried congressional appointments they were able to exercise a degree of independence from Washington. Officers interested in preserving their own reputations with their patrons in Congress could delay responding to Washington's orders or find political excuses for ignoring them altogether. Further undermining Washington's command were militia officers responsible to their state governors rather than to him. This structural disunity of command made Washington feel politically vulnerable and made it appear to him that confidence in his leadership was less than it actually was.

How else to explain his behavior in the Conway affair? Congress in 1777 was considering the appointment of Thomas Conway to inspector general of the army. This was a position of great importance because the inspector general was responsible for implementing a uniform system of training and discipline. (In Washington's mind, an inspector general could serve as an alternative locus of power in the army.) Conway, an Irishman trained in the French military who carried an air of overweening superiority, had privately disparaged Washington's abilities to General Horatio Gates, the commander of the northern army and a man who resented Washington's reputation. The coincidence of these events meant only one thing to Washington: some of his nominal subordinates and their advocates in Congress were conspiring to unseat him. This was the sort of mischief he thought was an inevitable result of his incomplete authority. Washington weathered the "crisis." Indeed, many historians believe that the "Conway Cabal" can be attributed entirely to Washington's overly sensitive ego.[46] The truth of the business is, nonetheless, less important than what Washington *perceived* as true. It was the latter that helped convince him of the necessity of a responsible executive.

The New Precedent:
A Responsible Chief Executive

Washington's presidency reflected this concern for administrative centralization. There would be no divided responsibility or ambiguity as to who was the chief executive. This is not to say that Washington failed to delegate. Military command had convinced him of the value of having talented lieutenants and staff officers to implement his plans. As president he was perfectly content to have surrogates, principally Alexander Hamilton, promote the administration's policies.

This style of administration has led many to conclude that Washington was not a president in the activist mold, or, less charitably, that Washington was little more than a stooge for Hamilton's grand machinations.[47] I will leave for others the daunting task of probing the psychological depths of the relationship between Hamilton and Washington. But from the standpoint of his conception of what a chief executive should be, Washington's conduct was perfectly consistent with his own long-held notions of administrative centralism. No matter how much discretion he chose to delegate to his subordinates Washington always held the reins of responsibility very tightly. Although he remained aloof from the details of government operations he insisted that his department heads inform him of every aspect of their daily activities, especially with regard to how their actions might affect his own authority. Washington could be quite jealous of his own authority and would chastise any subordinates who acted outside their official capacities. Close attention to the reports of his secretary of war led him to comment: "Who is Mr. Rosecrantz? And under what authority has he attended the councils of the Indians at Buffalo Creek? . . . No person should presume to speak to the Indians on business of a public nature except those who derive their Authority and receive their instructions from the War office."[48] In short, Washington was completely aware of what sort of actions his subordinates were embarking on (at least in their official capacities). If he chose not to rein in Hamilton it was not out of diffidence or dotty befuddlement; it was because Hamilton's plans for the federal government conformed perfectly well with his own.[49]

His revolutionary years had also impressed upon him the age-old administrator's bugaboo, "saying it doesn't make it so." More than once, opportunities were lost and battles jeopardized because Washington's orders were not effectively communicated down the chain of command: "Unless orders are attended to, and executed, they are of no consequence, and the greatest disorders will ensue"; officers should "see themselves that they are executed—if everyone in his own department would exert himself for this purpose, it would have the most happy effect."[50] When he became president he issued similar guidance to his administrative subordinates:

> Let me, in a friendly way, impress the following maxims upon the executive officers. In all important matters, to deliberate maturely, but to execute promptly and vigourously. And not to put things off until the Morrow which can be done, and require to be done to day. Without an adherence to these rules, business will never be *well*

done, or done in an easy manner: but will always be in arrear, with one thing treading upon the heels of another.[51]

These illustrations of Washington's administrative style would have little importance in a study of Washington's contribution to American constitutional development were it not for one often overlooked detail of considerable importance. There was nothing in the text of the Constitution that allocated *exclusive* responsibility for the work of subordinate executive officers to the president. He could "Commission all the Officers of the United States"; he could "appoint . . . all other Officers of the United States" (subject to limitations by Congress); and he could "require the Opinion, in writing of the principal Officer in each of the executive Departments, upon any Subject relating to the Duties of the respective Offices." But the Constitution did not expressly make these officers responsible to him alone. Indeed, there was substantial opinion and precedent to suggest that responsibility for department heads was to be shared by Congress and the president. Under the provisions of the Confederation, department heads had reported to Congress. Under the new Constitution the attorney general was clearly an executive officer, but a claim could be made that Congress's constitutional authority to insist on "a regular Statement and Account of the Receipts and Expenditures of all public Money" was cause to place the secretary of treasury at least partially within its jurisdiction. Congress's shared responsibility for making treaties and raising and supporting armies could give it a similarly based claim on the secretaries of state and war.

Washington, supported by the "strong presidency" faction in Congress, insisted that the president alone should assume responsibility for the actions of administrative officers. They successfully argued that the constitutional admonition that the president "take Care that the Laws be faithfully executed" would be null if an executive had to share his responsibilities with the legislature. If having a single executive held any advantage it was that he could more efficiently administer the laws and at the same time be held personally responsible for their execution.

Washington did not relish accepting responsibility for failure. To assure that he would not often be placed in such a position Washington applied two lessons as president that he had learned during his days as commander-in-chief of the Continental Army. First, he insisted on personally selecting all of his key subordinates. The Constitution gives the president the power to nominate, but it also gives the Senate the power to confirm. But the precise meaning of those provisions was left unclear by the framers. Might, for example, the Senate insist on "advising" the president on nominees as well as "consenting" to the president's choices? Might the "advise and consent" provision also mean that the Senate must be consulted before the president removed any of his appointees from office?

Washington clarified the ambiguity in favor of the responsible-executive principle. When the Senate first exercised its power of refusal—it rejected one Benjamin Fishbourne, Washington's nominee for customs officer for Savannah, Georgia—Washington accepted the Senate's constitutional prerogative, though with some irritation. The incident is often cited as the first example of senatorial courtesy in that Senator Gunn of Fishbourne's home state of Georgia appears to have led the opposition. But Washington's response served as another equally important precedent. He conceded that whatever "the reasons which induced your dissent, I am persuaded that they were such as you deemed sufficient."[52] He would not challenge the Senate's authority to say no, nor would he require the Senate to show just cause for its refusal. But another precedent was also validated. The president would not allow the Senate to play any role in suggesting nominees for the executive department. He continued to solicit suggestions from those he trusted, some of them Congressmen. But he would not permit involvement *as a matter of right* by the Senate in naming his lieutenants. If this point were conceded Washington would have to subject his own reputation to subordinates whose political loyalties and reliability he had little confidence in. "I shall not, whilst I have the honor to Administer the government, bring a man into office, of consequence knowingly whose political tenets are adverse to the measures which the *general* government are pursuing; for this, in my opinion, would be a sort of political Suicide."[53] No president should, he thought, have to tolerate a Gates or a Conway in his own "family."

More even than loyalty to the presidency, Washington demanded *personal* loyalty from his subordinates. Washington's volatile, nearly reckless behavior on learning of Benedict Arnold's treason (he abandoned important military discussions and rushed immediately to West Point at great risk to himself and, therefore, the command structure of the army) has perplexed many biographers. After all, both sides in the war suffered their share of traitors. Arnold's treason triggered Washington's well-known fury precisely because Arnold had been one of his most trusted lieutenants. His treason reflected poorly on Washington's executive judgment. As president, Washington wanted no Arnolds to sully his reputation. Personal loyalty became a selection criterion (though certainly not the only one) for all of his high-level nominees.[54] Unlike the model of the British cabinet (especially under Walpole), where various factions and competing political personalities were represented, all of the president's men *were* the president's men—a practice followed by most presidents ever since.

Given George Washington's standing with the public, personal disloyalty was never really an issue during his administration. When Jefferson sensed that his political sentiments and activities were out of step with the president's he chose to resign rather than be deemed disloyal. His replacement as secretary of state, Edmund Randolph, soon found himself in precisely the sort of situation his predecessor had hoped to avoid. Information had come to Washington (information that many believe was carefully selected and manipulated by Hamilton's allies) that Randolph had taken a bribe from the French to oppose the Jay Treaty. Washington coldly confronted Randolph with the accusation. Flustered, Randolph offered a limp explanation and then abruptly and angrily resigned. Recent scholarship suggests that Randolph was the injured party, but excessive fear of betrayal created a blind spot for Washington.[55] Nevertheless, with few exceptions political appointees from Alexander Hamilton to John Dean and Oliver North have henceforth been selected as much for their loyalty to the president as for their competence. This was the constitutional price if presidents were to be held accountable for the actions of their subordinates.

The Two Presidencies and the Case of the Unpaid Dragoons

Twenty-five years ago Aaron Wildavsky postulated the existence of two presidencies. The "domestic policy presidency" was characterized by high levels of partisanship, interbranch competition, and bargaining.

Presidents found it difficult to achieve their domestic goals and often had to settle for incremental accomplishments. Presidents could still lead, but they had to accommodate the significant constitutional and political prerogatives of Congress in doing so. Wildavsky noted that even relatively successful presidents were often frustrated in their attempt to establish a coherent legislative program.

On matters of military and foreign policy, however, the picture looked quite different. Presidents were generally much more likely to be given their head in such matters. Partisanship tended to be more muted; the president's constitutional prerogatives were at least equal to Congress's. The practical consideration that the nation must speak with one voice in the international arena; the need for foreign policy to be based on coherent, long-term commitments; and the superior intelligence-gathering capability of the executive branch all combined to give the president preeminence in foreign policy. Thus, Wildavsky painted a portrait of the modern president that revealed presidential dominance in foreign policy but presidential-congressional bargaining in domestic policy—two presidencies.[56] Wildavsky's conclusions were meant to apply only to modern presidencies, but strong evidence suggests that Washington already had a constitutional conception of the presidency that anticipated Wildavsky's observation.

This distinction can be illustrated by examining Washington's use (and nonuse) of the veto power. At the Philadelphia Convention, Washington advocated a veto power with few limits. He voted against a resolution that would have reduced the congressional majority needed to override a presidential veto from three-fourths to two-thirds (the resolution was approved despite his opposition).[57] Other proposals at the Convention considered the possibility of linking the judiciary or the Senate with the president in a Council of Revision. The veto power was ultimately placed exclusively with the chief executive, but the implication of these discussions was that the veto was to be exercised as a check on "unconstitutional" or improper legislation. Washington, who attended every session of the convention, must have been aware of this intention of the framers.

The president, then, had a constitutionally explicit veto power. But questions remained. Under what circumstances could the veto be exercised? Was it to be applied only against legislation of questionable constitutionality? Or could a president veto statutes whose policy aims he deemed detrimental to the national interest? Washington's advisers often encouraged this latter interpretation and urged him to use the veto as a policy tool. Such use would have established a precedent for presidential involvement in, and perhaps even dominance over, the legislative process. It might have even signaled the onset of a presidential model of government. But with one important exception, Washington declined these invitations.

For example, as a matter of justice Washington strongly believed that tariffs and duties should be based on the principle of reciprocity. Nations that interfered with or discriminated against American trade should not be entitled to the same treatment as the "good friends" of the United States. Thus, when he received, in July 1789, a tonnage bill that did not contain these discriminations, he considered not signing the bill as an indication of his displeasure. But he did *not* consider vetoing it. He eventually signed the bill when he was assured that Congress was already considering a revision that would satisfy many of his objections.[58]

A few weeks later Congress was considering another bill that struck Washington as unjust, and once again he declined to play the role of legislative leader. Congress was about to pass legislation providing that all congressmen be paid six dollars a day. Six years earlier, in his famous Circular Letter to the States, Washington had argued that governmental rewards should be proportionate "to the aids the public derives from them," an argument that led him to suggest that greater rewards for officers, either in severance pay or bounty lands, were justified.[59] Writing now to Madison, Washington expressed his view that senators (perhaps because of their added constitutional responsibilities) ought to receive higher pay than representatives and asked whether a veto would be appropriate.[60] Little more is known about the affair than this one cryptic note—except that no veto occurred.

While Washington thus declined to use his veto power to nullify policies he disagreed with, the controversy over the assumption bill indicated that he was willing to consider vetoing legislation he supported if its *constitutionality* were questioned. As a general and as a private citizen, Washington had long advocated the full payment of the national debt; early in his presidency he had even drafted his own plan for financing the debt, but he seems to have withdrawn it in favor of Hamilton's more comprehensive, sophisticated plans.[61] In the cabinet debate about Hamilton's funding plan, Washington never questioned its wisdom. The plan repaid the national debt at full value and did so in a way that clearly encouraged participation by the federal government in the development of national economic life, both long-held goals of Washington. But he voiced great concern over the bill's constitutionality. Although he signed the bill, it is clear that he viewed the president as having a special guardianship of the Constitution—this in the days before John Marshall was to take the first tentative steps toward asserting such a role for the Supreme Court.

Washington's endorsement of this special constitutional role explains his first veto. The census of 1790 yielded a population figure that when divided by the constitutional criterion of one representative per 30,000 persons authorized a House of Representatives of 120 members. But after allocating to each state one representative for every 30,000 persons, there obtained only 112 representatives. The congressional plan allocated the remaining seats to the eight states with the largest remainders (that is, with the largest population "balances" after seats had been allocated under the one seat per 30,000 rule). These "bonus" seats would have disproportionally favored the northern states. Sectional feeling ran high. Even his cabinet was divided. Hamilton and Knox (northerners) supported the bill; Jefferson and Randolph (southerners) opposed it. Washington decided to veto the bill but explained that his action was dictated solely by his regard for the Constitution. His message to Congress explained that "the Constitution has . . . provided that the number of representatives shall not exceed 1 for every 30,000 . . . and the bill has allotted to eight of the states more than 1 for every 30,000."[62]

Washington, then, understood the constitutional relationship between Congress and the president as one in which Congress held preeminent constitutional standing to make law. Several "strong presidency" men insisted that the chief executive could veto acts of Congress if in his view the national interest commanded it. This would have made the president's power analogous to the royal prerogatives held by the king and many of the colonial governors. But Washington refrained from using his veto in such a manner on domestic policy, not because he could not, but because he would not. He believed the policy preferences of Congress on domestic matters should prevail unless a clear constitutional provision commanded his intervention not only because he chose to take a strictly literalist view of the Constitution, but because to do otherwise would arouse the suspicions and jealousies of those who saw monarchist tendencies lurking in the new constitutional arrangements. He summarized his ideas to his old friend Edmund Pendleton:

> You do me more than Justice when you suppose that from motives of respect to the Legislature (and I might add from my interpretation of the Constitution) I give my signature to many Bills with which my Judgment is at variance. . . . From the nature of the Constitution, I must approve all parts of a Bill, or reject it in toto. To do the latter can only be Justified upon the clear and obvious ground of propriety; and I never had such confidence in my own faculty of judging as to be over tenacious of the opinions I may have imbibed in doubtful cases.[63]

Should we assume from all of this that Washington felt constitutionally bound to assume the role of a "weak" president, completely deferential to the whims of the legislature and unwilling to exercise policy leadership? Wildavsky's insight suggests that we should look closer. And, indeed, when we examine Washington's words and deeds with regard to foreign and military affairs we find a very different picture. Here, Washington willingly accepted a much more activist notion of presidential power.

First, Washington had considerably more "confidence in [his] own faculty of judging" the propriety of legislation regarding military and foreign affairs. The subjects had occupied much of his life for the previous twenty-five years. Few other Americans (and certainly even fewer congressmen) had the breadth and depth of personal experience with these matters, nor did any (not even Hamilton) match his commitment to the virtues of a single-minded, coherent, foreign policy. Second, in Washington's literalist reading of the Constitution there were few points of entry that would allow the president to challenge Congress's primacy in domestic politics. But foreign policy and military affairs were another matter. Here, his constitutional literalism led him to envision a leadership role for the president. The Constitution stipulated that the "president shall be Commander in Chief of the Army and Navy," that he shall have the power "to make treaties," to "appoint ambassadors,'' to ''receive ambassadors,'' and to protect each state ''against invasion.'' Even the proviso in the presidential oath that required him to ''preserve, protect and defend the Constitution of the United States'' implied added presidential responsibilities. Washington was not interested in monarchical authority; he still preferred a consensual mode of governance. But he was more likely to insist on his own *constitutional* prerogatives when diplomatic and defense related issues were at stake.

We can see this difference in perspective at work in Washington's oft-overlooked second veto. In the final days of his second term Congress passed a bill to reduce the size and cost of the military establishment. In what amounted to an item veto (that is, he vetoed the entire bill, but only because he objected to one particular provision), Washington rejected the bill because it included the dismissal of two specific companies of light cavalry (dragoons). His explanation to Congress focused on two *policy* objections. First, these units were serving at outposts on the western frontier. Travel and communication delays being what they were, it would be weeks before the troops could be notified of the decision, organized for demobilization (soldiers do not simply drop their gear in the mud and leave), and sent home. Yet if the president signed the bill, their pay would end immediately. As a soldier of the Revolution who had been constantly plagued by the grievances of unpaid troops, Washington was not about to have his administration be the source of similar indignities. Yet if he paid the troops in the interim, he would be overriding Congress's spending authority—a power exclusively granted to Congress by the Constitution.

Washington's second appeal also was based purely on practical (policy) considerations that he felt confident in asserting. The provision dismissing the dragoons was simply bad military policy. The frontier was the last place to turn for military reductions. Replacements would surely be needed, and re-mobilization would prove far less economical in the long run than maintaining the status quo. Congress agreed and immediately passed a new bill without the objectionable item. Congress has found it difficult to resist a firmly convinced president on military and diplomatic matters ever since.

6 / The Unintentions of a Framer

The story of George Washington's role in the founding of our constitutional traditions is not one of unrelenting success. As President he aspired to much that went unfulfilled during his two terms in office. In several significant ways, in fact, constitutional practices developed quite differently from what he had envisioned. But even here, Washington's role in the development of new and important constitutional forms was substantial, albeit unintended.

The frustrations that Washington suffered can be explained at least in part by the following observation: as Washington came more and more to embody the ideal of American heroism and public service, he came less and less to embody the ideals of American politics. As his personal standing advanced, the representativeness of his political values receded.

This may seem a curious claim. But it is based on a view that the early constitutional period (indeed, perhaps even the writing and ratification of the Constitution itself) represented a transitional period in American political history. According to Gordon Wood, before 1787 the dominant political tradition in American politics was classical republicanism. With the new Constitution, that tradition began to surrender its hegemony over how Americans thought (and acted) about politics to a new tradition, still republican in its spirit, but more liberal in its application.[1]

Nearly all Americans in the 1790s could be called republicans. They shared enough core values—support for constitutionalism and the rule of law, a belief in the social contract, self-government through institutions of representation, a commitment to liberty—that many Old World traditionalists saw these new Americans as all-of-a-piece. But while they shared a common political language, there were still fundamental differences in the way conservative, classical republicans and other republicans—some liberal, some democratic, some even radical—viewed their world.

For example, where conservatives saw the principal mission of republican government to be the promotion of virtue, liberals saw it as the protection of liberty. Where conservatives concerned themselves with generating public-spiritedness among citizens, liberals focused on safeguarding the private liberties of free men. Where conservatives favored mixed government and political unity, liberals preferred divided government and checks against excessive power. Where conservatives believed in the existence of something called the public interest, liberals acknowledged that private interest was both natural and largely uncontrollable. Where conservatives still believed that even republican governmental institutions should reflect the natural divisions within society, liberals believed that all republican institutions should be grounded in the "people." Where conservatives believed that order was a necessary condition for social harmony and economic prosperity, liberals saw the spirit of liberty as the more essential condition.

These dichotomies are, to some extent, archetypal. They define "ideal types"—what a "pure" classical republican and a "pure" liberal republican might look like in the 1790s. One ought not to make too much of these distinctions because most Americans, including Washington himself, drew upon both traditions. Practical experience tends to play havoc with ideological purity. Thus, while Washington was in most ways a classical republican, he had come to believe that a national republic might prosper better by binding the *interests* of citizens to itself (a more "liberal" notion), rather than by relying merely on some hoped-for improvement in the virtue of those citizens (a more "classical" aspiration). His many travels to the West and his extensive interests there (especially his entrepreneurial vision of a Potomac Canal) had convinced him that economic advantage, not just virtue and liberty, was what animated people on the frontier.

As important as the West, or his own particular idea of the West, was in shaping his political views, for George Washington the experience that directed much of his post-1787 thinking was, once again, the war, particularly the circumstances and frustrations of coordinating the military campaign for independence. His was a singular vantage point that set him apart from all other Americans. Even the members of his military "family"—men such as Hamilton, David Humphreys, and

John Laurens—or his nationalist political allies in Congress—Madison, Alexander McDougall, Robert Morris, James Duane, and others—could only share that experience at its edges, where it blurred into and was shaded by their own experiences.

Other Americans learned very different lessons from the war. Many spent those years going about their business, concerned only with how the conflict affected their families and themselves. Still others had come to political age after the war. Nor was the war the only thing that colored American's perceptions of politics. Their religious faith or the social values they held in common with their neighbors or the way they earned their living were often more important in shaping their political character than either the war or the tenets of republican ideology. In short, by 1789 the United States already contained a diversity of ideas, interests, and experiences that made Washington's vision of a virtuous, harmonious, prosperous union only one vision among many. It is not surprising, then, that Washington was compelled to accept the development of some constitutional traditions very different from the precedents he had hoped to initiate. At the height of his personal popularity he was engaged in a politics of nostalgia, seeking, in many respects unsuccessfully, to hold back the tide of liberal republicanism in favor of a classical vision of politics that was already on the wane.

A Cooperative Presidency

Among the constitutional traditions held in highest regard today are the twin structures undergirding the national government: separation of powers and checks and balances. Few constitutional debates today proceed very far without partisans seeking to justify their claims with an appeal to some particular reading of those two principles. Few now doubt that separation of powers and checks and balances are "good" principles and that they are each an essential element of a broadly accepted constitutional tradition. The language and spirit of the Constitution now seems to us self-evident. The Founders wanted to create a strong national union. Thus they endowed the central government with powers sufficient to accomplish its important ends. But to guard against the abuse of those powers they divided them among three separate political institutions and created provisions whereby each branch could involve itself in the others' business—a system based on "separate institutions sharing power."[2]

What we often fail to acknowledge is that this orthodox view reflects the perspective only of the victorious version of republicanism. Not all of the Founders fully subscribed to this view. As noted earlier, Washington had confided that there were some aspects of the Constitution that he was "persuaded never will, obtain my *cordial* approbation."[3] One of those things for which Washington had little enthusiasm was checks and balances. His own notions about republicanism emphasized, instead, the idea of mixed government. Drawn from classical antecedents and modified by the British constitutional tradition, mixed government was premised on the principle that each of the three "natural" orders within society—the monarchy, the aristocracy, and the people—should be represented within the government because each, indeed, retained some recognizably distinct interests. But the theory of mixed government also assumed that a genuine "public interest" could be discovered and advanced by the cooperation of the three orders. The British model of the king-in-parliament served as an example of the energy and unity that were possible in a mixed-government state. The king, guided by his ministers in the Lords (aristocracy) and the Commons (the people), could act only on those matters that generally served to protect the interests and privileges of *all* Englishmen. The system seemed to offer the advantages of republican government (a jealous regard for liberty, virtue, and the public interest), while maintaining a state sufficiently unified and energetic to achieve the common purposes of its people.

To many Americans, Britain was the seedbed of republicanism, and they saw much in its mixed-government system to commend it to the emerging American strain. Perhaps the best example of mixed-government thinking in the founding period can be seen in Alexander Hamilton's plan for government offered at the Philadelphia Convention. Recognizing that America had no hereditary monarchy and no ascriptive aristocracy, he proposed to create new, "artificial," orders in an elected presidency and an elected Senate, each to serve during good behavior, as well as another assembly popularly elected for limited terms. Hamilton was urging the convention to adopt a functional equivalent of Britain's mixed-government system, acknowledging "that the British Govt. was the best in the world."[4] But Hamilton's proposal was not taken up by the delegates, most of whom recognized that it was a form of constitutional monarchy no longer likely to generate popular consent.[5]

The newer orthodoxy, drawn from liberal strains of republicanism, warmly embraced the principle of checks and balances. James Madison in *Federalist* no.51 best exemplifies the "new science of politics."[6] Mixed government, with its emphasis on uniting the different social orders to cooperate for the common good, seemed to make little sense in a society without clearly demarcated classes. It was to be replaced with a new system in which political power would be checked and balanced by a division of powers into different departments, each held accountable in some way by the same class—the people. Nor was all this a purely federalist notion. Many antifederalists shared the new orthodoxy with respect to the principle of *balanced*, as opposed to *mixed*, government. If anything, the antifederalists were fearful that the Constitution did not go far enough in erecting sufficient safeguards against the abuse of power. They called for more checks, not fewer.[7]

For Washington, much of this new "science of politics" was anathema. He believed that the crisis of the confederacy had come about not because the national government lacked balance or had insufficient checks on its power. On the contrary, Washington was convinced that the central government needed *fewer* limitations on its power; that it needed *fewer* obstacles to its efficient operation; that it required, in a word, *energy*. The carefully wrought theories of Montesquieu and Hume may have been attractive to many of his better-read contemporaries. But Washington, who had been exposed to the paralyzing effects of an overly limited central government both during and after the Revolution, wanted a constitution that granted powers, not one that constrained them. He thought it foolhardy in the extreme to replace a government constrained by the petty, parochial jealousies of the states with one equally stalemated by excessive internal checks and balances. "No man is a warmer advocate for proper restraints and wholesome checks in every department than I am; but I have never yet been able to discover the propriety of placing it absolutely out of the power of men to render essential Services, because a possibility remains of their doing ill."[8]

But Washington remained a committed constitutionalist. Good republicans of all varieties accepted the authority of law, particularly law established through the consent of constituent assemblies, and Washington was, as we have seen, no exception.[9] These two norms—his broad republican commitment to the rule of law (epitomized by the new Constitution) and his more classical republican desire for harmony in government (in *opposition* to the very checks and balances established in that Constitution)—posed a difficult problem for the president. How could a president with strong nationalist feelings and a commitment to energetic government govern effectively under a Constitution that raised substantial barriers to the accomplishment of those goals?

The answer to that question reveals George Washington as a constitutional interpreter of considerable creativity. Moreover, the logic of his interpretation was both sensible and consistent. As we have seen, whenever his responsibilities as president were textually stipulated by the Constitution, Washington nearly always scrupulously followed the letter of the law, sometimes to absurd lengths. On the other hand, when the Constitution was silent or ambiguous, his classical inclination toward unity and cooperation led him to ignore the implicit boundaries between himself, the other branches of the national government, and the American people. A few examples—some successful, some not—will illustrate how Washington sought to use the presidency as symbol and representative of unity and national consolidation.

The Idea of a Consultative Presidency

Once again, Washington's experiences as revolutionary commander-in-chief provide a context for understanding his commitment to energy and unity in the national government. During the war he never once questioned that the army was an instrument for accomplishing a *political* purpose—independence. Expediency dictated that there be complete unity of purpose among the Congress, the states, and the army. Throughout the war Washington continually sought to involve as many individuals and political agencies in the common effort as possible. One could, of course, argue that Washington was simply trying to diffuse responsibility for the war effort in case things went badly (and they did go badly for much of the war). But consultation was essential to the character of a mixed government, especially a republican one; thus, it is not surprising that Washington sought to graft several consultative practices onto the constitutional presidency.

Councils of War were common occurrences at Washington's headquarters during the war. Here, his youthful experiences as an officer in the prewar Virginia militia are worth noting. He had served under two seasoned British commanders, General Braddock and Colonel Forbes, who used Councils of War to plan strategy and discuss tactical alternatives. Washington was impressed with the practice, not least perhaps because he found that his own advice was often taken seriously by his more "professional" superiors. But in addition, responsibility for the success of the subsequent operations could be shared, and each officer could be made aware of the purposes of the planned campaign so as to coordinate his efforts toward its success.

When the Continental Congress appointed Washington as commander-in-chief the delegates wanted to maintain direct control over the war effort. To that end they fully intended to keep the general on a short leash. Among the "friendly" suggestions offered by Congress was that Washington rely on a Council of War whenever considering strategy. Because Congress appointed all of the other general officers, a council would assure that the various congressional factions were represented at Washington's headquarters. War policy could not, therefore, emerge without a substantial consensus among the generals. In fact, Washington heartily endorsed the practice. He continued to use councils even after Congress had ceded its supervision of military operations to Washington in the periods of his "dictatorship." Washington was not lacking in confidence or self-regard, so his willingness to accede to councils (and there are instances in which advice from his councils dissuaded him from his own initial plans) might at first seem out of character. Washington recognized, however, that without the support of his own staff, victory in the field would be problematic. A council recommendation carried with it a sense of shared responsibility and common purpose that a general order issued by a commander-in-chief could never attain. If everyone's reputation were contingent upon the achievement of a common objective there would be ample glory to go around.

Washington made a conscious effort to incorporate these lessons into his conception of the presidency. The most successful example of his commitment to unified, cooperative government that has found its way into our constitutional tradition is the idea of a cabinet. Under the new Constitution Congress was authorized to create executive departments to see to the daily business of government. But might their responsibilities go beyond administration? Might they advise the president on other important public matters? The most that the Constitution said was that the president "may require the Opinion, in writing, of the principal Officer in each of the executive Departments, upon any subject relating to the Duties of their respective Offices." Construed narrowly, this meant only that the president might insist on a written accounting from officers who otherwise stood apart from his authority—a formal, compartmentalized view of government operations inconsistent with the notion of mixed government and shared responsibility.

Washington, instead, chose to draw upon his wartime experiences for a precedent. As commander-in-chief he faced a mountain of paperwork (running the army was a bureaucratic enterprise far larger even than his presidency). To help in this daunting task Washington surrounded himself with a singular assemblage of enormously talented young men, his "family" as he preferred to call them. It was a remarkable group—the brilliant Alexander Hamilton, the impulsive Marquis de Lafayette, the diplomatic David Humphreys, and the poetic John Laurens were but a few—all dedicated to serving the great general. Washington could ask advice on any political question (and he was compelled to deal with many), and he could expect useful counsel from several of his young assistants.

As president, Washington referred to his experience with the Councils of War and with his personal staff and tried to adopt elements of both. He refused to use his cabinet secretaries purely as departmental administrators. He preferred, instead, to utilize their collective talents as a presidential "family." Thus, while each cabinet member had specific administrative duties he was also a minister without portfolio, free to advise the president on any matter of public concern. Matters of foreign policy, for example, would not be the exclusive bailiwick of the secretary of state, Thomas Jefferson. Washington would also solicit the opinions (occasionally in writing, but more often in conversation) of his other cabinet members (Hamilton, Randolph, Knox) regardless of their departmental responsibilities. He would even look to trusted friends outside the executive branch such as John Jay and James Madison. Moreover, he used his cabinet as a genuine consultative body, occasionally making up his mind only after a full discussion with all of his ministers.

Most presidents of the early 1800s adhered to Washington's practice, but as a constitutional precedent his notions of a free-floating cabinet eventually withered away. The increasingly burdensome administrative duties of departmental secretaries have made their expertise more specialized and their time more scarce. Moreover, as a more liberal, interest-oriented philosophy of government developed later in the nineteenth century, department heads often became advocates of the interests represented within their particular agencies.[10] This bias made them less attractive as presidential counselors because they and their agencies were not necessarily "interested" in harmony and common purpose. However, modern presidents *have* found indispensable Washington's idea of a body of political advisers dedicated to serving the president, as the mushrooming growth of the White House staff suggests.

The Case of the Reluctant Judges

Where some supporters of the Constitution maintained that separation of powers set up impregnable barriers (or "high walls" to use Jefferson's analogy) between the branches, Washington preferred to conceive of those barriers as a semipermeable membrane. To liberal republicans the existence of these barriers promoted ongoing conflict and tension, perhaps even jealousy, among the branches of the federal government. The logic of Madison's *Federalist* certainly seemed to bear this out: "The great security against a gradual concentration of the several powers in the same department, consists in giving to those who administer each department the necessary and constitutional means and personal motives to resist encroachments of the others. . . . Ambition must be made to counteract ambition."[11] But Washington advocated harmony, not conflict; cooperation, not tension; common purpose, not institutional jealousy. And he sought at every opportunity to bend and stretch the Constitution in ways that minimized the new theory of balance.

An incident early in Washington's second term illustrates the growing incompatibility of classical republicanism with its newer varieties. Washington was committed to a policy of noninvolvement in European affairs. Yet he found his administration besieged by Americans (and Frenchmen—Citizen Genet was already working his political wiles) who insisted that the president be more supportive of the French and their revolution. Washington resisted. His conservative nature was offended by the extremes of the French Revolution. He deeply resented the involvement of the French in the internal politics of America.[12] And he wanted to maintain decent trade relationships with all of the Old World; favoritism in the deepening Anglo-French conflict might harm that policy. But most significant of all, Washington feared that the French were trying to maneuver the United States into a joint war against Britain. This was a dark scenario, indeed, because it would once again make the United States the plaything of Europe, subject most certainly to the efforts of an angry, vindictive Britain to reimpose its colonial authority. War was the last thing that a newly emergent nation needed. The country and the Constitution needed breathing space.

A policy of neutrality thus made perfect sense to Washington. But there was a small problem. The French properly insisted that they still had a treaty with the United States. The military alliance of 1778 that had been so indispensable to Washington's final success at Yorktown had never been revoked. It called for the sort of mutual assistance that might well draw the United States into war or, at the very least, require a foreign policy favorable to France (and therefore sure to alienate Great Britain). As a practical matter the treaty posed no particular obstacle to Washington's foreign policy. He had often commented that governments could be trusted to adhere to treaties only so long as their provisions coincided with each government's interests. But as the president of the United States he was firmly committed to evenhanded enforcement of the laws; and there was no question that the treaty was still the law of the land. As a matter of principle it would have been awkward for Washington to argue that treaties negotiated by the Continental Congress were not obligatory as a matter of law (and honor!), while the financial obligations of that government were assumable in full and enforceable under law.

So Washington's constitutional dilemma lay in trying to find a way to enforce the letter of the French treaty while maintaining his policy of neutrality. If he were to pull off this legal finesse, he would need the cooperation and support of the other branches of government. So, in addition to the advice of his cabinet and other trusted advisers, Washington sought the counsel of the Supreme Court. He was particularly interested in the views of John Jay, the chief justice. Jay had served for a time as the secretary for foreign affairs under the Confederation and was as experienced in diplomacy as any man in the country. Washington had good reason, then, to believe that Jay could offer valuable insights into the history of Franco-American relations. The president sent the Court a list of twenty-nine questions concerning the application of the French treaty.[13] The wording of many of the questions left little doubt that the president wanted the Supreme Court to validate a legal interpretation of the treaty that would endorse his neutrality policy.

Washington saw nothing untoward in this request. He had often consulted with individual justices before, especially Chief Justice Jay, on political matters. Three years earlier, the British had petitioned the president to permit them to march some troops across the frontier from Detroit to New Orleans. (The British wanted to make a show of strength against the Spanish there.) Washington knew that there was little that he could do militarily to prevent such a march, but he did not wish to give official consent to such a provocative request. He asked the heads of each of the departments *and* the chief justice to present their recommendations for a course of action. Washington considered this a time that required unity and mutual support among the great organs of government. Jay apparently agreed; he replied almost immediately.[14] This was not the only "advisory opinion" that Washington received. Washington encouraged Jay to write to the president regularly "and to pray that your ideas may not be confined to matters merely Judicial, but extended to all other topics which have, or may occur to you as subjects for general or private Communications."[15] When the president left the capital on one of his tours in 1791, he authorized the cabinet secretaries, the vice president, *and the chief justice* to consult with each other on pressing matters of government.[16] Moreover, Washington had already induced the Chief Justice to serve on a commission to manage the national debt fund (a purely *executive* function).

Washington understood all of this to mean that the Constitution was not hostile to the notion of interbranch cooperation, particularly between the executive and the judiciary. Was it any wonder, then, that in the face of a threat to the dignity and independence of the United States orchestrated by foreign powers Washington believed a president ought to receive the best available advice from whatever quarter it might come? Patriotism and the public interest demanded no less, separation of powers notwithstanding. Thus it was a considerable shock when the Supreme Court at last responded to the president's queries:

> We have considered the previous question . . . regarding the lines of separation drawn by the Constitution between the three departments of the government. These being in certain respects checks upon each other and our being judges of a court in the last resort, are considerations which afford strong arguments against the propriety of our extra-judicially deciding the questions alluded to especially as the power given by the Constitution to the president, of calling on the heads of departments for opinions seems to have been *purposely* as well as expressly united to the *executive* departments [my emphasis].[17]

The Court's response was fully consistent with the theory of separation of powers. What if the federal government enforced the treaty in accordance with the Court's advice? And what if that enforcement led to litigation over the appropriateness or constitutionality of the executive's actions? How could the Court impartially hear such a "case or controversy" if it had already advised the president as to the treaty's proper interpretation? Ironically then, Washington, the advocate of mixed government, had unintentionally set the stage for one of the first and strongest precedents supporting separation of powers—that the judicial branch shall not offer advice on matters pending before the executive (or the legislature).

Yet the precedent is less pervasive than modern scholars contend. Less than a year later, Washington appointed John Jay as special envoy to Great Britain, where he negotiated the controversial treaty bearing his name. Yet despite the Court's earlier pronouncement, Jay did not resign the chief justiceship, conceding, perhaps, that a president's call to serve the national interest transcended the claims of strict separation—a view more consistent with Washington's sentiments.[18] Indeed, despite the now-famous Supreme Court reply of 1793 several modern presidents have continued to call upon federal judges to provide them with advice or to perform executive functions. Franklin Roosevelt consulted with Felix Frankfurter even after the latter had been appointed to the Supreme Court, as did Lyndon Johnson with Abe Fortas.[19] Johnson appointed Earl Warren to head the commission that investigated the assassination of John Kennedy (a particularly egregious breech of the separation principle in that the Supreme Court could well have had to deal with litigation emerging from the murder), and Ronald Reagan induced Warren Burger to chair the commission charged with celebrating the bicentennial of the Constitution.

Washington must have been disappointed that his actions triggered a constitutional *rule* regarding executive-judicial relations that favored separation; but he insisted on sufficient *exceptions* to that rule that modern judges do not uniformly hang up the phone when the president calls.

The Creek Treaty Affair

Washington's idea of a "consultative presidency" was not confined to the judiciary. He wanted the new constitutional government to speak and act as much as possible with one voice. The Senate was the principal object of his efforts at cooptation. Washington's grand plan bore a strong resemblance to the king-and-council form characteristic of the British parliamentary system. A constitutionally defined and limited monarch ruled with the advice of a small group of ministers drawn from Parliament. These ministers would attend the king whenever important issues were at hand, retaining, of course, their links with Parliament. These prior consultations assured (or so it was presumed) that when the government chose to act it would have the sort of cooperation and national harmony indispensable to energetic leadership.

Washington was attracted to the idea of drawing the Senate into his circle for several reasons. First, it was a small group (only twenty-two senators at the outset of his first term—North Carolina and Rhode Island had yet to ratify the Constitution). Second, it was composed of the "better sort of men" because of its method of appointment. He thought that state legislatures were likely only to select men with significant experience and national reputations. Third, he thought the

Senate probably would be free of local, parochial interests, or that it would at least reflect those interests to a lesser degree than the House. Finally, the Senate had certain constitutional responsibilities, principally the "advise and consent" power, that suggested the possibility for close partnership with the president. What better instrument for combining with the president in pursuit of his nationalist vision?

The early months of his administration saw several attempts by Washington to institute procedures that would bridge the constitutional separation between the president and the Senate. For example, there were plans for establishing a special chamber where the Senate could meet with the president (at *his* call) for consultations, especially on diplomatic matters. Sensitive to the protocol problems involved in direct presidential-Senate consultations, particularly with regard to the "awkward situation" respecting the role of the vice president, Washington thought that a permanent meeting place, separate from Congress's usual chambers, would be appropriate. When he was reviewing plans for the new capital city, he suggested that "Whenever the Government shall have buildings of its own, an executive Chamber will no doubt be provided, where the Senate will generally attend the president."[20] Thus would the bonds between the president and the Senate be further cemented.

He hoped that these meetings would conform to the style and manner of his revolutionary Councils of War. He was comfortable with that format and thought it valuable in unifying military command. In a typical council Washington presented a broad strategic objective to his generals as well as a series of tactical problems, each usually phrased as a question. Generals were free to offer whatever analyses or comments they thought fit, and a consensus nearly always emerged. Occasionally, the commander-in-chief was dissuaded from his proposed course of action by the weight of the arguments. The vital elements in the success of these councils were the openness of the discussions and the immediacy of the results. Washington left each council believing that he and all of his generals understood equally well what the military strategy of the Continental Army was.

Washington believed that all consultations between the president and the Senate regarding treaties, ministerial appointments, and other diplomatic matters should be conducted orally. He was not opposed in principle to written communications *to* the Senate, particularly when dealing with non-diplomatic appointments. The Senate's responsibility there was simply to say yes or no; extended communications were unnecessary. But Washington's understanding of "advice and consent" was that treaties and questions of foreign policy required "advice" as well as "consent." A long, perhaps interminable, series of written memoranda between the chief executive and the Senate about complex questions would not serve the national interest well because of the inevitable delays and institutional posturing. "In all matters respecting Treaties, oral communications seem indispensably necessary—because in these a variety of matters are contained, all of which not only require consideration, but some of them may undergo much discussion—to do which by written communications would be tedious without being satisfactory."[21] The Senate was uncomfortable with Washington's plan. Senators seemed especially uneasy over the matter of "oral communications."

The Senate's uneasiness was well founded. Some indication of precisely how Washington wished to coopt the Senate came less than two weeks later with the onset of the Creek Treaty affair. A border dispute had arisen between Georgia and the Creeks (getting the states to conform to federal treaties with Indians proved to be a continual problem in Washington's administration), and Washington determined to send emissaries to enter into new negotiations with the Creeks and other southeastern tribes. But what sort of instructions should be provided to these emissaries? Invoking the council of war model, Washington called on the Senate to advise him on an appropriate strategy. With Secretary of War Henry Knox and Vice President John Adams in tow, Washington appeared before the Senate in person.[22] In his message to the Senate, he said: "As it is necessary that certain principles should be fixed *previously* to forming instructions for the Commissioners; the following questions arising out of the foregoing communications, are stated by the president of the United States, and the *advice* of the Senate requested thereon [my emphases]."[23] Would the Senate, he inquired, provide him with its "advice and consent" to a series of eleven questions? Vice president Adams then read the rather involved questions to a befuddled and unprepared Senate.

Things quickly deteriorated into broad farce. One senator rose and, citing the noise from passing carriages, asked that the questions be read again. William Maclay, self-appointed guardian of the people's liberties and a man deeply suspicious of Washington and his Federalist friends, initiated a series of motions designed to delay the proceedings and to insist on a full written disclosure of the president's plans. Washington's legendary temper now added further confusion to the moment. He angrily responded that Maclay's proposals would defeat "every purpose of my coming here" and then stormed out the chamber.[24] He is reputed to have declared that "he would be damned if he ever went there again."[25]

Washington should not, however, have been surprised by the Senate's reticence regarding oral consultations. The president had presumed that he could repeat the success of his wartime councils. But he overlooked important practical and constitutional differences between his general staff and the Senate. His generals had all been well versed in the practical realities of the war. They had faced the same enemy, dealt with the same day-to-day logistical difficulties, and most, important of all, shared the same "institutional memory" of the war. They knew what had gone on before and had learned, collectively, whatever lessons were to be learned. Therefore, every general understood precisely the problems the commander-in-chief faced and had a substantial body of experience to draw upon. In short, like a gathering of nuclear physicists who speak in a jargon mysterious to outsiders but perfectly plain to themselves, the generals spoke the same language. The senators, by contrast, found themselves confronted with a series of complex "but if" propositions that must have seemed perfectly alien to them. Here was the president asking their advice on something that they had never discussed and about which no background information had been provided. Moreover, he gave every impression of wanting the senators' advice *now*! No wonder they wanted time to consider the president's requests.

The second factor standing in the way of Washington's vision of consultative government was his misunderstanding of the Senate's constitutional standing. His generals had all been his subordinates. While the councils had been an attempt to develop a sense of shared responsibility, there was no disputing the hierarchical nature of the meetings. The commander-in-chief called the generals at a time and to a place of his choosing. They responded to questions of his selection. And they understood that, in the end, the authority to make any decisions rested solely with Washington. Washington's attempt to cast the Senate into this same mold was sure to fail. The Senate, after all, had its own constitutional standing as a coequal branch of government; it was in no way subordinate to the president. The formidable appearance of Washington with his "lieutenants" Knox and Adams must have unnerved some of the senators. They clearly felt pressured (Maclay referred to the episode as one in which "the president wishes to tread on the necks of the Senate"), and even the president's supporters in the Senate were discomfited by the royalist manner of the proceedings. Many of the senators were themselves Founders, having participated either at the Philadelphia Convention or their state ratifying conventions. And *their* interpretation of the document led many of them to believe that the Senate was not to be a mere instrument of the president. The Senate had powers and responsibilities of its own, powers that existed in part as a counterbalance to monarchical tendencies in the executive branch. Those responsibilities could not be blithely ignored even for the sake of efficiency. Washington's mixed-government interpretation was clearly out of synch with the constitutional times. Liberal republicanism with its suspicion of concentrated power and a preference for the checking function in presidential-Senate relationships was in the ascendant.

Most constitutional scholars see the Creek Treaty incident as an important precedent in strengthening the principle of separation of powers, an outcome quite the opposite of Washington's intention.[26] Indeed, never again would a president appear before the Senate for a face-to-face exchange of ideas. And never again would a president utilize oral communications as part of the advice and consent process. Henceforth, both parties would communicate their concerns in writing.

But this conventional interpretation is only partially accurate. Washington, in fact, returned two days later and put the same questions to the Senate. This time the senators consented to give the president the advice he sought, and they granted it by oral discussions and voice votes in the president's presence. But both parties disliked the process, and written consultations became the rule thereafter. The conventional interpretation sometimes goes further, suggesting that the incident signaled a precedent whereby future presidents would conduct foreign policy at their own initiative and leave the Senate the responsibility of conducting only *post hoc* assessments. While this has become the contemporary practice, Washington never completely abandoned his attempts to incorporate the Senate into a conciliar partnership. Even after the disappointing Creek Treaty business he continued to ask the Senate for their recommendations on "talking points" *before* committing the United States to negotiations, though he thereafter communicated only by written memoranda.[27]

However, by 1793 Washington conceded that his aspirations for a "special relationship" with the Senate had gone aground. Faced with increasing partisanship in Congress (and, for a time, within his own "family") Washington became less willing to trust the Senate to act in the national interest. With the Neutrality Proclamation he announced, without consultation with the Senate, that the foreign policy of the United States would henceforth be initiated by the president. With Jay's Treaty two years later he ended his efforts to consult with the Senate before treaty negotiations. Instead, the treaty was delivered to the Senate for their advice and consent, but in a way that made it clear that the Senate's role was now confined exclusively to "consent." It meant an abandonment of his vision of mixed government and his hopes for a consultative presidency. The foreign policy leviathan represented in the "two presidencies" moved closer to fruition, but it was not a development that Washington could have been pleased about.

Some Questions of Privilege

We can see further examples of Washington's efforts to establish a consultative presidency when we examine his reaction to congressional requests for information from the executive branch. In a system predicated upon separation of powers we would expect a president to assert the traditional prerogatives of a sovereign monarch against the encroachments of the legislature. Information intended for the president's eyes and ears would be solely at his disposal and beyond the legal grasp of any other governmental institution. Permitting, say, the House to obtain access to papers relative to the workings of the presidency would imply the subordination of the latter to the former.

When the Watergate crisis was at its zenith, there was a flurry of scholarly interest in the constitutional roots of executive privilege. Could Congress, pursuant to its constitutional authority to legislate in matters relative to campaign reform (the ostensible purpose for which the Senate's Ervin Committee was first formed) or to impeach officers of the United States, compel a president to turn over his personal papers and effects? Could Congress compel the testimony of members of the president's inner circle? Could the president, consistent with the principle of separation of powers, refuse such requests on constitutional grounds? As is often the case in matters of constitutional interpretation many looked to history for answers. They were particularly interested in the first precedents laid down in Washington's time. The president and many members of Congress were framers of the Constitution; their resolution of these questions would be greatly instructive, perhaps even definitive, in helping to determine whose constitutional claim in the Watergate crisis, Nixon's or Congress's, was the stronger. Not surprisingly each side discovered precedents from the Washington administration favorable to its own interpretations. But proponents of the most prevalent view argued that Washington successfully established the principle of limited, though not absolute, privilege.[28]

I believe, however, that a careful reading of each instance in which George Washington responded to a congressional request for information will indicate that he was less interested in invoking executive privilege (as might be defensible under a strict interpretation of the separation principle) than in promoting a spirit of comity between the two branches. Contemporary presidents have energetically defended their prerogatives; but it is not Washington's constitutional interpretation that they follow but their own. If a Nixon or Reagan or Truman can successfully insist on a privileged status under the Constitution, it is but one more sign of Washington's frustrated constitutional aspirations. Washington had wanted to leave a constitutional legacy of cooperation, not confrontation.

When, in 1790, the president's emissaries concluded a treaty with the Creeks (the same negotiations that had triggered Washington's ill-starred invitation to the Senate to serve as an advisory council) the question arose as to how much information should be provided to the Senate. Just the treaty? The treaty plus whatever background materials the president deemed relevant? Or all materials relative to the negotiations? Washington first consulted his cabinet. Their advice was that the president could constitutionally withhold any materials whose release he deemed harmful to the national interest or to his own executive power. That advice is often cited as an example of Washington's support for a rather expansive privilege. But this was only his cabinet's *advice.* When put to the test, Washington preferred to be guided by his own concern for unity within the national government. A strict adherence to a claim of privilege could shatter his hopes for cooperation. Therefore, he decided to submit, along with the treaty and his personal written recommendation for approval, all other related papers. He considered "that an *unreserved* . . . communication" of all such papers was "indispensably requisite for the information of Congress [my emphasis]."[29] His only stipulation was that any information that might jeopardize the national interest be reviewed in closed session. The Senate's constitutional authority to "advise and consent" gave it a textual claim to the information; the general public had no such claim.

Washington proved equally willing to share unpopular or embarrassing information with Congress. The St. Clair incident was nothing if not embarrassing. Washington had appointed Arthur St. Clair to command an expedition of militiamen against Indians of the Ohio Valley. Following his preference for seeking out men who had served with him in the Revolution Washington believed St. Clair to be a good choice. But St. Clair was routed, losing more than nine hundred of his men and leaving a trail of abandoned equipment. It was a national humiliation. Congress insisted on an investigation into this purely executive operation and, intent on discovering scapegoats for the disaster, asked the president to provide papers relating to the incident. To the surprise of those who invoke Washington as the progenitor of executive privilege he acceded to the House's request "for such persons, papers, and records as may be necessary to assist their inquiries."[30] He expressed some concern that a president *might* need to keep certain sensitive papers secret in the national interest; but his inclination toward interbranch cooperation and his desire to promote confidence in the new Constitution and its presidency led him to err on the side of openness. In the end, *no* papers were withheld.

St. Clair was not the only source of embarrassment to the president. For some time the growing Jeffersonian faction in Congress had focused their conspiracy theories and partisan fervor on the persona of Alexander Hamilton. In 1794 Hamilton's critics at last believed they had "the goods" on him. They asked him to appear before Congress to answer charges of financial mismanagement and misapplication of public funds. Washington made it clear that while he would not compel Hamilton to testify, he considered cooperation with Congress an important hallmark of his administration. Realizing that his political career was at stake Hamilton appeared before the Congress, where he defended his conduct quite successfully. We might well wonder about Washington's motivations in this. Had he chosen, to use John Ehrlichman's pithy phrase, to leave Hamilton "twisting slowly in the wind" in order to safeguard his own political reputation? Or had he acted for principled constitutional reasons, recognizing that Congress's request could easily be justified through its power of the purse? The documentary record is not helpful here. But Washington's behavior established a constitutional precedent that has remained difficult for executive officers, from Hamilton to Robert Haldeman to Oliver North, to ignore.

The imperious Gouverneur Morris was also a thorn in the side of the president. A man of extreme opinions, Morris did not suffer fools lightly—a characterization that the Anglophilic Morris was eager to ascribe to the French. As minister to France Morris wrote dispatches to Washington that dripped with insulting, derogatory portrayals of French leaders. Morris's stormy relationship with the French became the focus of much gossip in the capital and fueled Jeffersonian suspicions that Federalist foreign policy was antirepublican and Francophobic. At last, the Senate asked the president to provide all of the correspondence between Morris, the French government, and the State Department, apparently with an eye to embarrassing the Federalists and forcing Morris's ouster. For the first time, Washington was reluctant to comply with the Senate's request. Some of the messages in question were addressed to Washington personally, not as president, and he doubted that the Senate could constitutionally command them. In addition, Washington thought that the incendiary comments by Morris would only inflame passions and embarrass the United States in the international community. Nevertheless, after making his case to the Senate he submitted all but one of the dispatches they had asked for. Several obvious deletions had been made—not unlike Richard Nixon's celebrated "expletive deleted" transcripts. Washington maintained that releasing this information (in the main, Morris's gratuitous insults) would be harmful to the "national interest" without contributing to any useful public purpose. The Senate did not protest, perhaps because Washington indicated that Morris would be recalled.[31]

The foreign policy arena, particularly as it affected Franco-American relations, proved a continual challenge to Washington's expectations for a harmonious, cooperative national government. Jeffersonian republicans grew increasingly suspicious of the administration's motives, just as Federalists increasingly questioned the patriotism of their critics. Thus Washington began to harbor doubts that a system of mixed government could really govern effectively in the national interest. He came to trust Congress less, to rely on Federalist advisers (especially Hamilton) to the exclusion of almost all others, and to insist on presidential prerogatives in some matters (e.g., the neutrality proclamation, negotiations over the Jay Treaty) where he had previously sought to establish bridges between the executive and legislative branches. In the Morris affair he even seriously considered "stonewalling" the Congress, though in the end he convinced himself (his advisers strongly counseled him to resist Congress's entreaties) that this would be an unwise constitutional precedent.

The dispute over the Jay Treaty provided one more test of Washington's now-wavering commitment to consultative government. In the months after the Senate's approval of the treaty popular reaction against it widened, spurred in many instances by Jeffersonians who saw the treaty's controversial provisions as signs of a sinister conspiracy to undermine the promises of the American Revolution. The House of Representatives, seeking to reopen the controversy, requested that the president "lay before the House, a copy of the instructions to the Minister of the United States [Jay] who negotiated the treaty . . . together with the correspondence and other documents relative to that Treaty, excepting such of the said papers as any existing negotiation may render improper to be disclosed." The House justified its request by noting that implementation of the treaty required the expenditure of public funds, $90,000 to be precise, for which the House had joint responsibility with the Senate. Jeffersonian representatives believed that a detailed examination of the negotiation record would reveal the duplicitous conduct of the Federalists. Most of the motion's supporters were looking to pillory Jay and Hamilton, not the president. Many understood that Washington had come to support the treaty reluctantly as the best that could be attained under the circumstances.[32]

It was a shock (and a moment of much Federalist rejoicing), then, when Washington took strong offense at the request and absolutely refused to comply with it. Again, many scholars point to this as one of the earliest and strongest precedents for executive privilege. But Washington's message to the House reveals that he made no such extravagant claim. His denial was based not on a general claim of executive prerogative, but rather on a constitutional interpretation that narrowed the House's role in foreign affairs. First, he insisted that the Constitution, not partisan considerations, could be the only basis for resolving the interbranch dispute. Second, he argued that the Constitution authorized *only the Senate* to "advise and consent" to treaties. The Founders had deemed that a small body like the Senate was better able to exercise this checking function while maintaining a veil of secrecy beneficial to the national interest. Adding the House to treaty deliberations would expand the circle of political information and imperil the national interest by making secrecy next to impossible. Third, the Philadelphia Convention specifically rejected any House involvement in the treaty-making process. (Washington here was invoking his special standing as a Founder-at-the-scene.) Fourth, a bicameral Congress had been established as a fundamental constitutional compromise. The House had no authority to unilaterally amend the Constitution so as to minimize or eliminate the special responsibilities delegated to a chamber based on equality of the states (the Senate). To do so would imperil the delicate constitutional consensus. Fifth, the House had not previously contested the primacy of the president and Senate. In effect, this emergent constitutional *tradition* now precluded the House from raising the argument anew. Finally, the House would only be constitutionally entitled to these papers if it were conducting an impeachment investigation. Since the House had not couched its request in these constitutional terms, then he (the president) was not obliged to comply.

This certainly *sounds* like a ringing justification for executive privilege. But two points should be noted. First, Washington even here did not invoke an absolute privilege. Where the House could lay claim to a textual provision in the Constitution (pursuant to its impeachment powers, for example) Washington implied that the president was powerless to resist. He would be obliged to turn over the disputed papers. Second, Washington had already laid all of the papers in question before the Senate! Despite the Founders' concern for secrecy, the particulars surrounding the treaty were widely known because of the debates conducted in the Senate. No representative could seriously argue that Washington's refusal had prevented the House from examining those materials. In sum, this was hardly the sort of presidential "stonewall" that it is made out to be. Washington assuredly wanted to avoid further partisan warfare and preserve his own reputation. He had come to believe that opponents of the treaty were using the occasion only to "raise a general ferment" against constitutional government.[33] But in the end he excluded only the House from the treaty process, not the Senate.

The point, of course, is not that Washington never sought to exercise presidential prerogatives. As the Morris incident and the events surrounding the Jay Treaty suggest, Washington did invoke them on occasion. When his constitutional duties were clear, as when engaging in diplomacy with foreign governments, he could assert his prerogatives as jealously as any modern president. What sets Washington apart, however, is his willingness to cooperate with Congress whenever possible and to avoid actions that would divorce the presidency from the other institutions of national government. Executive openness, not executive privilege, was his constitutional practice. Washington would no doubt be disheartened to learn that contemporary presidents have interpreted the legacy of his administration quite differently.

The Impartial Magistracy

He would be even more disheartened, however, at the role political parties have come to play in the American constitutional tradition. There is no greater contrast between the older, classical vision of republicanism and the newer, liberal tradition than in how each views parties or factions. The Constitution of 1787 took no notice of parties. Even the slightest whiff of partisan aroma was enough to send many of Washington's generation scurrying to the parapets, eager to repel the "baneful spirit of party." Parties implied the existence of interests concerned more with the advancement of the self or of the group than with the community as a whole. Classical republicanism held that politics was dedicated to the attainment of "the good"—of the one, true, genuine public interest. This public interest could be discerned only by employing experience and careful, disinterested reason to the resolution of great public questions. The pursuit of virtue allowed for no consideration of the particular or the self-interested. Partisanship, therefore, was a noxious, unrepublican lesion on the body politic to be excised whenever it surfaced.

No man exemplified these views more adamantly than George Washington. In his Farewell Address he could still maintain that partisanship was the greatest threat to republican liberty and order:

> The alternate domination of one faction over another, sharpened by the spirit of revenge natural to party dissention . . . is itself a frightful despotism. But this leads at length to a more formal and permanent despotism. The disorders and miseries, which result, gradually incline the minds of men to seek security and repose in the absolute power of an Individual: and sooner or later the chief of some prevailing faction more able or fortunate than his competitors, turns this disposition to the purposes of his own elevation, on the ruins of Public Liberty.[34]

Partisanship, in other words, was a practice that would lead inevitably to the reimposition of the very tyranny against which republican Americans had fought.

Parties also "enfeebled" government administration, agitated the community with rumors and unwarranted jealousies, fomented "riot and insurrection," opened "the door to corruption and foreign influence," and encouraged citizens to pursue party patronage rather than disinterested public service.[35]

Yet the legacy of the Washington administration regarding partisanship and parties presents a curious paradox. Despite his passionate pleadings to refrain from factionalism Washington's presidency served, with the exception of the first year or two, as a lightning rod for partisanship—partisanship of a virulence that might well astonish modern-day Democrats and Republicans.[36] While Washington decried the formation of permanent political parties, his years in office saw partisanship obtain a tenacious foothold in American politics.[37] Thus, while president Washington had hoped to establish a political tradition consistent with the classical republican aspirations of impartiality and unity in pursuit of the national interest, he left office in 1797 immersed in a national politics dominated by parties and factions. The story of that failure in large part represents the story of the failure of classical republicanism.

It was no surprise that when George Washington took the oath as first president, he brought with him a loathing of the spirit of party. The previous dozen years had convinced him of the perils of partisanship. It mattered little to Washington whether the factionalism emerged from the parochial interests of individual states, from the petty posturings of self-interested politicians, from the regional prejudices already taking root in America, or from those suspicious of the patriotism of others. To him, the nation was poised on the brink of anarchy, and only a higher call to virtue, disinterestedness, and the common good could rescue the great republican experiment in America.

He wanted to be, and he wanted the office to be, "above party."[38] In his first Inaugural Address he promised that "no local prejudices, or attachments; no seperate views, nor party animosities, will misdirect the comprehensive and equal eye which ought to watch over this great Assemblage of communities and interests."[39] Today, the mantle of party leadership comes with the office of president. Washington, however, sought to create a presidency whose primary role was that of a chief magistrate, impartial and inured to the demands of any interest or faction. He could hardly expect to build the "national character" that he was so concerned about if, in his own conduct, he fell victim to the party disease. He laid out his conception of a republican presidency to James Wilson, one of the Philadelphia delegates most responsible for shaping the executive branch: "I presume it will be unnecessary for me to say that I have entered upon my office without the constraint of a single *engagement*, and that I never wish to depart from that line of conduct which will always leave me at full liberty to act in a manner which is befitting an impartial and disinterested magistrate."[40]

In what sense, specifically, did Washington believe he had to be "impartial"? From what did he have to distance himself? These questions are best explained by an examination of his views on the sources of faction. Many of Washington's generation saw class cleavage as the root cause of conflict in American politics. Even Madison, who tried to attribute the causes of faction to many impulses, concluded that the "most common and durable source of factions has been the various and unequal distribution of property."[41] Washington certainly had little sympathy for debtors and even less for legislative efforts to alleviate their distress. Stay laws and other legislation aimed at renunciating debts, public or private, were inherently dishonest and incompatible with the virtues expected of a republican people. Yet a search of his voluminous personal correspondence finds few references that suggest that class differences were, for him, the principal source of faction.

He saw the spirit of party arising, instead, from two other sources. Washington's revolutionary experience had convinced him of the salience of sectionalism and parochial viewpoints as continuing threats to national unity. The debates in Philadelphia and his observations of the subsequent ratification struggles only reinforced his belief that many factions derived from the pursuit of local interest. He had long pleaded with the state governments and with anyone else who would listen to "forget their local prejudices and policies, . . . make those mutual concessions which are requisite to the general prosperity," and "sacrifice their individual advantages to the interest of the Community."[42]

Personalism was the other principal source of faction. He had witnessed it in Virginia, where figures like Patrick Henry, John Robinson, and Thomas Jefferson were often able to attract a coterie of followers and influence (or disrupt) the administration of government. During the war Washington constantly felt the breath of conspiracy at his back and believed that combinations of congressional delegates pursuing their own personal interests and reputations were the cause. These "personality factions," or cliques, were especially odious to Washington because they often were characterized in his mind by conspiratorial backroom politics and a reliance on demagogic appeals for popular support. He early on had characterized Shays's Rebellion, for instance, not as a case of genuine class conflict, but rather as a symptom of factional dispute among the Massachusetts elite: "There are surely men of consequence and abilities behind the curtain who move the puppets; the designs of whom may be deep and dangerous."[43]

If localism and personalism were the two principal threats to the national interest, then many of Washington's actions as president were dedicated to defusing those prejudices. He sought to minimize sectionalism in a number of ways, not the least of which was the example of his own conduct. He took great care, as in his extensive tours of each section of the country, to project an image of himself as an *American* president who happened to be from Virginia, not as a *Virginian* president of the United States. When Rhode Island finally acknowledged the impossibility of its continued isolation and entered the new Union, Washington quickly extended a formal welcome to the state's governor.

Washington assured him that Rhode Island would be treated without prejudice and as a full partner in the national republic. But he also pressed the governor to join with the president to "drive away the daemon of party spirit and local reproach."[44] He sought to further dispel Rhode Islanders' suspicions regarding the new union by making a special trip to the state almost immediately after its ratification. The purpose of this trip, as with his southern and eastern tours, was to convert his enormous personal popularity into a medium conducive to the growth of unionist sentiments. The more that Americans could think "nationally" and could trust the federal government's officers, the less would be the threat of sectionally driven partisanship.

His opposition to sectionalism was more than symbolic. He took great pains to demonstrate impartiality in his advocacy and administration of policy. When Congress initially sought to reapportion the House of Representatives in 1792, its formula would have distributed those seats in a way that favored several northern states. Washington was convinced early on that the plan was unconstitutional but was further distressed when it became an issue that divided North and South. This conflict put him in a painfully awkward position because, as he confided to Jefferson, "he feared that he should be thought to be taking sides with a southern party."[45] Another Virginian, David Stuart, had earlier warned that "a spirit of jealousy which may become dangerous to the Union, towards the Eastern States, seems to be growing fast among us." Washington counseled his friend to avoid such localist thinking. He maintained that the Union could not long survive if it continually favored one section of the country over another. Accommodation and compromise were to be the watchwords of his administration. This "impartial magistracy" meant that some Virginians would have to be disappointed from time to time; neither the presidency nor the union itself could long survive if either catered to factional impulses.[46] Washington ultimately vetoed the bill, but his carefully worded list of objections to Congress addressed constitutional issues only; he pointedly refrained from appealing to sectional considerations.[47]

Further evidence of his efforts at sectional impartiality can be seen in his pattern of executive appointments. The scores of would-be officeholders and their sponsors who besieged Washington with requests for positions led him to resort to a sort of "stock" letter: "I have . . . uniformly declined giving any decisive answer to the numerous applications which have been made to me; being resolved, whenever I am called upon to nominate persons for those offices which may be created, that I will do it with a sole view to the public good—and shall bring forward those who, upon every consideration . . . will in my judgment be most likely to answer that great end."[48] Some of these considerations were noted earlier: competence, previous elective office, experience in the revolutionary cause, political reliability (usually defined early on in Washington's administration as support for the Constitution). But another consideration had nothing to do with the personal qualities of the applicant. One way to minimize sectional jealousies was to assure each state that it was represented in the executive branch. No state should have grounds for claiming that the presidency was the private domain of Virginians or New Yorkers or Pennsylvanians. To this end Washington viewed geography as a valid political consideration in the appointment process. In 1795, for example, he thought it important to review his six-year record of executive and judicial appointments, perhaps trying to convince himself of his impartiality in such matters. The list is particularly intriguing because he categorized his appointees by state—clearly an effort to determine whether he was maintaining a proper geographical balance to his administration.[49]

Washington also feared that party cliques might coalesce around prominent personalities. Competition for power between these personal factions could easily undermine the political harmony that he desired. To prevent the growth of these cliques Washington adopted a strategy of cooptation and democratic centralism. His courting of Thomas Jefferson is illustrative. He was well aware that during the ratification struggle Jefferson's support for the Constitution had been reluctant and conditional—a principal concern being the document's lack of a Bill of Rights. Nor did Washington have the same affectionate feelings toward Jefferson as he had toward his other principal advisers, Hamilton, Knox, and Madison. Why then was Jefferson so heavily lobbied by Washington for inclusion in the first cabinet? In part he was responding to the entreaties of Madison who was close to both men. However, a strategy of cooptation provides an equally plausible explanation. Jefferson already had a substantial personal following, especially in the southern states. What better way to weaken an alternative center of partisan gravity than to invite Jefferson into the administration?

Washington repeated this same strategy with other persons who might have served as a focal point for faction. The case of Patrick Henry is especially interesting. Henry had long been an extremely flamboyant and effective Virginia politico whose reputation had become well known throughout the nation. He and Washington had been on opposing sides in 1788 when Henry's ardent antifederalism had nearly carried the day at Virginia's ratifying convention. But Henry's criticisms of the new government under president Washington had thereafter become more muted. When Randolph left the cabinet during the height of the Jay Treaty controversy, Washington invited his old rival to become secretary of state—an obvious attempt to coopt the loyalty of Henry and his supporters. Henry declined, but Washington's larger purpose was still served; Henry was never again a serious critic of the administration.[50]

Some might fear bringing one's enemies into one's house. But Washington's strategy of cooptation was made effective by an organizational style that relied on democratic centralism. Washington encouraged his advisers to offer their policy views freely and frankly. Even in the first days of Washington's administration, Hamilton would often take issue with Jefferson and Madison.[51] The president was little concerned with these disputes at first because his conservative instincts encouraged him to move deliberately in most things, particularly something as perilous as establishing a new form of government. He needed the best advice he could get. However, once the president had decided on a line of conduct it was incumbent on members of his administration to hew to the party (presidential) line. Hamilton and Jefferson both understood this and, for the first few months of his administration, went out of the way to bend their own views to the president's will once Washington had decided on a policy.

But when the Hamilton-Jefferson conflict deepened and began to spill over into Congress, Washington saw the ugly specter of party on the horizon. In long, very personal letters he pleaded with both men for a compromising attitude—one that could provide at least an outward appearance of unity. To Jefferson he observed "how much it is to be regretted then, that whilst we are encompassed on all sides with avowed enemies and insidious friends, that internal dissensions should be harrowing and tearing our vitals.'' The republic itself was at risk, and unless there were ''liberal allowances, mutual forbearances, and temporizing yieldings on *all sides*'' the noble experiment could yet fail.[52]

But the effort could not bridge the widening ideological rift. Jefferson soon sensed that he could not continue to join in the president's political agenda, nor could he in good conscience enforce those policies as an officer of the administration. British and colonial politics offered numerous examples of cabinet governments in which factional struggles were tolerated and even in some cases promoted. Robert Walpole had managed an extraordinary political career in Britain with just such a politics of inclusion, constructing his ministry from a coalition of numerous competing interests. Walpole maintained his authority by allowing himself to be the fulcrum in these factional struggles.[53] Jefferson, though, understood well the president's character. He knew that Washington, both out of commitment to classical republican ideology and out of a sense of personal insecurity, could not play Walpole's game. So Jefferson left at the beginning of Washington's second term in 1793 rather than conduct guerrilla warfare from within the administration.

Washington and the Paradox of Party

George Washington was a stalwart antiparty man. To the end of his days one of his most scathing indictments of a man's character was that the fellow was a ''partisan.'' His aversion to partisanship had been shaped by classical republican ideology, and his actions as president— his efforts to erect an impartial magistracy, his attempts to deflect sectionalism, his strategy of coopting potentially competing centers of political gravity—consistently sought to promote the national harmony essential to this classical vision. In many other respects Washington was a remarkably successful president. By his retirement in 1797 he had accomplished much of his constitutional agenda. Yet national government was riven by partisanship within months of his inauguration; and that party spirit only escalated during his eight years as president. Why, then, did Washington fail here, while elsewhere he was so successful?

The answer to that paradox rests with two fundamental flaws in Washington's constitutional vision. One was a failure to recognize the changed realities of American political life in his time. The second was a failure to perceive the partisan qualities of his own political character.

There is a common public perception that presidents are not creatures of principle—that they are not, for example, bound to fulfill their campaign promises. Voters who believe what they are told by such knaves, so the conventional wisdom goes, are fools. Even though we live in different times than our constitutional Founders the claim that presidents are disingenuous regarding their true motives and plans has always been a bit of an exaggeration. Most presidents, in fact, expend extraordinary energy in trying to fulfill their promises to the American people.[54] Washington was no exception. Throughout his presidency he rarely departed from the classical republican principles he had espoused publicly and privately for at least a generation. He was unable to recognize, however, that he was attempting to implement an ideal of republicanism that no longer captured the reality of American politics—if it *ever* had. His pursuit of consensus and harmony and his perception of an organically whole national political community were hopes, not realities. Factionalism, not unity, had characterized colonial and national politics at least since the beginning of the eighteenth century.[55]

Washington had come to political maturity during a period in Virginia politics (the 1750s and 60s) when factionalism was less contentious than at most other times in its history. A common concern with the Indians and the French in the West combined with the sly political leadership of the Walpolian Speaker, John Robinson, may have contributed much to this era of stability. This era of good feelings in Virginia did not last. But Washington took it as a sign that government without parties was not only desirable, but possible.

This aspiration was reinforced by his revolutionary experience. The war, in his mind, had been fought for one purpose, national independence. And in the pursuit of that noble end there could be no factions or parties. He retained the quixotic view that *national* politics (he had long since abandoned hope for the survival of nonpartisan republican governments in the states) could rise above party. He insisted that national government was sufficiently continental in scope that, in drawing on his own extraordinary popularity as an exemplar, a "national character" could be molded on republican principles.

His own experiences with the Continental Congress should have dissuaded him from this flawed vision, as that body was no less factional than any other American legislature. Washington simply refused to adapt his republicanism to accommodate parties. He refused to recognize, as Madison did, that factions and interests were the natural byproducts of liberty. By 1789 classical republicanism was already a politics of nostalgia and was being supplanted by the dynamics of liberalism. The Washington presidency is a useful signpost to indicate the inadequacy of the older, classical vision of republicanism to contain the new American politics.

Moreover, despite his sincere desire to serve as an impartial chief magistrate Washington was *never* really nonpartisan in the sense of being "impartial" toward the great public questions of the day. The oft-repeated characterizations of Washington as a kind of disaffected referee in the mighty Hamilton-Jefferson struggle over public policy in the new government, or as a politically naive president increasingly overwhelmed by events, or as a man who lacked any strong ideological convictions of his own simply are not true. Hamilton was the intellectual progenitor of the Federalist "party" and the architect of many of its most significant legislative accomplishments. But Washington did not need any persuasion from the younger man to guide him into the Federalist camp. As I have noted, Washington held Federalist sentiments before, during, and after his presidency. He did not become a committed Federalist only, as some accounts would have it, in 1793 after compromise with the Jeffersonians was no longer possible. Washington was never an impartial magistrate on matters of public policy. Yet he could not comprehend or allow for the criticisms of his Jeffersonian opponents in part because he could not recognize his own persistent partisanship on behalf of the Federalist agenda.

Despite his repeated protestations to the contrary, Washington's self-image as a nonpartisan force for national harmony could not conceal from the administration's critics his obvious enthusiasm for Federalist politics. He patiently listened to the views of Jefferson and Madison and Randolph, but his interpretation of "accommodation" was that Federalist policy (*his* policy) and the national interest were one and the same. One strains to find any significant examples of this president who claimed to be "above party" exercising his impartiality on behalf of Jeffersonian aims.

As a classical republican he could only equate criticism of government policy with criticism of the constitutional system. Increasingly, he grew to see the national political landscape as one composed of well-meaning, reasonable supporters of good government (i.e., Federalists) versus conspiratorial foes of the Constitution (i.e., Jeffersonian republicans). This "impartial magistrate" confided to Hamilton that "[t]he difference of conduct between the friends, and foes of order, and good government, is in nothg. more striking than that, the latter are always working, like bees, to distil their poison; whilst the former, depending, often times *too much*, and *too long* upon the sense, and good dispositions of the people to work conviction, neglect the means of effecting it."[56]

Washington perceived the tenets of republican ideology (portions of which were held by nearly *all* factions in the 1790s) as an endorsement of Federalist policies and *only* Federalist policies. If there was only one true national interest, and if that national interest was synonymous with Federalism, then opposition was both illegitimate and antirepublican. But Jeffersonians were justifiably skeptical of this link between republicanism and Federalism. Jefferson and his followers saw nothing inherently "virtuous" in Hamilton's funding program. There was nothing unquestionably "honorable" in the Jay Treaty. "Liberality" was not necessarily to be found in the excise tax and in no other alternative. These were all policies about which good republicans could, and did, disagree. This, of course, is nothing new. American presidents have always tried to cloak their substantive goals in the rhetoric of "national interest." We now accept the idea of the president as head of his party as well as head of government and consider it part of our constitutional tradition. Even though he feared the "baneful spirit of faction" Washington's presidency verified that constitutional government could survive, perhaps even thrive, on partisan competition—something that he had thought impossible under a republican constitution.

Washington's gradual "conversion" from impartial magistrate to Federalist president was neither paradoxical nor unexpected. Washington was trying to rescue an ideal of classical republicanism, based on harmony and national consensus, that no longer described the reality of American politics. He refused even to acknowledge the lesson of his own experiences—that faction was an integral part of the national character he so earnestly wished to shape. In the end, there was only a paradox of party in Washington's mind. There was no paradox in his actions. He was our first partisan president.

Epilogue:
George Washington and
the Constitutional Tradition

When George Washington stepped down from the presidency in the spring of 1797 the survival of the Constitution was still much in doubt. Never unreservedly optimistic about the "noble" experiment in republican self-government, the events of the previous eight years had left him deeply pessimistic about the prospects for that experiment. His political sensitivities had always been constructed as much out of fear as aspiration: fear of foreign powers, fear of intrigue and conspiracy, fear of the spirit of party and disharmony, fear of disorder and anarchy, fear even of man's capacity to live according to any constitution at all. The last years of his life were more and more given over to these fears. He became increasingly embittered by the elevated partisanship of national politics and by the personal invective that rained upon him in the last months of his administration.[1] He offered his unequivocal support to John Adams and his old Federalist friends in their struggle with the Jeffersonians and warmly endorsed the Alien and Sedition Acts as an appropriate means of protecting "the constitutional form of government."[2] He answered President Adams's call that he serve yet again as commander-in-chief of the federal army being mustered in anticipation of war with France. To Washington the "concord, peace, and plenty" that had welcomed the new constitutional government in 1789 was nowhere to be found in 1797.[3] Things seemed to be falling apart.

But even if we account for the tragedy of a bitter and bloody Civil War fought by both sides in part over constitutional principles, things did not fall apart. Despite Washington's fears, the republic and the constitutional tradition upon which it was constructed endured. And Washington, despite a relatively short twenty-five-year career in public life and his own oft-repeated protestations of inadequacy, should be credited with significant contributions to this legacy.

As commander-in-chief of the Continental Army George Washington remained steadfast in his commitment to republican principles. Throughout the war he subordinated himself to the lawful authority of Congress and the states, even in those times, and there were many, when he was convinced that the policies of the civilian governments impeded the successful prosecution of that war. When he was granted emergency powers he refrained from exercising them in any manner that might reflect dishonor on the army, himself, or the republican cause. When a series of mutinies and insurrections erupted within the army—mutinies directed more at the civilian governments than at the army's command structure—he hesitated not at all to pit soldier against soldier in the defense of those governments. When the frustrations of many of the army's most talented officers had festered to a point where a coup d'état was a real possibility, he stood almost alone among his comrades in reminding them of their republican duty.

Emerging nations in the last two centuries have often given birth to constitutional governments founded upon the most optimistic ideals and principles. But all too frequently those constitutional regimes are the victims of preemptive strikes by their military "protectors." History demonstrates the wisdom of the old opposition republicans who believed fervently that no republic could long thrive where a standing army (or in modern terms, a permanent military establishment) existed. Yet the United States stands out as a shining exception. Here, the professional military takes pride in its unswerving support of the Constitution and its tradition of political disengagement. No constitution could survive long enough to become a tradition without a depoliticized military. George Washington's role in establishing military subordination to popular government is incalculable. This alone would be sufficient to assure his inclusion on any list of essential Founders.

But Washington's constitutional contributions did not end with the conclusion of the war. When internal crises in the postwar years led him to fear for the success of the grand experiment in republican self-government he chose to risk his hard-won reputation, a thing most precious to a classicist like Washington, in support of a peaceful, *constitutional* solution. His decision to attend the Philadelphia Convention lent that body a legitimacy it would not otherwise have had. Given that the final product of that assembly was a new Constitution, where merely amendments to the existing one had been authorized, Washington's presence was probably indispensable. During the war his commitment to republican principles had already been tested as had that of no other American. Thus, those who opposed the new Constitution had to surmount a formidable obstacle; George Washington had helped to write it and had given it a warm endorsement. The enterprise still very nearly failed. Ratification in such key states as New York and Virginia was in doubt until the very end. Washington alone did not carry the ratification fight, but it stretches credulity to contemplate federalist success without Washington's participation and support.

In an effort to quickly situate the new Constitution as the legitimate core of the constitutional tradition he accepted the new office of president. Recognizing that "first forms" can often influence the direction of an embryonic constitutional tradition for generations to come, he assumed the presidency with an eye not merely toward safeguarding republican principles, but also toward incorporating his particular continentalist vision of republicanism. Like every president since, he did not fully succeed. But modern presidents, despite having to govern under conditions quite unlike those in Washington's time, must still confront a presidential structure that owes much to Washington's particular reading of the Constitution.

First, Washington accepted the view that a constitutional presidency was one that was subordinate to the rule of law. Washington never allowed his enthusiasms for particular policies (principally Federalist policies) or his fears of real and imagined crises to serve as an excuse for government by fiat. He occasionally questioned the wisdom of popularly directed government, fretted over public opinion's tardiness in recognizing the "true" state of affairs, and even wondered on occasion whether the republican experiment would succeed. But he never once allowed those doubts to color his official commitment to the Constitution. He fervently believed that the nation would be well served by a national university and a system of canals (most especially, his favored Potomac Canal). But he never presumed that the presidency endowed him with extralegal powers to enact those projects on his own authority in the "national interest." Activist presidents ever since have faced the formidable figure of Washington in arguing otherwise.

Washington also helped to establish the tradition of the president as an interpreter of the Constitution with coequal authority to the Congress and the Judiciary. In numerous incidents—the nullification of his own Supreme Court appointment because he viewed his nominee (a former senator) as disqualified under the Constitution, his withholding of treaty materials from the House because it lacked a constitutional claim to them, his willingness to share those same materials with the Senate because of their constitutionally mandated responsibilities, his use of the veto, his removal of executive officers without the Senate's approval, his assumption of primary responsibility for the making of foreign policy, and many others noted earlier—George Washington put forth a "presidential interpretation" of the Constitution that was ultimately acceded to by the other coordinate branches.

There were some exceptions. The Senate, for example, successfully resisted his efforts to attach it as a conciliar appendage of the presidency. But even here Washington prevailed often enough to create a constitutional climate in which subsequent presidents have been able to make similar successful appeals for senatorial support. To see evidence of the enduring weight of Washington's precedent, one need look no further than the willingness of Congress to accept George Bush's interpretation of the president's constitutional war powers and treaty powers as a justification for American involvement in the Gulf War.

Washington also helped to shape a conception of the executive branch that we have come to know as the "two presidencies." While he was not uninterested in domestic affairs, foreign policy and, to a lesser extent, domestic insurrections were the focus of most of his thinking and writing as president. His classical background and, particularly, the ideal of the "patriot king" made him view the presidency as bearing a special responsibility for the defense of the people. As such he was more interested in defining his constitutional prerogatives more broadly here—the declaration of neutrality, his secret instructions to John Jay for negotiating with the British, and his use of military force and executive fiat to suppress the Whiskey Rebellion are but a few examples—than in the domestic arena where Congress's constitutional arsenal was far more substantial.

By the same token Washington was *not* prepared to expand his foreign policy powers any further than the Constitution or the coordinate branches would permit. When Congress insisted on investigating his failures, e.g., the St. Clair disaster, he consented. When the Senate insisted on all papers relative to a treaty, he consented. When the Senate questioned the conduct of one of his ministers, Washington removed him. When Congress frustrated his military policy by not establishing a uniform national militia, he did not insist on having his way by any means necessary. He was willing to push and stretch the Constitution in order to safeguard the nation, but he was not willing to steer the Constitution toward an unrepublican monarchy. If republican government was not always, in his judgment, "good" government, then he was prepared to accept that as the price of constitutionalism.

He also planted the presidency foursquare behind his vision of a continental republic. The Constitution did not require the president to stand as the symbol of the nation. In fact, Congress, as the most representative of the three branches, could lay equal claim to that role. But neither did the Constitution *prohibit* the president from serving as the spokesperson and symbol of the American people. For Washington's continental aspirations to succeed he had to establish that the presidency was not the captive of any region or faction or interest. If the president could demonstrate that he represented all Americans then he would be well positioned to suppress state particularism and the sorts of regional jealousies that had made the bonds of union so tenuous under the Confederation.

He did not entirely succeed in implanting his vision of a continental republic. Supporters of nationalism and states' rights continued their uneasy détente under the new Constitution; Washington was only able to give the more nationalist Federalists a temporary advantage in that struggle. His grand plan for a westward-looking republic nurtured by the national government would have to wait. And we still have no national university.

But he did succeed in establishing the president as the custodian of the national idea. He showed himself in every state of the new union at a time when such travels were physically uncomfortable, even difficult. By circulating important addresses and proclamations in newspapers and pamphlets (what passed for a national news media in his time) he spoke directly to the American people, rather than through Congress or other constitutional intermediaries. He insisted, without serious objection from Congress, on serving as the spokesperson for and representative of the American people in the community of nations. His personal reputation assured that the presidency (and to some extent the national government itself) would be treated with awe and respect without resort to the unrepublican trappings of monarchy. Today, most American citizens respect the presidency (a call from the White

House still causes the heart of the most jaundiced local politician to flutter just a bit) and rarely challenge the authority of a president to speak for the nation even when they have little regard for the occupant of the office.

Where ought we, then, place the bust of George Washington in the pantheon of constitutional demigods? A bit above James Madison? A bit to the left of Abraham Lincoln? The influence of any one person upon the intricate web of historical events is unmeasurable. But it is not unimaginable. For example, other men might well have offered greater skills as a general. Horatio Gates, Philip Schuyler, and Charles Lee could claim greater experience than Washington. Benedict Arnold and Nathanael Greene had battlefield successes that compare well to Washington's. But Gates and Schuyler were preoccupied with positioning themselves for political advantage within Congress; Lee had nothing but contempt for republicans; Greene's relationship with Congress in his duties as quartermaster general can most charitably be described as unhappy; and Arnold's brief encounter with civilian government as the administrator of Philadelphia during a period of martial law was a performance that alienated nearly all of the city's citizens and triggered a court-martial. Could any of these men, if appointed commander-in-chief, have subordinated their pursuit of military objectives (or personal glory) to the larger public enterprise of building and preserving a republican form of government?

And what of Washington's performance at Philadelphia in 1787 and in the ratification struggle afterwards? The convention threatened to dissolve at several points that summer. Had the gathering been presided over by a figure less imposing than George Washington, would the delegates have gone home? Or would the compromises have taken on a decidedly less continental tilt—perhaps leaving the delegates in agreement only on the submission of the sort of recommendations for revision of the Articles for which they had originally been convened? And without Washington's highly visible proratification stance could the federalists have prevailed? I do not mean to suggest that Washington was the oarsman without which the American constitutional tradition would have foundered. There were enough Americans committed to self-government, constitutionalism, and republican principles to guarantee that some sort of constitutional tradition would have continued, perhaps one that could have been every bit as successful in its own way as the tradition that eventually emerged. But there is a good chance that it would have been different.

And what does it matter that George Washington was the first president? Would our modern presidency have a different cast to it had John Hancock or John Adams or Thomas Jefferson or Benjamin Franklin been the first to occupy that office? Would Hancock have conceded legislative initiative in the domestic arena? Would Franklin have pursued presidential leadership in foreign affairs as diligently as Washington? Would Adams have sought to be as conciliatory to his political opposition? Would the weight of precedent characteristic of their "first forms" have shifted the current of the American constitutional tradition in a different direction?

The constitutional tradition enjoyed by Americans of the twenty-first century bears little surface resemblance to the one envisioned by Washington. We are today the constitutional children of countless constitutional parents. Throughout its more than two-hundred-year history our Constitution has been shaped and recast by innumerable individuals, groups, institutions, events, and social forces. The Constitution is no more exclusively George Washington's offspring than it is Madison's or Jefferson's or Lincoln's or Franklin Roosevelt's. It is no more the product of the Founding Fathers than it is of subsequent generations of Americans who have governed themselves under its auspices. It is no more the embodiment of classical republicanism than it is of modern welfare liberalism. Yet the constitutional tradition as we know it today still bears the unmistakable signs of Washington's imprint—of his having chosen to direct the main current of that tradition in one direction or another. In the end, the thing "twas builded better than he knew."

Notes

Chapter One: The Conservative Revolutionary

1. *Notes of Debates in the Federal Convention of 1787 Reported by James Madison* (New York: Norton, 1969), 447. For a somewhat different interpretation of Dickinson's remarks (namely, that they illustrated the Founders' larger sense of history rather than any special concern for their own more contemporaneous experiences) see Douglass G. Adair, "Experience Must Be Our Only Guide: History, Democratic Theory, and the United States Constitution," in *The Reinterpretation of Early American History: Essays in Honor of John Edwin Pomfret*, ed. Ray A. Billington (San Marino, Calif: Huntington Library, 1966), 129–148.

2. GW to George William Fairfax, 30 June 1785, *Writings of George Washington, D.C.*, ed. John C. Fitzpatrick (Washington, D.C.: GPO, 1931–1944), 28:183. I have relied primarily on two sources for the writings of George Washington. Until recently, the thirty-seven-volume *Writings of George Washington*, edited by John Fitzpatrick under the auspices of the Washington Bicentennial Commission, was the most complete and definitive collection. A few additional letters have emerged since the Fitzpatrick project began, but it remains a monumental work. Fitzpatrick's greatest service was in locating and transcribing the many Washington letters in private collections and in other libraries. In the last ten years scholars at the University of Virginia have embarked on an even more ambitious enterprise—the publication (with extensive annotations) of *all* of Washington's correspondence and state papers. This includes not only Washington's writings (the sole focus of the Fitzpatrick edition) but also the even more voluminous correspondence *to* him. Because this project is so enormous only a small portion of Washington's writings have so far been published in this series. (Some of the difficulties faced by the editors of *The Papers of George Washington* are discussed in Don Higginbotham, "The Washington Theme in Recent Historical Literature," *Pennsylvania Magazine of History and Biography* 114 [1990]: 423–437.) Wherever possible, I have used *The Papers* as the best available source for Washington's words. In all other cases I have relied on the Fitzpatrick *Writings*.

3. Richard Hofstadter, *Anti-Intellectualism in American Life* (New York: Vintage, 1963).

4. For a more complete discussion of the role that an increasingly common body of law played as a force for colonial cohesion, see Lawrence M. Friedman, *American Law: An Introduction* (New York: Norton, 1984), 41–42; Kermit L. Hall, *The Magic Mirror: Law in American History* (New York: Oxford University Press, 1989), 45–48.

5. GW to Robert Dinwiddie, 10 June 1754, *The Papers of George Washington: Colonial Series*, ed. W. W. Abbot (Charlottesville: University Press of Virginia, 1983–   ), 1:134. Fitzpatrick dates this letter as 12 June 1754.

6. See Charles S. Sydnor, *Gentlemen Freeholders* (Chapel Hill: University of North Carolina Press, 1952); Dumas Malone, ''The Great Generation,'' *Virginia Quarterly Review* 23 (1947):108–122.

7. Washington was not above shading the bounds of ethics (and honorable behavior) in acquiring some of his lands. He pestered Virginia's government for years to pay him and his soldiers the land bounties they had been promised. Publicly, he always spoke on behalf of the ''loyal soldiers,'' but as the commanding officer, his personal stake of fifteen thousand acres was considerably larger than that of any of his troops. Moreover, he assigned the best of these western lands to himself, arguing that he had borne most of the costs of the surveys and had taken up much of his own time in lobbying for and then administering the grants. Later, he sought to purchase additional tracts by employing a ''stalking horse''—a third party who would seek to buy land as an agent of Washington. Washington feared that the asking price of land would rise significantly if he were revealed as the prospective buyer. Washington's land grabbing fell short of the behavior expected from a man of virtue, but in truth it was relatively benign compared to the activities of many of his gentry peers. For the most scathing treatment of Washington's dealings, see Bernhard Knollenberg, *George Washington: The Virginia Period, 1732–1775* (Durham, N.C.: Duke University Press, 1964).

8. No brief summary can do justice to the richness of the literature on Country ideology. Among the most useful and influential are Bernard Bailyn, *The Ideological Origins of the American Revolution* (Cambridge, Mass.: Harvard University Press, 1967), esp. 22–93; John M. Murrin, ''The Great Inversion, or, Court versus Country: A Comparison of the Revolution Settlements in England and America,'' in *Three British Revolutions: 1641, 1688, 1776*, ed. J. G. A. Pocock (Princeton, N.J.: Princeton University Press, 1980), 368–453; J. G. A. Pocock, ''Virtue and Commerce in the Eighteenth Century,'' *Journal of Interdisciplinary History* 3 (1972):119–134; James H. Hutson, ''Country, Court, and Constitution: Antifederalism and the Historians,'' *William and Mary Quarterly* 38 (1981):337–368.

9. Jack Greene juxtaposes ''metropolitan'' interests with ''peripheral'' interests to help explain the growing division between a centralizing British state and independent-minded colonial legislatures resistant to that effort. He also uses the terms to describe a more intramural conflict being played out *between* Americans attached to centralized colonial governments and their neighbors in the hinterlands. It is this latter notion of ''metropolitan'' that is used here. Jack

P. Greene, *Peripheries and Center: Constitutional Development in the Extended Polities of the British Empire and the United States, 1607–1788* (Athens: University of Georgia Press, 1986).

10. The definitions of "realty" and "personalty" used here follow those made in Charles Beard, *An Economic Interpretation of the Constitution of the United States* (New York: Macmillan, 1913), 19–51. Much of Beard's analysis of the founding period has been found wanting, but realty and personalty still accurately define the economic world as Washington and many in the Virginia gentry perceived it.

11. GW to John Parke Custis, 26 May 1778, *Writings*, 11:457.

12. A more complete treatment of Washington's attempts to rise within the ranks of this landed gentry can be found in Paul K. Longmore, *The Invention of George Washington* (Berkeley: University of California Press, 1988).

13. GW to Robert Cary and Company, 20 September 1765, *Papers: Colonial Series*, 7:398–402.

14. Bernard Mandeville, *The Fable of the Bees: Or, Private Vices, Publick Benefits*, ed. F. B. Kaye (Oxford: Clarendon Press, 1924).

15. Michael Kammen, "A Different 'Fable of the Bees': The Problem of Public and Private Sectors in Colonial America," in *The American Revolution: A Heritage of Change*, ed. John Parker and Carol Urness (Minneapolis, Minn.: Associates of John Ford Bell Library, 1975), 53–68.

16. Gordon S. Wood, "Interests and Disinterestedness in the Making of the Constitution," in *Beyond Confederation: Origins of the Constitution and American National Identity*, ed. Richard Beeman, et al. (Chapel Hill: University of North Carolina Press, 1987), 83–85.

17. Douglass G. Adair, "Fame and the Founding Fathers," in *Fame and the Founding Fathers: Essays by Douglass Adair*, ed. H. Trevor Colbourne (New York: Norton, 1974), 3–26; for an assessment of how well Washington succeeded in presenting an image of a public man dedicated to fame, see Barry Schwartz, *George Washington: The Making of an American Symbol* (New York: Free Press, 1987), esp. 119–148.

18. GW to Robert Dinwiddie, 29 May 1754, *Papers: Colonial Series*, 1:106.

19. GW to Earl of Loudoun, ? January 1757, *Writings*, 2:12.

20. Ibid., 18.

21. GW to Robert Dinwiddie, 10 June 1754, *Papers: Colonial Series*, 1:130.

22. GW to Robert Dinwiddie, 18 May 1754, ibid., 1:100.

23. GW to William Fitzhugh, 15 November 1754, ibid., 1:226.

24. A more complete account of the popular response to Washington's actions in the Braddock campaign can be found in Longmore, *Invention of George Washington*, 29–33.

25. Douglas S. Freeman, *George Washington*, 7 vols. (New York: Scribner's, 1948–1957), 3:448.

26. Pauline Maier, *The Old Revolutionaries: Political Lives in the Age of Samuel Adams* (New York: Knopf, 1980).

27. GW to Francis Dandridge, 20 September 1765, *Papers: Colonial Series*, 7:395.

28. The Resolves are generally considered the handiwork of George Mason with Washington as his most significant collaborator. Much of the language used in the resolutions reads like Mason, and he had been the most openly vocal of the Fairfax freeholders. Nettels argues for a more significant involvement by Washington while Sweig suggests that the circle of authorship was broader than Mason and Washington. See Curtis P. Nettels, *George Washington and American Independence* (Boston: Little, Brown, 1951), 90–92; Donald M. Sweig, "A New-Found Washington Letter of 1774 and the Fairfax Resolves," *William and Mary Quarterly* 40 (1983): 285–289.

29. GW to Bryan Fairfax, 4 July 1774, *Writings*, 3:228.

30. Ibid., 229.

31. GW to Bryan Fairfax, 20 July 1774, ibid., 3:232–233.

32. GW to Bryan Fairfax, 10 June 1774, ibid., 3:224.

33. GW to Bryan Fairfax, 24 August 1774, ibid., 3:242.

34. Bryan Fairfax to GW, 17 July 1774, ibid., 3:230n.

35. GW to Bryan Fairfax, 20 July 1774, ibid., 3:233.

36. Ibid., 233; Many other Americans had similarly concluded that taxation was the fulcrum that divided British and American ideas of the Anglo-American constitution. Both sides placed other constitutional arguments on the scale, but in the end most Patriots simply could not accept the "new" constitution's assertions about parliamentary control over taxation, nor could Parliament accept the American position of local sovereignty in such matters. See John Philip Reid, *Constitutional History of the American Revolution: The Authority to Tax* (Madison: University of Wisconsin Press, 1987).

37. GW to Bryan Fairfax, 4 July 1774, ibid., 3:229.

38. In truth, few Americans advocated outright independence in 1774. But these were tumultuous times, and straw men of all shades were invoked by both sides to characterize their opponents' positions. Then, as now, such characterizations often served to place an adversary in a defensive posture. Indeed, Washington's conservative impulses made it difficult for him to completely discount Fairfax's portrayal of some of the Patriots, hence his insistence on disavowing any support for such "independence-minded" men.

39. GW to Robert MacKenzie, 9 October 1774, *Writings*, 3:246–247.

40. Ibid., 3:246.

Chapter Two. The Republican General

1. Washington perceived the military struggle as a war for independence rather than a revolution. Only toward the very end of the war does the word "revolution" appear in his letters, and only then because the term was being used widely (though subject to ambiguous and idiosyncratic meanings) by

many of his correspondents—state political leaders, members of Congress, fellow officers—as part of the regular discourse of the day.

2. Several recent works have made much of Washington's admiration of the hero of Joseph Addison's eighteenth-century play, *The Tragedy of Cato*. Longmore, *Invention of George Washington*, 171-183; and Garry Wills, *Cincinnatus: George Washington and the Enlightenment* (Garden City, N.Y.: Doubleday, 1984), in particular, have argued that much of Washington's public behavior was patterned on the classical republican hero of the play.

3. British generals, of course, had their own reputations to protect and thus tended to inflate Washington's prowess as a military strategist. See Sir Henry Clinton, *The American Rebellion*, ed. William B. Wilcox (New Haven, Conn.: Yale University Press, 1954); Charles Lord Cornwallis, *An Answer to that Part of the Narrative of Lieutenant-General Sir Henry Clinton . . .* (London: J. Debrett, 1783); Sir William Howe, *The Narrative of Lieut. Gen. Sir William Howe* (London: H. Baldwin, 1780).

4. Gordon S. Wood, *The Creation of the American Republic, 1776-1787* (Chapel Hill: University of North Carolina Press, 1969), 46-124.

5. Interestingly, one of the revolutionary transformations of the war was the dramatic change in the public's perception of the term "republican." Before 1776 most Americans, including most revolutionaries, avoided using the terms "republican" or "republicanism." Classical taxonomies of government usually characterized republics as "democracies." Since democracy was generally thought of as a depraved or corrupted form of government, no public figure seeking legitimacy for his ideas would refer to them as republican. After 1776 republicanism became *de rigueur*. No one knows exactly why, but the best speculation seems to be that Americans had long endorsed the substance of republican ideology even as they distanced themselves from republican rhetoric. Once independence separated the states from the old constitution (as well as the old language and old forms that went with it) Americans were free to unapologetically call themselves republicans. See Willi Paul Adams, "Republicanism in Political Rhetoric before 1776," *Political Science Quarterly* 85 (1970): 397-421; Adams, *The First American Constitutions: Republican Ideology and the Making of the State Constitutions in the Revolutionary Era* (Chapel Hill: University of North Carolina Press, 1980), 6-26 and 99-117; Cecelia Kenyon, "Republicanism and Radicalism in the American Revolution: An Old-Fashioned Interpretation," *William and Mary Quarterly* 19 (1962):166.

6. GW to Congress, 24 September 1776, *Writings*, 6:107.

7. Ibid., 6:111.

8. GW to Lund Washington, 20 August 1775, *The Papers of George Washington: Revolutionary War Series*, ed. Philander D. Chase (Charlottesville: University Press of Virginia, 1985-   ), 1:336.

9. GW to Richard Henry Lee, 29 August 1775, ibid., 1:372.

10. GW to John Hancock (Congress), 21 September 1775, ibid., 2:24-30; GW to John Parke Custis, 22 January 1777, *Writings*, 7:53-54; GW to Richard Henry Lee, 29 August 1775, *Papers: Revolutionary War Series*, 1:372-375.

11. Ironically, the social character of the Continental Army was probably "better" in 1775–76 than later in the war. The initial fever of patriotism in the first year of the war attracted volunteers from a cross section of colonial society—merchants, farmers, artisans, clergymen, in short, men of "respectability." But the productive middle class could not be expected to enlist for the duration of the conflict, so the army more and more came to represent the underclass of America—the unemployed, convicts, indentured men, recruits who had been paid by "respectable" men to take their place, and bounty jumpers (men who would enlist for the cash bounty, desert, and then reenlist for another bounty in a new unit). James Kirby Martin, "A 'Most Undisciplined, Profligate Crew': Protest and Defiance in the Continental Ranks, 1776–1783," in *Arms and Independence: The Military Character of the American Revolution*, ed. Ronald Hoffmann and Peter J. Albert (Charlottesville: University Press of Virginia, 1984), 122–126. Charles Royster draws a much more favorable portrait of revolutionary soldiery, suggesting that they were not the ne'er-do-wells that Martin and others describe, nor were they devoid of patriotic motives for their service. See Royster, *A Revolutionary People at War: The Continental Army and American Character, 1775–1783* (Chapel Hill: University of North Carolina Press, 1979), esp. 373–378. But whatever the historical truth, Washington's perception of the social qualities of his enlisted troops was closer to Martin's assessment than Royster's.

12. GW to Jonathan Trumbull, 9 September 1776, *Writings*, 6:39; GW to Congress, 24 September 1776, ibidl, 6:110–111.

13. GW to Massachusetts Provincial Congress, 4 July 1775, *Papers: Revolutionary War Series*, 1:60.

14. GW to Congress, 24 September 1776, *Writings*, 6:108.

15. GW to Lund Washington, 20 August 1775, *Papers: Revolutionary War Series*, 1:335.

16. Richard H. Kohn, in particular, has argued that despite their specific grievances against Congress and the states most of Washington's officers supported the subordination of the army to civilian government. See Kohn, "American Generals of the Revolution: Subordination and Restraint," in *Reconsiderations on the Revolutionary War: Selected Essays*, ed. Don Higginbotham (Westport, Conn.: Greenwood Press, 1978), 104–123.

17. Stanley Elkins and Eric McKitrick, "The Founding Fathers: Young Men of the Revolution," *Political Science Quarterly* 76 (1961):181–216.

18. GW to Congress, 24 September 1776, *Writings*, 6:108.

19. GW to William Livingston, 12 July 1777, ibid., 8:442.

20. GW to Henry Laurens, 24 July 1778, ibid., 12:224.

21. GW to Board of War, 9 January 1779, ibid., 13:498.

22. GW to Committee of Conference, 20 January 1779, ibid., 14:27.

23. GW to Congress, 10 April 1778, ibid., 11:237–238.

24. GW to William Maxwell, 10 May 1779, ibid., 15:33.

25. Military historians have generated a rich literature on the strategic character of the Revolutionary War. A particularly useful debate on the question of

whether the war was a traditional conflict or an irregular one can be found in Hoffmann and Albert, eds., *Arms and Independence*. See, especially, the contribution of Don Higginbotham, "Reflections on the War of Independence, Modern Guerilla Warfare, and the War in Vietnam," 1–24.

26. GW to Joseph Reed, 28 May 1780, *Writings*, 18:436.

27. See Bailyn, *The Ideological Origins of the American Revolution*, 112–120.

28. Royster, *Revolutionary People at War*.

29. These fears, it seems, were not entirely unfounded. Richard Kohn and Kenneth Bowling both suggest that there were political factions within Congress, usually clustered around the ultranationalists Alexander Hamilton and Gouverneur Morris, who *did* use the threat of army insurrection as a means for manipulating Congress and the states for their own designs. See, Kohn, "The Inside History of the Newburgh Conspiracy: America and the Coup d'Etat," *William and Mary Quarterly* 27 (1970):187–220; and Bowling, "New Light on the Philadelphia Mutiny of 1783: Federal-State Confrontation at the Close of the War for Independence," *Pennsylvania Magazine of History and Biography* 101 (1977):419–450.

30. Forrest McDonald, *Novus Ordo Seclorum: The Intellectual Origins of the Constitution* (Lawrence: University Press of Kansas, 1985), 77. This was no abstract notion. During the army crisis of 1782–83 Washington was asked several times to overthrow the national government (it is unclear whether this effort was to extend to the states as well). These inducements, almost always emanating from his own officer corps, usually invited Washington to install himself as the head of a new government with the army's backing. Washington insisted with considerable passion that such an action would destroy the principles of the Revolution and all that the army had fought to preserve. For an interesting, if somewhat overly colorful, account of these events, see James Flexner, *George Washington* (Boston: Little, Brown, 1965–1972) 2:487–508. Also, see below, pp. 40–47.

31. General Orders, 21 October 1778, *Writings*, 13:118–119; General Orders, 1 March 1778, ibid., 11:8–10; General Orders, 30 March 1781, ibid., 21:159.

32. GW to Patrick Henry, 28 March 1778, ibid., 11:164.

33. Worthington Ford et al., eds., *Journals of the Continental Congress, 1774–1789* (Washington, D.C.: GPO, 1904–1937), 2:96–97.

34. The best account of this episode appears in Freeman, *George Washington*, 4:138–140. See also Flexner, *George Washington*, 2:102–103.

35. *Writings*, 5:274n.

36. GW to George Clinton, 8 October 1778, ibid., 13:50; GW to Charles Scott, 15 October 1778, ibid., 13:82; GW to William Livingston, 15 April 1778, ibid., 11:262–263

37. GW to Joseph Reed, 8 May 1779, ibid., 15:23.

38. The first proclamation granting these extraordinary powers to Washington was issued on 12 December, 1776. Congress resolved: "That, until the Congress shall otherwise order, General Washington be possessed of full power to order and direct all things relative to the department, and to the operations of

war." *Writings*, 6:354n. This delegation of power was both open-ended (Congress did not set any time limit on its grant) and plenary. His powers were not merely executive, but legislative and judicial as well. The second proclamation, issued 17 September, 1777, was more time-specific and geographically confined. But within his area of jurisdiction Washington's powers were still clearly dictatorial. "Resolved, That General Washington be authorized and directed to suspend all officers who shall misbehave, and to fill up vacancies in the American army, under the rank of brigadiers, until the pleasure of Congress shall be communicated; to take, wherever he may be, all such provisions and other articles as may be necessary for the comfortable subsistence of the army under his command, paying or giving certificates for the same; to remove and secure, for the benefit of the owners, all goods and effects, which may be serviceable to the enemy; provided, that the powers hereby vested shall be exercised only in such parts of these states as may be within the circumference of 70 miles of the head quarters of the American army, and shall continue in force for the space of 60 days, unless sooner revoked by Congress." *Writings*, 9:237n.

39. See the discussion in Wills, *Cincinnatus*, 17–23.

40. GW to William Shippen, Jr., 27 January 1777, *Writings*, 7:71.

41. GW to William Livingston, 15 April 1778, ibid., 11:262–263.

42. Proclamation, 20 December 1777, ibid., 10:175.

43. Proclamation, 24 January 1777, ibid., 7:61–63.

44. GW to Gouverneur Morris, 29 May 1778, ibid., 11:485.

45. Royster, *Revolutionary People at War*, 255–330.

46. GW to Congress, 27 May 1980, *Writings*, 18:416–419.

47. Circular to the New England States, 5 January 1781, ibid., 21:61–62; GW to Congress, 6 January 1781, ibid., 21:64–66.

48. GW to Robert Howe, 22 January 1781, ibid., 21:128–129.

49. Lewis Nicola to GW, 22 May 1782, ibid., 24:273n.

50. Louise Burnham Dunbar, *A Study of "Monarchical" Tendencies in the United States from 1776 to 1801* (Urbana: University of Illinois Studies in Social Sciences, 1923); GW to J. G. Gebhard, 5 November 1783, *Writings*, 27:231.

51. Lewis Nicola to GW, 22 May 1782, *Writings*, 24:273n.

52. GW to Lewis Nicola, 22 May 1782, ibid., 24:272–273.

53. The best account by far of the Newburgh Conspiracy can be found in Kohn, "The Inside History of the Newburgh Conspiracy."

54. The Newburgh Address, 11 March 1783, in *Basic Documents on the Confederation and Constitution*, ed. Richard B. Morris (New York: Van Nostrand, 1970), 43–46.

55. General Orders, 11 March 1783, *Writings*, 26:208.

56. GW to the Officers of the Army, 15 March 1783, ibid., 26:224–225.

57. Ibid., 226–227.

58. There is some dispute about whether these words were spoken before or after Washington's main address. Most accounts place the remark after the speech. In addition, the precise wording of Washington's extemporaneous com-

ment varies slightly among the witnesses. This particular version seems to be the most widely accepted one. It appears in *Writings*, 26:222n.

59. Wood, *Creation of the American Republic*, 499–506.

60. Ironically, Washington's idea was adopted, but without giving him the command he wanted. In fact, in this new joint colonial command he was made a subordinate of the governor of Maryland—hardly what Washington had had in mind! For a fuller accounting, see Freeman, *George Washington*, 2:125–168.

61. Marc Egnal, "The Origins of the Revolution in Virginia: A Reinterpretation," *William and Mary Quarterly* 37 (1980):401–428.

62. Most Patriots accepted the notion that military victory over the British was essential. But Patriots divided—fragmented is perhaps the more descriptive term—over other goals of the Revolution. As Carl Becker put it so cogently more than three-quarters of a century ago, the Revolution was not just to establish home rule; it was to determine who should rule at home. Becker, *History of Political Parties in the Province of New York, 1760–1776* (Madison: University of Wisconsin Press, 1909).

63. GW to Benjamin Harrison, 18 December 1778, *Writings*, 13:464.

64. GW to Benjamin Harrison, 30 December 1778, ibid., 13:466.

65. Ibid., 13:467.

66. E. Wayne Carp, *To Starve the Army at Pleasure* (Chapel Hill: University of North Carolina Press, 1984).

67. GW to Benjamin Harrison, 21 March 1781, *Writings*, 21:342.

68. GW to William Duer, 14 January 1777, ibid., 7:13.

69. Behavior such as this was not unique to revolutionary state governments. This phenomenon, the "free rider" problem, characterizes many social interactions. Given the alternative of receiving a particular benefit by paying for it or receiving the same benefit without paying for it (or better yet, getting another party to pay for it!), a rational actor will consistently choose the latter two alternatives. See Mancur Olson, *The Logic of Collective Action* (Cambridge, Mass.: Harvard University Press, 1965), 9–36.

70. "The States are not behind hand in making application for assistance notwithstanding scarce any one of them, that I can find, is taking effectual measure to compleat its quota of Continental Troops, or have even power or energy enough to draw forth their Militia; each complains of neglect because it gets not what it asks; and conceives that no other suffers like itself because they are ignorant of what others experience, receiving the complaints of their own people *only*. I have a hard time of it and a disagreeable task. To please every body is impossible; were I to undertake it I should probably please no body." GW to John Armstrong, 18 May 1779, *Writings*, 15:97.

71. Illustrative of this problem is a letter to the Governor of New Jersey. "I am extremely apprehensive that very disagreeable consequences may result from an increase of the standing pay of the militia. It would create an additional cause of discontent to the Soldiery, who would naturally draw a comparison between their situation and that of the Militia and would think it very hard and unjust that *these* should receive for temporary services a greater reward

than *they* for permanent ones." GW to William Livingston, 4 May 1779, *Writings*, 14:489–490.

72. GW to John Armstrong, 18 May 1779, ibid., 15:97.

73. Washington's troubles with Congress and the states over the appointment and promotion of officers is well documented elsewhere. See Don Higginbotham, *George Washington and the American Military Tradition* (Athens: University of Georgia Press, 1985); Louis C. Hatch, *The Administration of the Revolutionary Army* (New York: Macmillan, 1904); and Jonathan Gregory Rossie, *The Politics of Command in the American Revolution* (Syracuse, N.Y.: Syracuse University Press, 1975).

74. GW to John Sullivan, 27 December 1780, *Writings*, 20:488.

75. GW to James Varnum, 4 November 1777, ibid., 10:5.

76. GW to John Banister, 21 April 1778, ibid., 11:291–292.

77. An excellent summary of the dimensions of this debate from the perspectives of both the revolutionary generation and contemporary historians can be found in Jack N. Rakove, *The Beginnings of National Politics: An Interpretive History of the Continental Congress* (New York: Knopf, 1979), 163–191.

78. See E. Wayne Carp, "The Origins of the Nationalist Movement of 1780–1783: Congressional Administration and the Continental Army," *Pennsylvania Magazine of History and Biography* 107 (1983): 363–392; E. James Ferguson, "The Nationalists of 1781–1783 and the Economic Interpretation of the Constitution," *Journal of American History* 56 (1969):241–261; Merrill Jensen, *The New Nation: A History of the United States during the Confederation, 1781–1789* (New York: Knopf, 1950), 54–84. For significant modifications of the thesis that there was a cohesive nationalist movement in this period, see Lance Banning, "James Madison and the Nationalists, 1780–1783," *William and Mary Quarterly* 40 (1983):227–255; Rakove, *Beginnings of National Politics*, 307–324.

79. GW to Francis Lewis, 6 July 1780, *Writings*, 19:130–132.

80. Ibid.

81. See GW to Joseph Jones, 24 March 1781, ibid., 21:374; GW to William Fitzhugh, 25 March 1781, ibid., 21:375–376; GW to John Armstrong, 26 March 1781, ibid., 21:379–380.

82. GW to John Parke Custis, 28 February 1781, ibid., 21:320–321.

83. GW to Joseph Jones, 14 May 1780, ibid., 18:356–357.

84. *Papers: Revolutionary War Series*, 1:84.

Chapter Three: The Restive Correspondent

1. Cited in Flexner, *George Washington*, 2:469.

2. GW to John Augustine Washington, 15 June 1783, *Writings*, 27:12.

3. Farewell Orders to the Armies of the United States, 2 November 1783, ibid., 27:224.

4. GW to Thomas Johnson, 15 October 1784, ibid., 27:481.

5. GW to Henry Knox, 25 February 1787, ibid., 29:169–170.

6. As noted earlier (see Chapter 1), *dis*interestedness was a virtue in republican societies. *Dis*interested was not, as it is often used today, a synonym for *un*interested. Rather, it suggested that one's virtue and independence were such that one could rise above narrow self-interest and act out of a sense of the public good.

7. Washington often issued Circular Letters while acting as commander-in-chief. He communicated with Congress on an almost daily basis. But when he thought the message was important enough he wrote to the states directly. He would write a common letter and post it to each of the state chief executives, perhaps altering a few details to customize the letter or to address something applicable only to that state. Because of the length and importance of this final, farewell Circular Letter it took considerable time to produce thirteen copies. Thus, some states received their copies almost two weeks after the first posting.

8. Circular Letter to the States, 8 June 1783, *Writings*, 26:484–485.

9. Ibid., 26:486.

10. Ibid.

11. Ibid., 26:488–489.

12. Ibid., 26:487.

13. Ibid., 26:488.

14. Ibid.

15. Ibid., 26:487.

16. Ibid., 26:489–490.

17. See the earlier discussion describing Washington's opposition to that part of the Fairfax Resolves that called for a moratorium on the payment of legal debts to British creditors, p. 20.

18. GW to Lund Washington, 17 December 1778, *Writings*, 13:408.

19. Circular Letter to the States, 6 June 1783, ibid., 26:490.

20. Ibid., 26:493.

21. Ibid., 26:494.

22. Ibid., 26:486.

23. Ibid., 26:491.

24. Ibid., 26:487.

25. GW to Charles Carter, ? August 1754, *Papers: Colonial Series*, 1:197. There is some confusion over precisely when and to whom this letter was written. The Fitzpatrick *Writings* catalogued it as a letter to Thomas Lee, head of the Ohio Land Company; but Lee died in 1750. Washington had traveled down the Potomac in July and August of 1754 making the *Papers'* dating reasonable. However, Egnal points out that Washington's surveying duties took him into this area as early as 1749, when Lee was still alive, so it is not impossible that the idea of a Potomac Canal surfaced even earlier than 1754. See Egnal, ''Origins of the Revolution in Virginia'': 412n.

26. GW to Thomas Johnson, 20 July 1770, *Writings*, 3:19.

27. Charles H. Ambler, *George Washington and the West* (Chapel Hill: University of North Carolina Press, 1936), 174.

28. GW to James Duane, 7 September 1783, *Writings*, 27:133.

29. GW to Thomas Jefferson, 29 March 1784, ibid., 27:374.

30. GW to Benjamin Harrison, 10 October 1784, ibid., 27:475.

31. GW to Henry Knox, 5 December 1784, ibid., 28:4.

32. GW to Congress, 17 June 1783, ibid., 27:16–18. Washington at this point had still another concern: seeing that the disbanded but still greatly disenchanted army was finally paid. Making good on those bounty lands would not only fulfill Congress's obligation, it would place a potential source of political disenchantment a safe distance from the centers of government.

33. GW to Francis Vanderkemp, 28 May 1788, *Writings*, 29:504–505.

34. GW to the Secretary for War (Henry Knox), 18 June 1785, ibid., 28:168.

35. GW to Thomas Jefferson, 29 March 1784, ibid., 27:376.

36. GW to Edmund Randolph, 25 December 1786, ibid., 29:120.

37. GW to David Stuart, 30 November 1785, ibid., 28:328.

38. GW to James Wilson, 22 March 1782, ibid., 24:88. There are some interesting conjunctions in this relationship. Wilson became one of the most effective advocates at the Philadelphia Convention for just the sort of energetic national government that George Washington envisioned. Indeed, the presidency that Washington was later to occupy owed a sizable debt to Wilson's skills of persuasion. Wilson's student, Bushrod Washington, after being turned down for a federal judgeship by his uncle (out of the latter's desire to demonstrate his impartiality and lack of favoritism), was appointed to the Supreme Court of the United States by President John Adams. With John Marshall, Bushrod Washington interpreted the Constitution with such a sympathetic eye toward the defense of national prerogatives that the old man must surely have smiled just a bit. The two justices ardently defended Federalist policies and political theory on the bench well into the 1820s.

39. Bushrod Washington to GW, 27 September 1786, *Writings*, 29:21–22n.

40. Bushrod Washington to GW, 31 October 1786, ibid., 29:23–24n.

41. GW to Bushrod Washington, 30 September 1786, ibid., 29:22.

42. For much of his second term as president, George Washington complained bitterly about the activities of a group of organizations known as the Democratic-Republican societies. These organizations were critical of the policies of his administration, particularly its posture toward the revolution in France. Washington's occasionally vitriolic responses are often taken as a sign of a decline in his evenhandedness. That is certainly true up to a point, for the president was by then a thoroughgoing Federalist partisan. But his letters to Bushrod Washington indicate that his suspicions about extragovernmental factions appeared long before 1793 and extended even to groups whose views he was much more sympathetic to. See Eugene P. Link, *Democratic-Republican Societies, 1790–1800* (New York: Octagon, 1973).

43. GW to Philip Schuyler, 21 May 1776, *Writings*, 5:65–66.

44. GW to Henry Lee, 5 April 1786, ibid., 28:402.

45. Bushrod Washington to GW, 31 October 1786, ibid., 29:23–24n.

46. GW to Bushrod Washington, 30 September 1786, ibid., 29:22.

47. GW to Benjamin Harrison, 18 January 1784, ibid., 27:306.

48. Burke's most memorable explication of these issues is found in a speech he made in 1780 while defending himself against the charge that he had not adequately represented the interests of his Bristol constituents: "Parliament is not a *congress* of ambassadors from different and hostile interests, which interests each must maintain, as an agent and advocate, against other agents and advocates; but Parliament is a *deliberative* assembly of *one* nation, with *one* interest, that of the whole. . . . You choose a member, indeed; but when you have chosen him he is not a member of Bristol, but he is a member of *Parliament*." Cited in Charles O. Jones, *The United States Congress: People, Place, and Policy* (Homewood, Ill.: Dorsey Press, 1982), 182.

49. This is certainly not all there is to say about representation theories in the founding period. A far more comprehensive discussion of these changes can be found in Wood, *Creation of the American Republic*; Donald S. Lutz, "Popular Consent and Popular Control, 1776–1789," in *Founding Principles of American Government*, ed. George J. Graham, Jr., and Scarlett G. Graham, rev. ed. (Chatham, N.J.: Chatham House, 1984), 60–97; McDonald, *Novus Ordo Seclorum*, 143–184; and Lance Banning, *The Jeffersonian Persuasion: Evolution of a Party Ideology* (Ithaca, N.Y.: Cornell University Press, 1978), 92–114.

50. For a reminder of how alien Massachusetts's social and political climate was to Washington, see above, pp. 27–28.

51. See David Szatmary, *Shays' Rebellion: The Making of an Agrarian Insurrection* (Amherst: University of Massachusetts Press, 1980); Robert J. Taylor, *Western Massachusetts in the Revolution* (Providence, R.I.: Brown University Press, 1954), 103–167. For a more radical interpretation of the uprising, see Monroe Stearns, *Shays' Rebellion, 1786–7: Americans Take Up Arms against Unjust Laws* (New York: Franklin Watts, 1968).

52. Each town in Massachusetts was entitled to representation in the General Court, but each town was also obliged to support its representative on the court. Many of the smaller towns in the interior had concluded that their one representative was not worth the taxes necessary to support him. By 1786, economic conditions had worsened to the point that few of these western towns could afford to send representatives, leaving them grossly underrepresented in the General Court. J. R. Pole, *Political Representation in England and the Origins of the American Republic* (New York: St. Martin's Press, 1966), 227–244.

53. GW to David Humphreys, 22 October 1786, *Writings*, 29:27.

54. GW to David Humphreys, 26 December 1786, ibid., 29: 125–126.

55. GW to Henry Lee, 31 October 1786, ibid., 29:34–35.

56. There was never a doubt that Washington supported the aims of the convention. But he hesitated to accept a position as delegate principally for two reasons. One concern was that he had already declined, for personal reasons, to attend the Society of the Cincinnati meeting, which was scheduled to convene in Philadelphia at about the same time as the constitutional convention. He worried that his personal honor might be compromised and that his former comrades would take personal offense that their organization was less deserv-

ing of the general's attentions. Second (and this is more speculative because Washington does not speak directly to this concern), Washington was worried about risking his personal reputation on a venture whose success was doubtful. The Annapolis Convention had already failed to achieve its aims—though Madison and Hamilton had used the forum as an opportunity to call for the Philadelphia meeting. Might the Philadelphia convention be equally unsuccessful? And might that failure carry away with it any possibility that Washington could exercise some influence on the course of political events?

57. The notion of constitutional decay was common to much of the British opposition ideology that had been absorbed by many American republicans. A useful discussion of decay can be found in Lance Banning, "Republican Ideology and the Triumph of the Constitution," *William and Mary Quarterly* 31 (1974):167–188.

58. GW to Henry Lee, 31 October 1786, *Writings*, 29:34.

59. GW to Lafayette, 25 March 1787, ibid., 29:184.

Chapter Four: The Framer as Partisan

1. See Banning, "Republican Ideology," 187; Thomas C. Grey, "Origins of the Unwritten Constitution: Fundamental Law in American Revolutionary Thought," *Stanford Law Review* 30 (1978):843–893; and Donald S. Lutz, *The Origins of American Constitutionalism* (Baton Rouge: Louisiana State University Press, 1988).

2. GW to James Madison, 18 November 1786, *Writings*, 29:71.

3. Ibid., 72.

4. Negotiations between Maryland and Virginia to enter into a Potomac Canal compact came to include Pennsylvania because the best site for a connection to the Ohio River seemed to be through that state. With this tripartite compact under consideration, it became apparent to some that a whole range of interstate commerce and relations needed to be examined by all the states. Virginia took the lead in calling the Annapolis Convention of 1786 to consider these matters. But only five states sent delegates to the Convention and it concluded no substantive business. Washington saw the results of this low attendance as one more sign of the failure of the confederacy and, initially, used it as an excuse for not attending the Philadelphia Convention. Yet Hamilton and Madison had used the event as an opportunity to convince the few delegates in attendance to call for a constitutional convention to remedy defects in the federal form of government. Despite Washington's belief that the Annapolis Convention was yet another failure for the forces of sound government, Madison and Hamilton came away genuinely hopeful that the tide of sentiment and events was moving their way. Richard Morris, *Witnesses at the Creation: Hamilton, Madison, Jay, and the Constitution* (New York: Holt, Rinehart and Winston, 1985), 161–169.

5. Richard Neustadt, *Presidential Power: The Politics of Leadership from*

FDR to Carter (New York: John Wiley, 1980), 44–79. Neustadt's emphasis on reputation appears throughout the book, but it is most clearly expressed in chapters 4 and 5.

6. GW to Lafayette, 25 March 1787, *Writings*, 29:184.

7. GW to Henry Knox, 2 April 1787, ibid., 29: 193–194.

8. Max Farrand, ed., *The Records of the Federal Convention of 1787*, rev. ed., 4 vols. (New Haven, Conn.: Yale University Press, 1937), 1:20.

9. Most accounts believe that the disingenuous first resolution was added to the Virginia Plan at the last minute as a concession to Randolph. See Irving Brant, *James Madison: Father of the Constitution, 1787–1800* (Indianapolis, Ind.: Bobbs-Merrill, 1950), 24.

10. Farrand, *Records*, 1:24.

11. John P. Roche, "The Founding Fathers: A Reform Caucus in Action," American Political Science Review, 55 (1961):803.

12. GW to James Madison, 31 March 1787, *Writings*, 29:190–191.

13. Ibid., 29:191–192.

14. Madison had already been working on his "Vices of the Political System," a scathing indictment of the weaknesses of government under the Articles of Confederation. In addition, he had suggested in earlier letters to Edmund Randolph and Thomas Jefferson most of the proposals for constitutional change that were to find their way into the Virginia Plan. Thus, Washington did not initiate Madison's thinking on this matter. Washington's support was probably indispensable to the success of the plan at the Convention, and the Plan certainly coincided with many of Washington's oft-repeated concerns of the previous decade, but its authorship must be attributed principally to Madison. See "Vices of the Political System," April 1787; James Madison to Thomas Jefferson, 19 March 1787; and Madison to Edmund Randolph, 8 April 1787, *The Papers of James Madison*, ed. Robert A. Rutland et al. (Chicago: University of Chicago Press, 1975), 9:317–319, 348–358, 368–371.

15. James Madison to G. W., 16 April 1787, *Papers of James Madison*, 9:382–383.

16. Farrand, *Records*, 3:20–21.

17. Roche, "The Founding Fathers,"800.

18. Arthur N. Holcombe, "The Role of Washington in the Framing of the Constitution," *Huntington Library Quarterly* 19 (1956):323–324.

19. Farrand, *Records*, 2:644.

20. Ibid., 2:221.

21. Readers may be skeptical of the claim that Washington single-handedly moved the convention to adopt Gorham's proposal. Historians have long been aware that the records of the convention, even Madison's comprehensive retrospective notes, are incomplete. It is quite probable that there are aspects to the convention's business that will remain forever unknown to us. Thus my speculation is based on this admittedly partial record. Nevertheless, Washington appears to have been the only one to have spoken substantively on this issue, after which the delegates, perhaps taken by the force of his arguments or perhaps

merely expressing their respect for Washington, unanimously changed a provision they had unanimously supported a few weeks earlier.

22. For a more complete discussion of theories of representation in the founding period, see Wood, *Creation of the American Republic*, 162–181.

23. Washington's fears seem well founded. Several antifederalists pointed out the insufficiency of representation in the national Congress. To many of them even a district composed of thirty thousand persons was rather large in the context of the 1780s. The city of New York, after all, had fewer than twenty-five thousand inhabitants. But the issue was not central to the antifederalist case, perhaps because of Washington's judiciousness. See Speech of Melancton Smith, 20–21 June 1788, *The Anti-Federalist Papers and the Constitutional Convention Debates*, ed. Ralph Ketcham (New York: New American Library, 1986), 341–347.

24. Again, it is difficult to assess the precise impact that Washington had on ratification. We know that his reputation was significant enough that Luther Martin and other Maryland antifederalists had an awkward time trying to explain why their fellow delegates to the state ratifying conventions should not support an effort so closely associated with Washington. See Farrand, *Records*, 3:178, 190, 294. In his home state of Virginia the general's support in this closely divided state may have tipped the balance in favor of the federalists, or at least so some of the participants thought. As James Monroe commented to Thomas Jefferson, "Be assured [Washington's] influence carried this government." Cited in Freeman, *George Washington*, 6:140. For a useful one-volume source on the politics of the individual state ratifying conventions, see Michael A. Gillespie and Michael Lienesch, eds., *Ratifying the Constitution* (Lawrence: University Press of Kansas, 1989).

25. His letter to Alexander Hamilton, pleading with the New Yorker to return to the Convention, is the most famous illustration of Washington's trepidation about the outcome of the whole affair: "In a word, I *almost* despair of seeing a favourable issue to the proceedings of our Convention, and do therefore repent having had any agency in the business. . . . I am sorry you went away. I wish you were back. The crisis is equally important and alarming, and no opposition under such circumstances should discourage exertions till the signature is fixed." GW to Alexander Hamilton, 10 July 1787, *Writings*, 29:245–246.

26. See Max Farrand, *The Framing of the Constitution of the United States* (New Haven, Conn.: Yale University Press, 1913), 66.

27. There have been many useful analyses of the voting behavior at the convention. But the most sophisticated analysis (and the one used here) is in Calvin C. Jillson, *Constitution Making: Conflict and Consensus in the Federal Convention of 1787* (New York: Agathon Press, 1988).

28. Farrand, *Records*, 1:65.

29. Ibid., 1:97.

30. Ibid., 2:33–36.

31. GW to Lafayette, 28 April 1788, *Writings*, 29:479.

32. One observer has placed Washington among a group of presidential "radicals"—men dedicated to promoting a national chief executive with powers akin to a constitutional monarchy. Donald L. Robinson, "The Inventors of the Presidency," *Presidential Studies Quarterly* 13 (1983):8–25.

33. Farrand, *Records*, 1:164.

34. Charles F. Hobson, "The Negative on State Laws: James Madison, the Constitution, and the Crisis of Republican Government," *William and Mary Quarterly* 36 (1979):215–235.

35. GW to William Gordon, 8 February 1783, *Writings*, 27:52.

36. Rakove, *Beginnings of National Politics*, 337–338.

37. Farrand, *Records*, 2:280.

38. Beard, *An Economic Interpretation of the Constitution*, 144–146.

39. See, for example, Forrest McDonald, *We the People: The Economic Origins of the Constitution* (Chicago: University of Chicago Press, 1958).

40. GW to James Madison, 31 March 1787, *Writings*, 29:188–189.

41. GW to Battaile Muse, 18 September 1785, ibid., 28:269.

42. GW to Jabez Bowen, 9 January 1787, ibid., 29:139.

43. GW to Thomas Stone, 16 February 1787, ibid., 29:164.

44. Ibid., 29:164–165.

45. GW to Jonathan Trumbull, 20 July 1788, ibid., 30:21.

46. Madison mentions only that he (Madison) was the swing vote within the state's delegation. Mason and Randolph spoke against the motion. Both of them, while stating their opposition in principle to paper money, were concerned that the omission would tie the hands of the legislature and prevent it from acting in the public interest. Given Washington's antipathy to paper money it seems fair to assume that he would have been one of three votes (with Madison) necessary to counter Mason and Randolph in support of the motion. Farrand, *Records*, 2:308–310.

47. Ibid., 2:641–649.

48. This method of political analysis is common among political behavioralists. See, for example, Robert A. Dahl, *Modern Political Analysis* (Englewood Cliffs, N.J.: Prentice-Hall, 1963).

49. GW to Edmund Randolph, 8 January 1788, *Writings*, 29:358.

50. GW to David Stuart, 5 November 1787, ibid., 29:302.

51. Cited in Freeman, *George Washington*, 6:98.

52. The names used to describe particular political combinations in this period are always a bit confusing. When I use the term "federalists" it refers to those who supported ratification of the Constitution in 1787–88 or who stood for election in support of its principles in 1788. The "antifederalists" were those opposed to the Constitution of 1787. On the other hand, "Federalists" were the faction that began to coalesce around the specific policies of the Washington administration. The distinction between "federalists" and "Federalists" will become more apparent in chapters 5 and 6.

53. GW to Lafayette, 18 September 1787, *Writings*, 29:277.

54. See GW to Patrick Henry, 24 September 1787, ibid., 29:278–279; to Edmund Randolph, 8 January 1788, 29:357–358.

55. GW to David Humphreys, 10 October 1787, ibid., 29:287; to David Stuart, 17 October 1787, 29:290; to David Stuart, 30 November 1787, 29:323–324; to James Madison, 7 December 1787, 29:331.

56. GW to James Madison, 10 January 1788, *Writings*, 29:372–373.

57. An interesting illustration of Washington's astute political sense is his advice to a couple of Maryland delegates not to allow their convention to adjourn without a vote on ratification. New Hampshire had already adjourned its convention, and Washington believed that two such adjournments in rapid succession would lend significant momentum to the antifederalists. Two months later, he *encouraged* New York to consider just such an adjournment. He correctly sensed that the New York delegates would defeat the Constitution if it were put to an immediate vote; thus, he now saw time as an ally rather than an adversary. He perceived that other states, principally Virginia, were prepared to ratify, a situation that would leave New York the only significant state outside of the Union. That circumstance would surely compel New Yorkers to support the Constitution. In short, Washington was very much involved in the politics of the ratification process. See GW to Thomas Johnson, 20 April 1788, *Writings*, 29:463; to James McHenry, 27 April 1788, 29:471–472; to Charles Cotesworth Pinckney, 28 June 1788, 30:10.

58. GW to James Madison, 8 June 1788, *Writings*, 29:511.

59. GW to Lewis Morris, 13 December 1788, ibid., 30:157; to Charles Pettit, 16 August 1788, 30:41.

60. GW to Charles Pettit, 16 August 1788, ibid., 30:41.

61. GW to David Stuart, 1 July 1787, ibid., 29:238–239.

62. GW to Bushrod Washington, 10 November 1787, ibid., 29:312.

63. GW to James Madison, 2 March 1788, ibid., 29:431; to Richard Butler, 3 April 1788, 29:454; to Madison, 7 December 1787, 29:331; to Benjamin Lincoln, 26 October 1788, 30:118; to Henry Knox, 30 March 1788, 29:449–450; to Lincoln, 2 April 1788, 29:452; to John Armstrong, 25 April 1788, 29:466.

64. For a particularly useful and spirited discussion of the conspiratorial worldview common among Washington's generation, see Marshall Smelser, "The Federalist Period as an Age of Passion," *American Quarterly* 10 (1958): 391–419.

65. GW to Alexander Hamilton, 3 October 1788, *Writings*, 30:112; to James Madison, 23 September 1788, 30:100–101.

66. GW to Benjamin Fishbourne, 23 December 1788, ibid., 30:171; to Jonathan Trumbull, 4 December 1788, 30:149.

67. GW to David Stuart, 2 December 1788, ibid., 30:146–147; to Benjamin Lincoln, 14 November 1788, 30:125–126; to James Madison, 23 September 1788, 30:100–101; to Secretary at War, 1 January 1789, 30:173–174.

68. GW to Lafayette, 29 January 1789, ibid., 30:184.

69. Several biographers have noted that Washington usually accepted public offices according to a pattern in which he would first insist that he did not want

the office, then state that he lacked the qualifications or was in other ways un-deserving, wait for a sign of broad support along the lines of "only George can do it," and, at last, insist that only his sense of public duty had convinced him to accept the office against his personal disinclination. Wills, in particular, points out that this was the pattern whereby good Roman republicans accepted office. See, Wills, *Cincinnatus*; Longmore, *Invention of George Washington*; Barry Schwartz, "George Washington and the Whig Conception of Heroic Leadership," *American Sociological Review* 48 (1983):18–33; and Schwartz, *George Washington*.

Chapter Five: The Framer as Interpreter

1. Ralph Ketcham, *Presidents above Party: The First American Presidency, 1789–1829* (Chapel Hill: University of North Carolina Press, 1984), 8.

2. H. Jefferson Powell, "The Original Understanding of Original Intent," *Harvard Law Review* 98 (1985):885–948.

3. GW to John Adams, 10 May 1789, *The Papers of George Washington: Presidential Series*, ed. Dorothy Twohig (Charlottesville: University Press of Virginia, 1987–   ), 2:246–247. This letter was intended to solicit views on a number of issues related to the organization of the new presidency and was also sent to Hamilton, Madison, John Jay, and Robert Livingston.

4. V. O. Key coined this term to explain, particularly, the development and "persistence" of the two-party system in the United States. But the phrase could equally apply to many other constitutional customs that have become entrenched by persistent practice. Key, *Politics, Parties and Pressure Groups* (New York: Crowell, 1969).

5. One only needs to recall the pitifully absurd picture of Michael Dukakis "commanding" an M1 tank in the 1988 presidential campaign to see how wise John Adams and other presidents were in *not* following Washington's example. George Washington looked good on a horse; subsequent presidents might have cut a less imposing figure.

6. See Wills, *Cincinnatus*; and Schwartz, *George Washington*, 1–103.

7. It should be remembered that in 1788 electors cast *two* ballots for president. To guarantee a truly *national* presidency at least one vote had to be cast for a candidate not from the elector's home state. No provision existed for ordering the two votes, so we cannot be certain that Washington was every elector's *first* choice. Unanimity meant that every elector placed Washington on his "two-choice" ballot.

8. GW to James Madison, 5 May 1789, *Papers: Presidential Series*, 2:216–217.

9. First Inaugural Address, 30 April 1789, ibid., 2:175.

10. Thad Tate has pointed out that some of the domestic unrest of the Confederation period can be attributed to the feeling among many citizens that their state constitutions were *not*, in fact, genuinely republican constitutions. Most had been established by rump legislatures with little or no consent by

"the people," a situation that cast an air of illegitimacy upon their actions. Thad W. Tate, "The Social Contract in America, 1774-1787: Revolutionary Theory as Conservative Instrument," *William and Mary Quarterly* 22 (1965):375-391.

11. GW to Henry Lee, 31 October 1786, *Writings*, 29:33-34.

12. GW to Jonathan Trumbull, Jr., 4 December 1788, *Papers: Presidential Series*, 1:159.

13. Alexander Hamilton, James Madison, and John Jay, *The Federalist Papers* (New York: New American Library, 1961), 322.

14. Thanksgiving Proclamation, 3 October 1789, *Writings*, 30:427-428.

15. The best summary of the official correspondence regarding the *Little Sarah* affair is in *The Journal of the Proceedings of the President, 1793-1797*, ed. Dorothy Twohig et al. (Charlottesville: University Press of Virginia, 1981), 187, 190-193.

16. GW to John Hancock, 26 October 1789, *Writings*, 30:453.

17. Woodrow Wilson, *George Washington* (New York: Schocken, 1969), 282.

18. For an interesting account of the public response to one of these trips, see Archibald Henderson, *Washington's Southern Tour, 1791* (Boston: Houghton Mifflin, 1923).

19. There is some debate over how significant distilled whiskey was as a "cash crop" in the West. Forrest McDonald has suggested that whiskey was an insignificant commodity and that, therefore, the rebels' behavior must be explained on other grounds. But Thomas Slaughter and David O. Whiten, though not necessarily insisting that the economic impact of the excise was the sole causative factor motivating the rebels, offer evidence to the contrary. For a useful discussion of this and other historiographical disputes regarding the Whiskey Rebellion, see Thomas P. Slaughter, "The Friends of Liberty, the Friends of Order, and the Whiskey Rebellion: A Historiographical Essay," in *The Whiskey Rebellion: Past and Present Perspectives*, ed. Steven R. Boyd, (Westport, Conn.: Greenwood Press, 1985), 9-30.

20. GW to [Alexander Hamilton], 17 September 1792, *Writings*, 32:154.

21. GW to Henry Lee, 31 October 1786, ibid., 29:34.

22. GW to [Alexander Hamilton], 16 September 1792, ibid., 32:153.

23. Proclamation, 15 September 1792, ibid., 32:150-151.

24. Warren W. Hassler, Jr., *The President as Commander in Chief* (Menlo Park, Calif.: Addison-Wesley, 1971), 19-28.

25. Forrest McDonald suggests that Hamilton deliberately goaded the tax resisters into rebellion as part of a larger plan to "discredit and crush" the Jeffersonians "by identifying them with treason." McDonald, *The Presidency of George Washington* (Lawrence: University Press of Kansas, 1974), 145-147. Most other accounts see the rebellion as far more complex. See Thomas P. Slaughter, *The Whiskey Rebellion: Frontier Epilogue to the American Revolution* (New York: Oxford University Press, 1986).

26. GW to Charles Mynn Thurston, 10 August 1794, *Writings*, 33:465.

27. William Shakespeare, *Henry IV, Part I*, act 3, sc. 1.

28. Cited in Richard H. Kohn, "The Washington Administration's Decision to Crush the Whiskey Rebellion," *Journal of American History* 59 (1972): 583.

29. Proclamation, 25 September 1794, *Writings*, 33:507–508.

30. GW to Henry Lee, 20 October 1794, ibid., 34:6.

31. GW to the Senate, 28 February 1793, ibid., 32:362.

32. The Supreme Court was not the "jewel" appointment that it has today become. The justices heard few cases, had no permanent offices or courtroom, and often had to travel long distances to perform inconsequential duties. State judicial positions (or even federal district judgeships, which rarely required travel from their home state) were far more attractive to most political aspirants than the federal Supreme Court. Thus, it is no reflection on Washington that many of the people he asked to serve on the Court turned him down. The proportion of refusals became so embarrassing that he took to inquiring of a potential nominee's friends whether the person might be interested. For a useful history of the early Court, see David M. O'Brien, *Storm Center: The Supreme Court in American Politics*, 2d ed. (New York: Norton, 1990), 135–140.

33. Henry J. Abraham, *Justices and Presidents: A Political History of Appointments to the Supreme Court*, 2d ed. (New York: Oxford University Press, 1985), 75–76.

34. The reference here is not to the federal Constitution, but to the law of the land, in general, and to the Pennsylvania constitution, in particular. GW to Thomas Smith, 22 September 1786, *Writings*, 29:13.

35. Wills, *Cincinnatus*, 17–25.

36. First Annual Address to Congress, 8 January 1790, *Writings*, 30:491–494.

37. At one point he asked his secretary to review the progress of his previous "recommendations" to Congress. But his purpose does not seem to have been motivated by any concern with holding Congress accountable. Rather, it appears he merely wanted to avoid the embarrassment of making recommendations in his next annual address on matters Congress had already dealt with. GW to Tobias Lear, 7 October 1791, *Writings*, 31:384–385.

38. This address was initially drafted by David Humphreys, but Madison persuaded Washington to substitute a shorter, less stilted version that became the core of the first Inaugural Address. Unfortunately, Tobias Lear later cut up pieces of the Humphreys version to distribute as mementoes to the president's friends, the attraction being that the draft was in Washington's handwriting! Thus, there are only fragments of this address extant. See, *Papers: Presidential Series*, 2:152–173; Nathaniel E. Stein, "The Discarded Inaugural Address of George Washington," *Manuscripts* 10 (1958):2–17.

39. GW to Baron Poellnitz, 23 March 1790, *Writings*, 31:23–24.

40. Cited in Henry J. Abraham, *The Judicial Process*, 5th ed. (New York: Oxford University Press, 1986), 341 and n.

41. Freeman, *George Washington*, 6:302. A brief account of this affair is found in *Writings*, 31:169n.

42. *Papers: Revolutionary War Series*, 1:84.

43. Carp, "Origins of the Nationalist Movement," 382.

44. Rossie, *The Politics of Command in the American Revolution*, 164.

45. GW to Lund Washington, 30 September 1776, *Writings*, 6:138.

46. Particularly critical is Bernhard Knollenberg, *Washington and the Revolution: A Reappraisal* (New York: Macmillan, 1940), 108–128.

47. Forrest McDonald never openly claims this, but it is curious that his book on Washington's presidency contains a far more detailed analysis of Hamilton's plans for the national government than of the purposes and accomplishments of the president! See McDonald, *Presidency of George Washington*.

48. GW to [Henry Knox], 15 August 1792, *Writings*, 32:116–117.

49. Washington's leadership style, in fact, looks very much like the sort of "hidden-hand presidency" that Fred Greenstein so effectively ascribes to Dwight Eisenhower. The "hidden hand" refers generally to the practice of remaining in control of the political agenda through the use of surrogates, while the president preserves his public stature by appearing to be above the partisan political fray. Greenstein's approach led him to a much more favorable assessment of Eisenhower (that is, to a conclusion that Eisenhower accomplished many more of his policy goals—usually the characteristic of activist presidents) than many other presidential scholars. The same sort of analysis would, I believe, lead many to reassess the Washington-Hamilton relationship in light of the resultant achievement of Washington's longtime political goals. See Fred I. Greenstein, *The Hidden-Hand Presidency: Eisenhower as Leader* (New York: Basic Books, 1982).

50. General Orders, 16 August 1776, *Writings*, 5:442.

51. GW to [James McHenry], 13 July 1796, ibid., 35:138.

52. GW to the Senate, 6 August 1789, *Papers: Presidential Series*, 3:391–392. Angry at the Senate's action, Washington set forth in some detail his own reasons for the Fishbourne nomination.

53. GW to Henry Knox, 20 September 1795, *Writings*, 34:315.

54. Washington wrote often about the sorts of qualities he looked for in nominees. In addition to the dimension of personal and political compatibility with the president, he preferred men with experience in government (especially elective), men of general competence and public integrity, and men with proven loyalty to the Union (often defined as service in the Revolution or in writing or ratifying the Constitution). In addition, Washington was concerned with maintaining geographical balance among his appointments. For a useful summary of his appointment criteria and how they were used, see Leonard D. White, *The Federalists: A Study in Administrative History* (New York: Macmillan, 1948), 257–266.

55. Jerald A. Combs, *The Jay Treaty: Political Battleground of the Founding Fathers* (Berkeley: University of California Press, 1970), 152–188; and Irving Brant, "Edmund Randolph, Not Guilty," *William and Mary Quarterly* 7 (1950):180–198.

56. Aaron Wildavsky, "The Two Presidencies," *Trans-Action* 4 (1966):7–14.

57. Farrand, *Records*, 2:587.

58. GW to David Stuart, 26 July 1789, *Papers: Presidential Series*, 3:323–324. Fitzpatrick dates this letter as 1 July 1789.

59. Circular Letter to the States, 8 June 1783, *Writings*, 26:492–493.

60. GW to James Madison, ? August 1789, ibid., 30:394. The editors of the *Papers of George Washington* place this letter a bit later, somewhere around September 8. Twohig, *Papers: Presidential Series*, 3:406n.

61. Finance Plan, ? October 1789, *Writings*, 30:454–455.

62. GW to House of Representatives, 5 April 1792, ibid., 32:16–17; Harry C. Thomson, "The First Presidential Vetoes," *Presidential Studies Quarterly* 8 (1978):30.

63. GW to Edmund Pendleton, 23 September 1793, *Writings*, 33:96.

Chapter Six: The Unintentions of a Framer

1. This idea of a transition from a classical form of republicanism to a more liberal, largely Lockeian, form was most clearly expressed first in Wood, *The Creation of the American Republic*. The Wood thesis has been modified by others, principally Banning, *The Jeffersonian Persuasion*; and Drew R. McCoy, *The Elusive Republic: Political Economy in Jeffersonian America* (Chapel Hill: University of North Carolina Press, 1980), who place the transition period somewhat later, during the Jeffersonian era. Others take issue with the "republican synthesis" entirely, seeing Lockeian principles as the core tradition in American political thought throughout the founding period. See Thomas L. Pangle, *The Spirit of Modern Republicanism: The Moral Vision of the American Founders and the Philosophy of Locke* (Chicago: University of Chicago Press, 1988); Isaac Kramnick, "Republican Revisionism Revisited," *American Historical Review* 87 (1982):629–664; Gary J. Schmitt and Robert H. Webking, "Revolutionaries, Antifederalists, and Federalists: Comments on Gordon Wood's Understanding of the American Founding," *Political Science Reviewer* 9 (1979):195–229.

2. Neustadt, *Presidential Power*, 26.

3. See above, pp. 112–116.

4. Farrand, *Records*, 1:282–293 at 288.

5. Roche, "The Founding Fathers," 799–816.

6. See Michael Lienesch, *New Order of the Ages: Time, the Constitution, and the Making of Modern American Political Thought* (Princeton, N.J.: Princeton University Press, 1988), 130–137; Wood, *Creation of the American Republic*, 593–615; and Douglass G. Adair, "That Politics May Be Reduced to a Science: David Hume, James Madison, and the Tenth Federalist," *Huntington Library Quarterly* 20 (1957): 343–360.

7. Herbert Storing, *What the Anti-Federalists Were For* (Chicago: University of Chicago Press, 1981), 53–63; Cecelia M. Kenyon, "Men of Little Faith: The Anti-Federalists on the Nature of Representative Government," *William and Mary Quarterly* 12 (1955):3–43.

8. GW to Bushrod Washington, 10 November 1787, *Writings*, 29:312.

9. See my earlier comments on p. 73.

10. Marver Bernstein's history of the Interstate Commerce Commission asserts that certain kinds of bureaucratic agencies tend to be "captured" by their client groups over time. The agency heads become transformed into advocates for the client group rather than regulators acting in the public interest. Bernstein, *Regulating Business by Independent Commission* (Princeton, N.J.: Princeton University Press, 1955). Lowi carries this claim further and argues that the national government as a whole has been "captured"—that it serves only to perpetuate the advantages of certain privileged groups in American society. This philosophy of interest-group liberalism is, in Lowi's view, the inevitable offspring of Madison's "new science of politics." Theodore J. Lowi, *The End of Liberalism: The Second Republic of the United States*, 2d ed. (New York: Norton, 1979), esp. 3–63.

11. Madison, *Federalist* no.51.

12. "Is the Minister of the French Republic [Citizen Genet] to set the Acts of this Government at defiance, *with impunity?* and then threaten the Executive with an appeal to the People. What must the World think of such conduct, and of the Governmt. of the U. States in submitting to it?" GW to [Thomas Jefferson], 11 July 1793, *Writings*, 33:4.

13. Questions Proposed to Be Submitted to the Judges of the Supreme Court, 18 July 1793?, ibid., 33:15–19.

14. Queries to the Heads of the Departments, 27 August 1790, *Writings*, 31:102–103n.

15. GW to [John Jay], 4 September 1791, ibid., 31:354. Jay took Washington up on his offer. A few months later Jay offered his opinion that the Senate was acting improperly and that the president should resist that body's encroachments on his executive power. John Jay to GW, 27 January 1792, ibid., 31:500n.

16. George C. Edwards III and Stephen J. Wayne, *Presidential Leadership: Politics and Policy Making*, 2d ed. (New York: St. Martin's Press, 1990), 165.

17. Cited in Charles Warren, *The Supreme Court in United States History*, rev. ed., 2 vols. (Boston: Little, Brown, 1926), I:110–111.

18. Jay never returned to the Supreme Court after his diplomatic mission. He was elected governor of New York and submitted his resignation to Washington shortly after his return to the United States. But he was the sitting chief justice at the time of his appointment and service to the president.

19. See Max Freedman, *Roosevelt and Frankfurter: Their Correspondence, 1928–1945* (Boston: Little, Brown, 1968); and Bruce Murphy, *Fortas: The Rise and Ruin of a Supreme Court Justice* (New York: Morrow, 1988).

20. Conference with a Committee of the U.S. Senate, 10 August 1789, *Papers: Presidential Series*, 3:409.

21. Conference with a Committee of the U.S. Senate, 8 August 1789, ibid., 3:400–401.

22. The secretary of state would have been a more appropriate adviser than

the secretary of war, but Jefferson had not yet arrived from France to assume his duties.

23. GW to the Senate, 22 August 1789, *Papers: Presidential Series*, 3:523.

24. William Maclay, *Sketches of Debate in the First Senate of the United States* (Harrisburg, Pa.: Lane S. Hart, 1880), 122–126.

25. Daniel S. Cheever and H. Field Haviland, Jr., *American Foreign Policy and the Separation of Powers* (Cambridge, Mass.: Harvard University Press, 1952), 42–44.

26. See, for example, Edward S. Corwin, *The President: Office and Powers, 1787–1957*, 4th rev. ed. (New York: New York University Press, 1957), 209–210; Louis Henkin, *Foreign Affairs and the Constitution* (New York: Norton, 1972), 131; Cheever and Haviland, *American Foreign Policy*, 42–46; and Frank T. Reuter, *Trials and Triumphs: George Washington's Foreign Policy* (Fort Worth: Texas Christian University Press, 1983), 46–48.

27. See, for example, his letter to the Senate regarding a boundary dispute with Britain (9 February 1790) and his letter asking for preapproval of treaties with the Barbary pirates (8 May 1792), *Writings*, 31:7–8, 32:41–42.

28. See, for example, Abraham D. Sofaer, "Executive Privilege: An Historical Note," *Columbia Law Review* 75 (1975):1318–1321; Sofaer, "The Presidency, War, and Foreign Affairs: Practice under the Framers," *Law and Contemporary Problems* 40 (1976):12–18; and Gordon B. Baldwin, "The Foreign Affairs Advice Privilege," *Wisconsin Law Review* 1976 (1976):28–37.

29. GW to Congress, 12 August 1790, *Writings*, 31:91.

30. White, *The Federalists*, 80.

31. Sofaer, "Executive Privilege," 1318–1321.

32. GW to the Secretary of State, 22 July 1795, *Writings*, 34:244.

33. GW to Gouverneur Morris, 22 December 1795, ibid., 34:403.

34. Farewell Address, 19 September 1796, ibid., 35:227.

35. Ibid., 227–228.

36. Smelser, "The Federalist Period as an Age of Passion."

37. See Mary P. Ryan, "Party Formation in the United States Congress, 1789 to 1796: A Quantitative Study," *William and Mary Quarterly* 28 (1971):523–542; Ronald P. Formisano, *The Transformation of Political Culture: Massachusetts Parties, 1790s–1840s* (New York: Oxford University Press, 1983), 3–33; Richard McCormick, "Political Parties," in *Encyclopedia of American Political History*, ed. Jack P. Greene (New York: Scribner's, 1984), 3:939–948; John Zvesper, *Political Philosophy and Rhetoric: A Study of the Origins of American Party Politics* (Cambridge: Cambridge University Press, 1977).

38. Ralph Ketcham maintains that the first American presidents consciously modeled their administrations on the image of the "patriot king" espoused by Bolingbroke. Patriot kings represented the authentic national interest against the partisan maneuverings of self-interested parliamentary factions. A patriot president would fill a similar role in the new republic, safeguarding the national interest against the interests of the several states or against coali-

tions of political convenience in the Congress. Ketcham, *Presidents above Party*.

39. First Inaugural Address, 30 April 1789, *Papers: Presidential Series*, 2:175.

40. GW to James Wilson, 9 May 1789, *Writings*, 30:314.

41. *Federalist* no.10.

42. Circular Letter to the States, 8 June 1783, *Writings*, 26:487.

43. GW to David Humphreys, 26 December 1786, ibid., 29:126.

44. GW to Governor Fenner, 4 June 1790, ibid., 31:48.

45. Flexner, *George Washington*, 3:324.

46. GW to David Stuart, 28 March 1790, *Writings*, 31:28–30.

47. See above, p. 152, and Thomson, "First Presidential Vetoes."

48. GW to Robert Livingston, 31 May 1789, *Papers: Presidential Series*, 2:417.

49. List of Government Officers, *Writings*, 34:165–167; GW to Secretary of State, 27 September 1795, ibid., 34:315; see also Glenn A. Phelps, "George Washington and the Paradox of Party," *Presidential Studies Quarterly* 19 (1989):740.

50. GW to Edward Carrington, 9 October 1795, *Writings*, 34:331–332; GW to Patrick Henry, 9 October 1795, 34:335.

51. Madison was not a formal member of the cabinet. As a member of the House of Representatives he could not constitutionally hold any executive office. Madison served as Washington's eyes and ears in the Congress and as an important political adviser; Washington communicated with him regularly during the first years of his administration. This was a tacit violation of the separation principle, but presidents ever since Washington have similarly utilized "old friends" in the legislature as key advisers.

52. GW to Thomas Jefferson, 23 August 1792, *Writings*, 32:130–131; Washington expressed similar views in his letter to Hamilton three days later, 32:132–133.

53. J. A. W. Gunn, *Factions No More: Attitudes to Party in Government and Opposition in Eighteenth Century England* (London: Frank Cass, 1972).

54. Jeff Fishel, *Presidents & Promises: From Campaign Pledge to Presidential Performance* (Washington, D.C.: Congressional Quarterly, 1985).

55. See Bernard Bailyn, *The Origins of American Politics* (New York: Knopf, 1968); and Jackson T. Main, *Political Parties Before the Constitution* (Chapel Hill: University of North Carolina Press, 1973).

56. GW to Alexander Hamilton, 29 July 1795, *Writings*, 34:264.

*Epilogue: George Washington and
the Constitutional Tradition*

1. This personal criticism was particularly nettlesome for Washington because it was a challenge to his reputation. In contemporary American politics a "thick skin" is thought to be a prerequisite to the pursuit of public office. Liberalism presumes a relatively unconstrained arena of conflict in which diverse interests (and the candidates who represent those interests) are considered fair

game for public criticism. (See *New York Times v. Sullivan*, 376 U.S. 254, 1964, for an explication of this "checking" theory cast in constitutional terms.) But to a classical republican like Washington one's public reputation was the mark of his standing as a citizen. He could not ignore or set aside such personal criticism so easily.

2. See GW to Patrick Henry, 15 January 1799, *Writings*, 37:87–90.

3. First Annual Address to Congress, 8 January 1790, ibid., 30:491.

Selected Bibliography

Abraham, Henry J. *The Judicial Process*. 5th ed. New York: Oxford University Press, 1986.

———. *Justices and Presidents: A Political History of Appointments to the Supreme Court*. 2d ed. New York: Oxford University Press, 1985.

Adair, Douglass G. "Experience Must Be Our Only Guide: History, Democratic Theory, and the United States Constitution." In *The Reinterpretation of Early American History: Essays in Honor of John Edwin Pomfret*, ed. Ray A. Billington, 129–148. San Marino, Calif.: Huntington Library, 1966.

———. "Fame and the Founding Fathers." In *Fame and the Founding Fathers: Essays by Douglass Adair*, ed. Trevor Colbourne, 3–26. New York: Norton, 1974.

———. "That Politics May Be Reduced to a Science: David Hume, James Madison, and the Tenth Federalist." *Huntington Library Quarterly* 20 (1957):343–360.

Adams, Willi Paul. *The First American Constitutions: Republican Ideology and the Making of the State Constitutions in the Revolutionary Era*. Chapel Hill: University of North Carolina Press, 1980.

———. "Republicanism in Political Rhetoric before 1776." *Political Science Quarterly* 85 (1970):397–421.

Agresto, John. " 'A System without Precedent' –James Madison and the Revolution in Republican Liberty." *South Atlantic Quarterly* 82 (1983):129–144.

Alden, John R. *George Washington: A Biography*. Baton Rouge: Louisiana State University Press, 1984.

Ambler, Charles H. *George Washington and the West*. Chapel Hill: University of North Carolina Press, 1936.

Appleby, Joyce. *Capitalism and a New Social Order*. New York: New York University Press, 1984.

———. "Republicanism in Old and New Contexts." *William and Mary Quarterly* 43 (1986):20–34.

———. "What Is Still American in the Political Philosophy of Thomas Jefferson?" *William and Mary Quarterly* 39 (1982):287–309.

Bailyn, Bernard. *The Ideological Origins of the American Revolution*. Cambridge, Mass.: Harvard University Press, 1967.

———. *The Origins of American Politics*. New York: Knopf, 1968.

Baldwin, Gordon B. "The Foreign Affairs Advice Privilege." *Wisconsin Law Review* 1976 (1976):16–46.

Banks, Margaret A. "Attitudes in the Philadelphia Convention towards the British System of Government." *American Journal of Legal History* 10 (1966):15–33.

Banning, Lance. "James Madison and the Nationalists, 1780–1783." *William and Mary Quarterly* 40 (1983):227–255.

————. *The Jeffersonian Persuasion: Evolution of a Party Ideology.* Ithaca, N.Y.: Cornell University Press, 1978.

————. "The Practicable Sphere of a Republic: James Madison, the Constitutional Convention, and the Emergence of Revolutionary Federalism." In *Beyond Confederation: Origins of the Constitution and American National Identity*, ed. Richard Beeman, Stephen Botein, and Edward C. Carter II, 162–187. Chapel Hill: University of North Carolina Press, 1987.

————. "Republican Ideology and the Triumph of the Constitution." *William and Mary Quarterly* 31 (1974):167–188.

Beard, Charles. *An Economic Interpretation of the Constitution of the United States.* New York: Macmillan, 1913.

Becker, Carl. *History of Political Parties in the Province of New York, 1760–1776.* Madison: University of Wisconsin Press, 1909.

Beeman, Richard, Stephen Botein, and Edward C. Carter II, eds. *Beyond Confederation: Origins of the Constitution and American National Identity.* Chapel Hill: University of North Carolina Press, 1987.

Bell, Rudolph M. *Party and Faction in American Politics: The House of Representatives, 1789–1801.* Westport, Conn.: Greenwood Press, 1973.

Berger, Raoul. *Executive Privilege: A Constitutional Myth.* Cambridge, Mass.: Harvard University Press, 1974.

————. "The Presidential Monopoly of Foreign Relations." *Michigan Law Review* 71 (1972):1–58.

Bernstein, Marver. *Regulating Business by Independent Commission.* Princeton, N.J.: Princeton University Press, 1955.

Binkley, Wilfred E. *American Political Parties, Their Natural History.* 3d ed., rev. and enl. New York: Knopf, 1958.

Black, Barbara A. "The Constitution of Empire: The Case for the Colonists." *University of Pennsylvania Law Review* 124 (1976):1157–1211.

Boller, Paul F., Jr. "Washington and Civilian Supremacy." *Southwest Review* 39 (1954):9–22.

Bowling, Kenneth. "New Light on the Philadelphia Mutiny of 1783: Federal-State Confrontation at the Close of the War for Independence." *Pennsylvania Magazine of History and Biography* 101 (1977):419–450.

Bowman, Albert H. "Realism versus Moralism in Foreign Policy: Jefferson, Hamilton, and the Franco-British War." In *The President's War Powers: From the Federalists to Reagan*, ed. Demetrios Caraley, 5–28. New York: Academy of Political Science, 1984.

Bradley, Harold W. "The Political Thinking of George Washington." *Journal of Southern History* 11 (1945):469–486.

Branson, Roy. "James Madison and the Scottish Enlightenment." *Journal of the History of Ideas* 40 (1974):235–250.

Brant, Irving. "Edmund Randolph, Not Guilty." *William and Mary Quarterly* 7 (1950):180–198.

_____. *James Madison: Father of the Constitution, 1787–1800*. Indianapolis, Ind.: Bobbs-Merrill, 1950.

Brown, Richard D. "Shays's Rebellion and the Ratification of the Federal Constitution in Massachusetts." In *Beyond Confederation: Origins of the Constitution and American National Identity*, ed. Richard Becman, Stephen Botein, and Edward C. Carter II, 113–127. Chapel Hill: University of North Carolina Press, 1987.

Buel, Richard, Jr. *Securing the Revolution: Ideology in American Politics, 1789–1815*. Ithaca, N.Y.: Cornell University Press, 1972.

Caldwell, Lynton K. *The Administrative Theories of Hamilton and Jefferson*. New York: Russell & Russell, 1964.

Carp, E. Wayne. "The Origins of the Nationalist Movement of 1780–1783: Congressional Administration and the Continental Army." *Pennsylvania Magazine of History and Biography* 107 (1983):363–392.

_____. *To Starve the Army at Pleasure*. Chapel Hill: University of North Carolina Press, 1984.

Chambers, William N. "Parties and Nation-Building in America." In *Political Parties and Political Development*, ed. Joseph P. LaPalombara and Myron Weiner, 79–106. Princeton, N.J.: Princeton University Press, 1966.

_____. "Party Development and the American Mainstream." In *The American Party Systems: Stages of Political Development*. 2d ed., ed. William N. Chambers and Walter Dean Burnham, 3–32. New York: Oxford University Press, 1975.

Chambers, William N., and Walter Dean Burnham, eds. *The American Party Systems: Stages of Political Development*. 2d ed. New York: Oxford University Press, 1975.

Channing, Edward. "Washington and Parties, 1789–1797." *Massachusetts Historical Society Proceedings* 47 (1913):35–44.

Charles, Joseph. *The Origins of the American Party System*. Williamsburg, Va.: Institute of Early American History and Culture, 1956.

Cheever, Daniel S., and H. Field Haviland, Jr. *American Foreign Policy and the Separation of Powers*. Cambridge, Mass.: Harvard University Press, 1952.

Clinton, Sir Henry. *The American Rebellion*, ed. William B. Wilcox. New Haven, Conn.: Yale University Press, 1954.

Colbourne, H. Trevor. *The Lamp of Experience: Whig History and the Intellectual Origins of the American Revolution*. New York: Norton, 1974.

Collier, Christopher, and James Lincoln Collier. *Decision in Philadelphia: The Constitutional Convention of 1787*. New York: Random House, 1984.

Combs, Jerald A. *The Jay Treaty: Political Battleground of the Founding Fathers*. Berkeley: University of California Press, 1970.

Cornwallis, Charles Lord. *An Answer to That Part of the Narrative of Lieutenant-General Sir Henry Clinton* . . . London: J. Debrett, 1783.

Corwin, Edward S. *The President: Office and Powers, 1787–1957*. 4th rev. ed. New York: New York University Press, 1957.

————. "The Progress of Constitutional Theory between the Declaration of Independence and the Meeting of the Philadelphia Convention." *American Historical Review* 30 (1925):511–536.

Cress, Lawrence D. "Republican Liberty and National Security: American Military Policy as an Ideological Problem, 1783–1789." *William and Mary Quarterly* 38 (1981):73–96.

Cronin, Thomas E., ed. *Inventing the American Presidency*. Lawrence: University Press of Kansas, 1989.

Cunliffe, Marcus. *American Presidents and the Presidency*. London: Eyre and Spottiswoode, 1969.

————. *George Washington: Man and Monument*. Boston: Little, Brown, 1982.

Dahl, Robert A. *Modern Political Analysis*. Englewood Cliffs, N.J.: Prentice-Hall, 1963.

Davis, Joseph L. *Sectionalism in American Politics, 1774–1787*. Madison: University of Wisconsin Press, 1977.

Diamond, Martin. "The Declaration and the Constitution: Liberty, Democracy, and the Founders." *Public Interest* 41 (1975):39–55.

Diggins, John P. *The Lost Soul of American Politics: Virtue, Self-Interest, and the Foundations of Liberalism*. Chicago: University of Chicago Press, 1984.

Dorfman, Joseph. "The Regal Republic of John Adams." *Political Science Quarterly* 59 (1944):227–247.

Draper, Theodore. "Hume & Madison: The Secrets of Federalist Paper No. 10." *Encounter* 58 (1982):34–47.

Dunbar, Louise B. *A Study of "Monarchical" Tendencies in the United States from 1776 to 1801*. Urbana: University of Illinois Studies in Social Sciences, 1923.

Edwards, George C., III, and Stephen J. Wayne. *Presidential Leadership: Politics and Policy Making*. 2d ed. New York: St. Martin's Press, 1990.

Egnal, Marc. "The Origins of the Revolution in Virginia: A Reinterpretation." *William and Mary Quarterly* 37 (1980):401–428.

Eliott, Jonathan, ed. *The Debates in the Several State Conventions, on the Adoption of the Federal Constitution*. 5 vols. Philadelphia: J. B. Lippincott, 1907.

Elkins, Stanley, and Eric McKitrick. "The Founding Fathers: Young Men of the Revolution." *Political Science Quarterly* 76 (1961):181–216.

Erler, Edward J. "The Problem of the Public Good in *The Federalist*." *Polity* 13 (1981):649–667.

Farrand, Max. *The Framing of the Constitution of the United States*. New Haven, Conn.: Yale University Press, 1913.

_____, ed. *The Records of the Federal Convention of 1787*. Rev. ed., 4 vols. New Haven, Conn.: Yale University Press, 1937.

Feer, Robert A. "Shays's Rebellion and the Constitution: A Study in Causation." *New England Quarterly* 42 (1969):388–410.

Ferguson, E. James. "The Nationalists of 1781–1783 and the Economic Interpretation of the Constitution." *Journal of American History* 56 (1969):241–261.

_____. "Political Economy, Public Liberty, and the Formation of the Constitution." *William and Mary Quarterly* 40 (1983):389–412.

_____. *The Power of the Purse: A History of American Public Finance, 1776–1790*. Chapel Hill: University of North Carolina Press, 1961.

_____. "State Assumption of the Federal Debt during the Confederation." *Mississippi Valley Historical Review* 38 (1951):403–424.

Ferling, John E. *The First of Men: A Life of George Washington*. Knoxville: University of Tennessee Press, 1988.

Fishel, Jeff. *Presidents & Promises: From Campaign Pledge to Presidential Performance*. Washington, D.C.: Congressional Quarterly, 1985.

Flexner, James Thomas. *George Washington*. 4 vols. Boston: Little, Brown, 1965–1972.

Ford, Worthington et al., eds. *Journals of the Continental Congress, 1774–1789*. Washington, D.C.: GPO, 1904–1937.

Formisano, Ronald P. "Federalists and Republicans: Parties, Yes—System, No." In *The Evolution of American Electoral Systems*, ed. Paul Kleppner et al., 33–43. Westport, Conn.: Greenwood Press, 1981.

_____. *The Transformation of Political Culture: Massachusetts Parties, 1790s–1840s*. New York: Oxford University Press, 1983.

Freedman, Max. *Roosevelt and Frankfurter: Their Correspondence, 1928–1945*. Boston: Little, Brown, 1968.

Freeman, Douglas Southall. *George Washington*. 7 vols. New York: Scribner's, 1948–1957.

Friedman, Lawrence M. *American Law: An Introduction*. New York: Norton, 1984.

Frisch, Morton J. "Hamilton's Report on Manufactures and Political Philosophy." *Publius* 8 (1978):129–139.

Gillespie, Michael A., and Michael Lienesch, eds. *Ratifying the Constitution*. Lawrence: University Press of Kansas, 1989.

Goldwin, Robert A., and William A. Schambra, eds. *How Capitalistic Is the Constitution?* Washington, D.C.: American Enterprise Institute, 1982.

_____, and _____, eds. *How Democratic Is the Constitution?* Washington, D.C.: American Enterprise Institute, 1980.

Goodman, Paul. "Perspectives on the Presidency and the Parties in the 1790s." *Reviews in American History* 3 (1975):71–76.

Greene, Jack P. *Peripheries and Center: Constitutional Development in the Extended Polities of the British Empire and the United States, 1607–1788*. Athens: University of Georgia Press, 1986.

_____. "Political Mimesis: A Consideration of the Historical and Cultural

Roots of Legislative Behavior in the British Colonies in the Eighteenth Century." *American Historical Review* 75 (1969):337–360.

Greenstein, Fred I. *The Hidden-Hand Presidency: Eisenhower as Leader*. New York: Basic Books, 1982.

Grey, Thomas C. "Origins of the Unwritten Constitution: Fundamental Law in American Revolutionary Thought." *Stanford Law Review* 30 (1978):843–893.

Guggenheimer, Jay C. "The Development of the Executive Departments, 1775–1789." In *Essays in the Constitutional History of the United States*, ed. J. Franklin Jameson, 116–185. Boston: Houghton Mifflin, 1889.

Gummere, Richard M. *The American Colonial Mind and the Classical Tradition*. Cambridge, Mass.: Harvard University Press, 1963.

Gunn, J. A. W. *Factions No More: Attitudes to Party in Government and Opposition in Eighteenth Century England*. London: Frank Cass, 1972.

Hall, Kermit, L. *The Magic Mirror: Law in American History*. New York: Oxford University Press, 1989.

Hamilton, Alexander. *The Papers of Alexander Hamilton*, ed. H. C. Syrett et al., 26 vols. New York: Columbia University Press, 1961–1979.

Hart, James. *The American Presidency in Action, 1789: A Study in Constitutional History*. New York: Macmillan, 1948.

Hartz, Louis. "American Political Thought and the American Revolution." *American Political Science Review* 46 (1952):321–342.

Hassler, Warren W., Jr. *The President as Commander in Chief*. Menlo Park, Calif.: Addison-Wesley, 1971.

Hatch, Louis C. *The Administration of the Revolutionary Army*. New York: Macmillan, 1904.

Henderson, Archibald. *Washington's Southern Tour, 1791*. Boston: Houghton Mifflin, 1923.

Henderson, H. James. "Quantitative Approaches to Party Formation in the United States (with reply by Mary P. Ryan)." *William and Mary Quarterly* 30 (1973):307–324.

Henkin, Louis. *Foreign Affairs and the Constitution*. New York: Norton, 1972.

Higginbotham, Don C. *George Washington and the American Military Tradition*. Athens: University of Georgia Press, 1985.

———. ed. *Reconsiderations of the Revolutionary War: Selected Essays*. Westport, Conn.: Greenwood Press, 1978.

———. "Reflections on the War of Independence, Modern Guerrilla Warfare, and the War in Vietnam." In *Arms and Independence: The Military Character of the American Revolution*, ed. Ronald Hoffmann and Peter J. Albert, 1–24. Charlottesville: University Press of Virginia, 1984.

———. *War and Society in Revolutionary America: The Wider Dimensions of Conflict*. Columbia: University of South Carolina Press, 1988.

———. *The War of American Independence: Military Attitudes, Policies and Practice, 1763–1789*. New York: Macmillan, 1971.

_____. "The Washington Theme in Recent Historical Literature." *Pennsylvania Magazine of History and Biography* 114 (1990):423–437.

Hobson, Charles F. "The Negative on State Laws: James Madison, the Constitution, and the Crisis of Republican Government." *William and Mary Quarterly* 36 (1979):215–235.

Hoffmann, Ronald, and Peter J. Albert, eds. *Arms and Independence: The Military Character of the American Revolution.* Charlottesville: University Press of Virginia, 1984.

Hofstadter, Richard. *The American Political Tradition and the Men Who Made It.* New York: Knopf, 1948.

_____. *Anti-Intellectualism in American Life.* New York: Vintage, 1963.

_____. *The Idea of a Party System, 1780–1840.* Berkeley: University of California Press, 1969.

Holcombe, Arthur N. "The Role of Washington in the Framing of the Constitution." *Huntington Library Quarterly* 19 (1956):317–334.

Howe, Sir William. *The Narrative of Lieut. Gen. Sir William Howe.* London: H. Baldwin, 1780.

Hughes, Emmet John. *The Living Presidency.* Baltimore, Md.: Penguin, 1972.

Hutson, James H. "Country, Court, and Constitution: Antifederalism and the Historians." *William and Mary Quarterly* 38 (1981):337–368.

Jackson, Carlton. *Presidential Vetoes, 1792–1945.* Athens: University of Georgia Press, 1967.

Jensen, Merrill. "The Idea of a National Government during the American Revolution." *Political Science Quarterly* 58 (1943):356–379.

_____. *The New Nation: A History of the United States during the Confederation, 1781–1789.* New York: Knopf, 1950.

Jillson, Calvin C. "Constitution-Making: Alignment and Realignment in the Federal Convention of *1787.*" *American Political Science Review* 75 (1981):598–612.

_____. *Constitution-Making: Conflict and Consensus in the Federal Convention of 1787.* New York: Agathon Press, 1988.

Johnson, Herbert A. "Toward a Reappraisal of the 'Federal' Government: 1783–1789." *American Journal of Legal History* 8 (1964):314–325.

Jones, Charles O. *The United States Congress: People, Place and Policy.* Homewood, Ill.: Dorsey Press, 1982.

Jones, Robert F. *George Washington.* Rev. ed. New York: Fordham University Press, 1986.

_____. "George Washington and the Establishment of a Tradition." In *Power and the Presidency,* ed. Philip C. Dolce and George H. Skau, 13–23. New York: Scribner's, 1976.

_____. "George Washington and the Politics of the Presidency." *Presidential Studies Quarterly* 10 (1980):28–35.

Kammen, Michael. "A Different 'Fable of the Bees': The Problem of Public and Private Sectors in Colonial America." In *The American Revolution: A Heri-*

tage of Change, ed. John Parker and Carol Urness, 53–68. Minneapolis, Minn.: Associates of John Ford Bell Library, 1975.

_____. *Sovereignty and Liberty: Constitutional Discourse in American Culture*. Madison: University of Wisconsin Press, 1988.

Kelly, Alfred H., Winfred A. Harbison, and Herman Belz. *The American Constitution: Its Origins and Development*. 7th ed., 2 vols. New York: Norton, 1991.

Kenyon, Cecelia. "Alexander Hamilton: Rousseau of the Right." *Political Science Quarterly* 73 (1958):161–178.

_____. "Men of Little Faith: The Anti-Federalists on the Nature of Representative Government." *William and Mary Quarterly* 12 (1955):3–43.

_____. "Republicanism and Radicalism in the American Revolution: An Old-Fashioned Interpretation." *William and Mary Quarterly* 19 (1962):153–182.

Kerber, Linda K. "The Federalist Party." In *History of United States Political Parties*. Vol. I, *1789–1860, From Factions to Parties*, ed. Arthur M. Schlesinger, 3–29. New York: Chelsea House, 1973.

Kernan, Michael. "A President without Precedent." *Smithsonian* 20 (1989):94–103.

Ketcham, Ralph, ed. *The Anti-Federalist Papers and the Constitutional Convention Debates*. New York: New American Library, 1986.

_____. *From Colony to Country: The Revolution in American Thought, 1750–1820*. New York: Macmillan, 1974.

_____. *Presidents above Party: The First American Presidency, 1789–1829*. Chapel Hill: University of North Carolina Press, 1984.

_____, and Nathaniel Stein. "Two New Letters Reveal Madison's Role; Unmask 'Ghost' of Washington's Unused Inaugural." *Manuscripts* (Spring 1959):54–60.

Key, V. O. *Politics, Parties and Pressure Groups*. New York: Crowell, 1969.

Knollenberg, Bernhard. *George Washington: The Virginia Period, 1732–1775*. Durham, N.C.: Duke University Press, 1964.

_____. *Washington and the Revolution: A Reappraisal*. New York: Macmillan, 1940.

Koch, Adrienne. *Power, Morals, and the Founding Fathers: Essays in the Interpretation of the American Enlightenment*. Ithaca, N.Y.: Cornell University Press, 1961.

Kohn, Richard H. "American Generals of the Revolution: Subordination and Restraint." In *Reconsiderations on the Revolutionary War: Selected Essays*, ed. Don Higginbotham, 104–123. Westport, Conn. Greenwood Press, 1978.

_____. "The Inside History of the Newburgh Conspiracy: America and the Coup d'Etat." *William and Mary Quarterly* 27 (1970):187–220.

_____. "The Washington Administration's Decision to Crush the Whiskey Rebellion." *Journal of American History* 59 (1972):567–584.

Kramnick Isaac. *Bolingbroke and His Circle: The Politics of Nostalgia in the Age of Walpole*. Cambridge, Mass.: Harvard University Press, 1968.

_____. "The 'Great National Discussion': The Discourse of Politics in 1787." *William and Mary Quarterly* 45 (1988):3–32.

_____. "Republican Revisionism Revisited." *American Historical Review* 87 (1982):629–664.

LaPalombara, Joseph G., and Myron Weiner, eds. *Political Parties and Political Development.* Princeton, N.J. Princeton University Press, 1966.

Learned, Henry Barrett. *The President's Cabinet: Studies in the Development and Structure of an American Institution.* New Haven, Conn.: Yale University Press, 1912.

Lieberman, Carl. "George Washington and the Development of American Federalism." *Social Science* 51 (1976):3–10.

Lienesch, Michael. "The Constitutional Tradition: History, Political Action, and Progress in American Political Thought, 1787–1793." *Journal of Politics* 42 (1980):2–30.

_____. "Historical Theory and Political Reform: Two Perspectives on Confederation Politics." *Review of Politics* 45 (1983): 94–115.

_____. "Interpreting Experience: History, Philosophy, and Science in the American Constitutional Debates." *American Politics Quarterly* 11 (1983): 379–401.

_____. *New Order of the Ages: Time, the Constitution, and the Making of Modern American Political Thought.* Princeton, N.J.: Princeton University Press, 1988.

Link, Eugene P. *Democratic-Republican Societies, 1790–1800.* New York: Octagon, 1973.

Lipset, Seymour Martin. *The First New Nation: The United States in Historical and Comparative Perspective.* New York: Basic Books, 1963.

Longmore, Paul K. *The Invention of George Washington.* Berkeley: University of California Press, 1988.

Loss, Richard. *The Modern Theory of Presidential Power: Alexander Hamilton and the Corwin Thesis.* New York: Greenwood Press, 1990.

Lowi, Theodore J. *The End of Liberalism: The Second Republic of the United States.* 2d ed. New York: Norton, 1979.

Lutz, Donald S. *The Origins of American Constitutionalism.* Baton Rouge: Louisiana State University Press, 1988.

_____. "Popular Consent and Popular Control, 1776–1789." In *Founding Principles of American Government.* Rev. ed., ed. George J. Graham, Jr., and Scarlett G. Graham, 60–97. Chatham, N.J.: Chatham House, 1984.

Maclay, William. *Sketches of Debate in the First Senate of the United States.* Harrisburg, Pa.: Lane S. Hart, 1880.

Madison, James. *Notes of Debates in the Federal Convention of 1787 Reported by James Madison.* New York: Norton, 1969.

_____. *The Papers of James Madison,* ed. Robert A. Rutland et al. Chicago: University of Chicago Press, 1962– .

Maier, Pauline. "The Beginnings of American Republicanism, 1765–1776." In

The Development of a Revolutionary Mentality, 99–117. Washington, D.C.: Library of Congress, 1974.

———. *From Resistance to Revolution: Colonial Radicals and the Development of American Opposition to Britain, 1765–1776*. New York: Knopf, 1972.

———. *The Old Revolutionaries: Political Lives in the Age of Samuel Adams*. New York: Knopf, 1980.

Main, Jackson T. *The Anti-Federalists: Critics of the Constitution, 1781–1788*. New York: Norton, 1974.

———. "The One Hundred." *William and Mary Quarterly* 11 (1954):354–367.

———. *Political Parties before the Constitution*. Chapel Hill: University of North Carolina Press, 1973.

Malone, Dumas. "The Great Generation." *Virginia Quarterly Review* 23 (1947):108–122.

Mandeville, Bernard. *The Fable of the Bees: Or, Private Vices, Publick Benefits*, ed. F. B. Kaye, 2 vols. Oxford: Clarendon Press, 1924.

Markowitz, Arthur. "Washington's Farewell and the Historians: A Critical Review." *Pennsylvania Magazine of History and Biography* 94 (1970):173–191.

Marks, Frederick W., III. *Independence on Trial: Foreign Affairs and the Making of the Constitution*. Baton Rouge: Louisiana State University Press, 1973.

Marshall, John. *The Life of George Washington*. 5 vols. London: Crissy, 1804–1807.

Marshall, Jonathan. "Empire or Liberty: The Antifederalists and Foreign Policy, 1787–1788." *Journal of Libertarian Studies* 4 (1980):233–254.

Martin, James Kirby. "A 'Most Undisciplined, Profligate Crew': Protest and Defiance in the Continental Ranks, 1776–1783." In *Arms and Independence: The Military Character of the American Revolution*, ed. Ronald Hoffmann and Peter J. Albert, 119–140. Charlottesville: University Press of Virginia, 1984.

Mason, Alpheus Thomas. "*The Federalist*—A Split Personality." *American Historical Review* 57 (1951):625–643.

Matson, Cathy D., and Peter S. Onuf. *Union of Interests: Political and Economic Thought in Revolutionary America*. Lawrence: University Press of Kansas, 1990.

Matteson, David M. *Washington and the Constitution*. Washington, D.C.: George Washington Bicentennial Commission, 1931.

Maurer, Maurer. "Military Justice under General Washington." *Military Affairs* 28 (1964):8–16.

McCormick, Richard. "Political Parties." In *Encyclopedia of American Political History*, ed. Jack P. Greene, 3:939–948. New York: Scribner's, 1984.

McCoy, Drew R. "American Political Ideology in the 1790s: Two Approaches." *Reviews in American History* 6 (1978):496–502.

———. *The Elusive Republic: Political Economy in Jeffersonian America*. Chapel Hill: University of North Carolina Press, 1980.

McDonald, Forrest. "The Anti-Federalists." *Wisconsin Magazine of History* 46 (1963):206–214.

_____. *E Pluribus Unum: The Formation of the American Republic, 1776–1790*. Boston: Houghton Mifflin, 1965.

_____. *Novus Ordo Seclorum: The Intellectual Origins of the Constitution.* Lawrence: University Press of Kansas, 1985.

_____. *The Presidency of George Washington.* Lawrence: University Press of Kansas, 1974.

_____. *We the People: The Economic Origins of the Constitution.* Chicago: University of Chicago Press, 1958.

McDougal, Myres S., and Asher Lans. "Treaties and Congressional-Executive or Presidential Agreements: Interchangeable Instruments of National Policy." *Yale Law Journal* 54 (1945):181–351, 534–615.

Meyers, Marvin, ed. *The Mind of the Founder: Sources of the Political Thought of James Madison.* Indianapolis, Ind.: Bobbs-Merrill, 1973.

Miller, John C. *Crisis in Freedom: The Alien and Sedition Acts.* Boston: Little, Brown, 1951.

_____. *The Federalist Era, 1789–1801.* New York: Harper & Brothers, 1960.

Miller, Randall M. "The Founding of a Father: John Adams and the Appointment of George Washington as Commander-in-Chief of the Continental Army." *Maryland Historian* 4 (1973):13–23.

Morgan, Edmund S. *The Birth of the Republic, 1763–1789.* Chicago: University of Chicago Press, 1956.

_____. *The Genius of George Washington.* New York: Norton, 1980.

_____. *Inventing the People: The Rise of Popular Sovereignty in England and America.* New York: Norton, 1988.

Morris, Richard B., ed. *Basic Documents on the Confederation and Constitution.* New York: Van Nostrand, 1970.

_____. "Washington and Hamilton: A Great Collaboration." *Proceedings of the American Philosophical Society* 102 (1958):107–116.

_____. *Witnesses at the Creation: Hamilton, Madison, Jay, and the Constitution.* New York: Holt, Rinehart and Winston, 1985.

Murphy, Bruce. *Fortas: The Rise and Ruin of a Supreme Court Justice.* New York: Morrow, 1988.

Murrin, John M. "The Great Inversion, or, Court versus Country: A Comparison of the Revolution Settlements in England and America." In *Three British Revolutions: 1641, 1688, 1776*, ed. J. G. A. Pocock, 368–453. Princeton, N.J.: Princeton University Press, 1980.

Nettels, Curtis P. *The Emergence of a National Economy, 1775–1815.* New York: Holt, Rinehart and Winston, 1962.

_____. *George Washington and American Independence.* Boston: Little, Brown, 1951.

Neustadt, Richard. *Presidential Power: The Politics of Leadership from FDR to Carter.* New York: John Wiley, 1980.

O'Brien, David M. *Storm Center: The Supreme Court In American Politics.* 2d ed. New York: Norton, 1990.

Olson, Mancur. *The Logic of Collective Action*. Cambridge, Mass.: Harvard University Press, 1965.

Onuf, Peter S. "Liberty, Development, and Union: Visions of the West in the 1780s." *William and Mary Quarterly* 43 (1986):179–213.

―――――. "Reflections on the Founding: Constitutional Historiography in Bicentennial Perspective." *William and Mary Quarterly* 46 (1989):341–375.

―――――. "Toward Federalism: Virginia, Congress, and the Western Lands." *William and Mary Quarterly* 34 (1977):353–374.

Padover, Saul. "George Washington—Portrait of a True Conservative." *Social Research* 22 (1955):199–222.

Page, Benjamin I., and Mark P. Petracca. *The American Presidency*. New York: McGraw-Hill, 1983.

Palmer, R. R. *The Age of the Democratic Revolution: A Political History of Europe and America, 1760–1800*. Vol. I, *The Challenge*. Princeton, N.J.: Princeton University Press, 1959.

Pangle, Thomas L. *The Spirit of Modern Republicanism: The Moral Vision of the American Founders and the Philosophy of Locke*. Chicago: University of Chicago Press, 1988.

Peterson, Paul. "The Meaning of Republicanism in *The Federalist.*" *Publius* 9 (1979):43–75.

Phelps, Glenn A. "George Washington and the Building of the Constitution: Presidential Interpretation and Constitutional Development." *Congress & the Presidency* 12 (1985):95–110.

―――――. "George Washington and the Founding of the Presidency." *Presidential Studies Quarterly* 17 (1987):345–363.

―――――. "George Washington and the Paradox of Party." *Presidential Studies Quarterly* 19 (1989):733–746.

―――――. "George Washington: Precedent Setter." In *Inventing the American Presidency*, ed. Thomas E. Cronin, 259–281. Lawrence: University Press of Kansas, 1989.

Pocock, J. G. A. *The Machiavellian Moment: Florentine Political Thought and the Atlantic Republican Tradition*. Princeton, N.J.: Princeton University Press, 1975.

―――――. "Virtue and Commerce in the Eighteenth Century." *Journal of Interdisciplinary History* 3 (1972):119–134.

Pole, J. R. "Historians and the Problem of Early American Democracy." *American Historical Review* 67 (1962):626–646.

―――――. *Political Representation in England and the Origins of the American Republic*. New York: St. Martin's Press, 1966.

Pomper, Gerald. "Conflict and Coalitions at the Constitutional Convention." In *The Study of Coalition Behavior*, ed. Sven Grennings, E. W. Kelley, and Michael Leiserson, 209–225. New York: Holt, Rinehart and Winston, 1970.

Powell, H. Jefferson. "The Original Understanding of Original Intent." *Harvard Law Review* 98 (1985):885–948.

Prescott, Arthur Taylor. *Drafting the Federal Constitution*. New York: Greenwood Press, 1968.

Rakove, Jack N. *The Beginnings of National Politics: An Interpretive History of the Continental Congress*. New York: Knopf, 1979.

———. "The Structure of Politics at the Accession of George Washington." In *Beyond Confederation: Origins of the Constitution and American National Identity*, ed. Richard Beeman, Stephen Botein, and Edward C. Carter II, 261–294. Chapel Hill: University of North Carolina Press, 1987.

Ranney, Austin, and Willmoore Kendall. *Democracy and the American Party System*. New York: Harcourt, Brace, 1956.

Reid, John Philip. *Constitutional History of the American Revolution: The Authority to Tax*. Madison: University of Wisconsin Press, 1987.

Reuter, Frank T. *Trials and Triumphs: George Washington's Foreign Policy*. Fort Worth: Texas Christian University Press, 1983.

Riemer, Neal. "The Republicanism of James Madison." *Political Science Quarterly* 69 (1954):45–64.

Riesman, Janet A. "Money, Credit, and Federalist Political Economy." In *Beyond Confederation: Origins of the Constitution and American National Identity*, ed. Richard Beeman, Stephen Botein, and Edward C. Carter II, 128–161. Chapel Hill: University of North Carolina Press, 1987.

Risch, Erna. *Supplying Washington's Army*. Washington, D.C.: Center of Military History, 1981.

Risjord, Norman K. *Chesapeake Politics, 1781-1800*. New York: Columbia University Press, 1978.

———, and Gordon DenBoer. "The Evolution of Political Parties in Virginia, 1782-1800." *Journal of American History* 60 (1974):961–984.

———. "Virginia Federalists." *Journal of Southern History* 33 (1967):486–517.

Robinson, Donald L. "The Inventors of the Presidency." *Presidential Studies Quarterly* 13 (1983):8–25.

———. *"To the Best of My Ability": The Presidency and the Constitution*. New York: Norton, 1987.

Roche, John P. "The Founding Fathers: A Reform Caucus in Action." *American Political Science Review* 55 (1961):799–816.

Rossie, Jonathan Gregory. *The Politics of Command in the American Revolution*. Syracuse, N.Y.: Syracuse University Press, 1975.

Rossiter, Clinton. *Alexander Hamilton and the Constitution*. New York: Harcourt, Brace and World, 1964.

———. *The First American Revolution: The American Colonies on the Eve of Independence*. San Diego: Harcourt Brace Jovanovich, 1981.

Royster, Charles. *A Revolutionary People at War: The Continental Army and American Character, 1775-1783*. Chapel Hill: University of North Carolina Press, 1979.

Ryan, Mary P. "Party Formation in the United States Congress, 1789 to 1796: A Quantitative Study." *William and Mary Quarterly* 28 (1971):523–542.

Schlesinger, Arthur M., ed. *History of United States Political Parties*. Vol. I, *1789–1860, From Factions to Parties*. New York: Chelsea House, 1973.

Schmitt, Gary J., and Robert H. Webking. "Revolutionaries, Antifederalists, and Federalists: Comments on Gordon Wood's Understanding of the American Founding." *Political Science Reviewer* 9 (1979):195–229.

Schwartz, Barry. "George Washington and the Whig Conception of Heroic Leadership." *American Sociological Review* 48 (1983):18–33.

———. *George Washington: The Making of an American Symbol*. New York: Free Press, 1987.

———. "Social Change and Collective Memory: The Democratization of George Washington." *American Sociological Review* 56 (1991):221–236.

Shalhope, Robert E. "Southern Federalists and the First Party Syndrome." *Reviews in American History* 8 (1980):45–51.

Shevory, Thomas C. "John Marshall as Republican: Order and Conflict in American Political History." In *John Marshall's Achievement: Law, Politics, and Constitutional Interpretation*, ed. Thomas C. Shevory, 75–93. New York: Greenwood Press, 1989.

Shy, John. *A People Numerous and Armed: Reflections on the Military Struggle for American Independence*. New York: Oxford University Press, 1976.

Slaughter, Thomas P. "The Friends of Liberty, the Friends of Order, and the Whiskey Rebellion: A Historiographical Essay." In *The Whiskey Rebellion: Past and Present Perspectives*, ed. Steven R. Boyd, 9–30. Westport, Conn.: Greenwood Press, 1985.

———. *The Whiskey Rebellion: Frontier Epilogue to the American Revolution*. New York: Oxford University Press, 1986.

Smelser, Marshall. "The Federalist Period as an Age of Passion." *American Quarterly* 10 (1958):391–419.

———. "George Washington and the Alien and Sedition Acts." *American Historical Review* 59 (1954):322–334.

Smith, James Morton. *Freedom's Fetters: The Alien and Sedition Laws and American Civil Liberties*. Ithaca, N.Y.: Cornell University Press, 1956.

Smith, Louis. *American Democracy and Military Power*. Chicago: University of Chicago Press, 1951.

Sofaer, Abraham D. "Executive Privilege: An Historical Note." *Columbia Law Review* 75 (1975):1318–1321.

———. "The Presidency, War, and Foreign Affairs: Practice under the Framers." *Law and Contemporary Problems* 40 (1976):12–38.

Stearns, Monroe. *Shays' Rebellion, 1786–7: Americans Take Up Arms against Unjust Laws*. New York: Franklin Watts, 1968.

Stein, Charles W. *The Third-Term Tradition*. New York: Columbia University Press, 1943.

Stein, Nathaniel E. "The Discarded Inaugural Address of George Washington." *Manuscripts* 10 (1958):2–17.

Storing, Herbert. *What the Anti-Federalists Were For*. Chicago: University of Chicago Press, 1981.

Stourzh, Gerald. *Alexander Hamilton and the Idea of Representative Government.* Stanford, Calif.: Stanford University Press, 1970.

Sweig, Donald. "A Capital on the Potomac: A 1789 Broadside and Alexandria's Attempts to Capture the Cherished Prize." *Virginia Magazine of History and Biography* 87 (9179):74–95.

———. "A New-Found Washington Letter of 1774 and the Fairfax Resolves." *William and Mary Quarterly* 40 (1983):283–291.

Sydnor, Charles S. *Gentlemen Freeholders.* Chapel Hill: University of North Carolina Press, 1952.

Szatmary, David. *Shays' Rebellion: The Making of an Agrarian Insurrection.* Amherst: University of Massachusetts Press, 1980.

Tate, Thad W. "The Coming of the Revolution in Virginia: Britain's Challenge to Virginia's Ruling Class, 1763–1776." *William and Mary Quarterly* 19 (1962):323–343.

———. "The Social Contract in America, 1774–1787: Revolutionary Theory as Conservative Instrument." *William and Mary Quarterly* 22 (1965):375–391.

Taylor, Robert J. *Western Massachusetts in the Revolution.* Providence, R.I.: Brown University Press, 1954.

Thach, Charles C. *The Creation of the Presidency, 1775–1789.* Baltimore, Md.: Johns Hopkins University Press, 1922.

Thomas, Robert E. "The Virginia Convention of 1788: A Criticism of Beard's *An Economic Interpretation of the Constitution.*" *Journal of Southern History* 19 (1953):63–72.

Thomson, Harry C. "The First Presidential Vetoes." *Presidential Studies Quarterly* 8 (1978):27–32.

Twohig, Dorothy, et al., eds. *The Journal of the Proceedings of the President, 1793–1797.* Charlottesville: University Press of Virginia, 1981.

Ulmer, S. Sydney. "Sub-Group Formation in the Constitutional Convention." *Midwest Journal of Political Science* 10 (1968):288–303.

Ver Steeg, Clarence L. "The American Revolution Considered as an Economic Movement." *Huntington Library Quarterly* 20 (1957):361–372.

Warren, Charles. *The Making of the Constitution.* Boston: Little, Brown, 1929.

———. *The Supreme Court in United States History.* Rev. ed., 2 vols. Boston: Little, Brown, 1926.

Washington, George. *The Diary of George Washington, From 1789 to 1791,* ed. Benson J. Lossing. Freeport, N.Y.: Books for Libraries Press, 1972.

———. *The Papers of George Washington: Colonial Series,* ed. W. W. Abbot. 7 vols. to date. Charlottesville: University Press of Virginia, 1983– .

———. *The Papers of George Washington: Presidential Series,* ed. Dorothy Twohig. 3 vols. to date. Charlottesville: University Press of Virginia, 1987– .

———. *The Papers of George Washington: Revolutionary War Series,* ed. Philander D. Chase. 4 vols. to date. Charlottesville: University Press of Virginia, 1985– .

———. *Writings of George Washington,* ed. John C. Fitzpatrick. Washington, D.C.: GPO, 1931–1944.

White, Leonard D. *The Federalists: A Study in Administrative History.* New York: Macmillan, 1948.

Wildavsky, Aaron. "The Two Presidencies." *Trans-Action* 4 (1966):7–14.

Wills, Garry. *Cincinnatus: George Washington and the Enlightenment.* Garden City, N.Y.: Doubleday, 1984.

_____. *Explaining America: The Federalist.* New York: Doubleday, 1981.

_____. *Inventing America: Jefferson's Declaration of Independence.* New York: Doubleday, 1978.

Wilson, Frederick T. *Federal Aid in Domestic Disturbances: 1787–1903.* Reprint. New York: Arno Press, 1969.

Wilson, Woodrow. *George Washington.* New York: Schocken, 1969.

Wood. Gordon S. *The Creation of the American Republic, 1776–1787.* Chapel Hill: University of North Carolina Press, 1969.

_____. "Interests and Disinterestedness in the Making of the Constitution." In *Beyond Confederation: Origins of the Constitution and American National Identity,* ed. Richard Beeman, Stephen Botein, and Edward C. Carter II, 69–109. Chapel Hill: University of North Carolina Press, 1987.

Wright, Esmond. *Washington and the American Revolution.* New York: Collier, 1962.

Zvesper, John. "The Madisonian Systems." *Western Political Quarterly* 37 (1984):236–256.

_____. *Political Philosophy and Rhetoric: A Study of the Origins of American Party Politics.* Cambridge: Cambridge University Press, 1977.

Index